RUMOUR IN ORLEANS

RUMOUR IN ORLEANS

by

EDGAR MORIN

in collaboration with
Bernard Paillard, Evelyne Burguière, Claude Capulier,
Suzanne de Lusignan, Julia Vérone

Translated from the French by
PETER GREEN

ANTHONY BLOND

First published 1971 in Great Britain by
Anthony Blond Limited,
56 Doughty Street,
London W.C.1

218 51441 7

Printed in Great Britain by
Clarke, Doble & Brendon Ltd., Plymouth

CONTENTS

ORLEANS. Orléans is the capital of the Loiret *département* (pop. 430,000). The actual town has 88,000 inhabitants, while the overall population (sixteen *communes*) is 170,000 (1968). In 1953 the overall population was only 90,000, and during the past decade it has increased by 60,000 inhabitants. Orléans lies midway between Eastern and Western France, and 110 kilometres south of Paris.

Economic activities are varied (industry, trade, services) and none of them markedly developed in relation to the others. Orléans is, on many counts, an average town—a fact which has won it the lasting attention of the public opinion polls.

'The Loiret *département* is that of the "golden mean". Balance, harmony—such are the words that best describe us.'

Pocket guidebook, *Orléans et le Loiret*
(Editions P.P., 1969), p. 9.

SYNTHESIS

by Edgar Morin

INTRODUCTION

A rumour of vanishing women that shook an entire town,
though not one disappearance was actually reported to the
police; the near certain belief, held by thousands of
Orléans' citizens, that a white slave traffic was being run
from the very heart of town, in the fitting-rooms of six
dress shops—all Jewish—though neither press, radio nor
television had one word to say in support of it; a kind of
medieval panic that for several days held a modern town
in its grip, in the age of the mass media; a fantastic sexual
threat that suddenly conjured up the grim spectre of anti-
Semitism—here was a story that fascinated me when I
first read the accounts of it in *Le Monde*, *L'Express* and
Le Nouvel Observateur. I had the impulse to make it the
subject of an on-the-spot investigation, an exercise in that
'occurrential' or 'clinical' sociology which I endeavour to
promote in my section of the Centre for the Study of Mass
Communications (*Ecole pratique des Hautes Etudes, sixième
section*). This section concerns itself with what I term 'contemporary sociology' (*sociologie du présent*), the principles
of which are set out in an appendix to the present work
(see below, pp. 265 ff.).

However, the official organisations which have manna
to bestow upon sociological research not only take little
interest in those problems that are of all-absorbing interest to me, but cannot earmark funds in advance for

11

the investigation of a totally unforeseen incident. I had
therefore given up all hope of plunging into the strange
events reported from Orléans when, at the beginning of
July, the Jewish Social Foundation approached me, and
offered to finance just such an investigation. I would like to
take this opportunity of thanking M. Kaufmann, who was
responsible for this decision, Léon Poliakov, who suggested
the idea of a sociological enquiry to him, and my friend
Gérard Rosenthal, who arranged what proved to be an
extremely profitable meeting between us.

After four days of preliminary study of the affair, a team
consisting of Evelyne Burguière, Claude Capulier, Suzanne
de Lusignan, Edgar Morin, Bernard Paillard and Julia
Vérone descended on Orléans. A month had elapsed since
the occurrence. The rumour had been broken up and,
seemingly, put out of circulation; at the same time a veil of
secrecy had been thrown over it. The adolescent girls who
had incubated the rumour were chary of giving anything
away to 'grown-ups'. The people of Orléans as a whole
were on their guard against outsiders, smart Parisians who
might sneer at them. There was also the fear, when these
unknown investigators arrived, that prosecutions were
liable to be brought for 'spreading false information'.

We derived much help, at the outset, from the militant
anti-racialist groups, the journalists of the provincial press,
and the actual victims of the rumour, whom we invited, on
arrival, to meet us over what might be termed a 'sociological dinner'. Over the hors-d'oeuvres both sides were
embarrassed, nervous and full of inhibitions. By the time
we had reached the dessert however, everyone was talking
freely—and truthfully. We briefly enjoyed the exquisite
privilege of interrogating a police officer and confessing a
priest. But from the start, our real problem was to get
away from such official or militant circles, and to penetrate
that twilight zone where the rumour had actually fermented, spreading thence—with quite incredible force—
throughout the entire town. We therefore abandoned any

idea of using tape-recorders (those I had brought were left in the boot of my car). Instead we worked through interviews, selecting people either at random, by means of chance encounters, or else in a sequence, with one acquaintance passing us on to the next. Above all, our five young investigators operated a kind of 'sociological dragnet', combing the teenagers' bars, the hairdressing salons, and other such meeting places.

The very first contacts we made showed us that, contrary to the beliefs of the militant groups, officialdom and the victims themselves, the rumour was by no means dead; it had, rather, been transformed into a swarm of mini-rumours and micro-myths. Though the affair was, on the face of it, closed, in fact it still flourished, in an indirect, underground fashion, infiltrating the town's subconscious at the same time as it was being digested by the traditional structure of the *polis*.

We suddenly became aware that our enquiry, far from being held too late, was taking place at a particularly advantageous moment. We would be able to follow the entire life-cycle of a rumour, from its germination to its ultimate breakdown. In one sense the whole thing *had* finished, which meant that it could be examined in histcrical retrospect. But in another sense nothing was ended; and it was that which made a live, on-the-spot enquiry possible. Thus we worked simultaneously at two levels, hot and cold as one might say—or, combining the two, we followed a warm trail: the warmth of embers.

Such an investigation both stimulates and modifies its own orientation, strategy and hypotheses *in situ*. One aspect of it—the side which calls for improvisation, flair, a nose for deduction and a sense of adventure—comes very close to journalistic reportage. Yet in ways the two are very different. The sociological enquiry organises its evidence more systematically, and employs more sophisticated techniques of investigation. Instead of an article for the press, the researcher is writing a personal journal.

Above all, there is the rôle played, in any investigating
team, by the constant exchange of views and criticisms
between its various members (not to mention self-
criticism in the individual). Considerable time is also
allowed for the very necessary process of reflection between
field-work and the final publication of one's conclusions.
If our on-the-spot enquiries yielded a rich harvest in a very
short space of time, this was largely attributable to the
constant pooling of fresh information by all team members,
and the virtually non-stop discussion that this produced.
Such an approach presupposed sympathy, mutual interests, frankness—friendship, in fact—between the various
members of the group, and, at the same time, a passionate
interest in the people we encountered, the endless new
problems to which such interviews gave rise: in short, an
almost obsessional urge to *know*, to discover the truth of
the matter.

To put it another way, this type of research calls not
only for quasi-cynical curiosity, but also for full subjective
involvement on the part of the investigator, who needs to
identify himself, emotionally and emphatically, with the
situation and personal beliefs which he is called upon to
explore. His feelings must not, it is true, blunt his intellectual awareness; yet the latter must learn to go with
the former, though without being thrown off balance by
them, like a surfer skimming along on the crest of a wave.

This is the sphere in which our undertaking sought its
strategy, guidance, as well as its stimulation and self-
discipline. Here, too, it falls into a different category from
the normal sociological enquiry no less than from journalistic reportage.

Our three days of investigation *in situ* were followed by
a joint review of the material we had accumulated, a
discussion of all hypotheses advanced, a period of reflection, and, finally, an attempt to formulate some sort of
report on the phenomenon we had been studying. This
part of our investigation—a process of increasing com-

plexity, involving several fresh starts—kept us fully occupied for nearly two months. Its outcome was the present volume, which we now offer to the general public—though well aware that it still lacks sufficient objectivity or coolness of judgment.

In a work such as this, based on a rapid 'dragnet' survey, there are bound to be many errors (minor, one hopes) and some serious omissions. We shall be extremely grateful to anyone, in Orléans or elsewhere, who lets us have information, corrections or criticisms that we can incorporate in a second edition, if one should be called for.

As a pendant to the report proper, we also include the researchers' field-notes, though unfortunately in a somewhat fragmentary condition. Our intense on-the-spot activity in Orléans meant that we lacked the time to keep full day-to-day diaries, as we had hoped to do. As regards Bernard Paillard and myself, the moment we got back we plunged into the task of sifting and analysing the evidence we had amassed, and it proved psychologically impossible to rethink this material into the form in which it was before we broke down its elements by passing them through our sociological *moulinette*, whence they emerged with a completely fresh pattern and structure. Furthermore, we could not consider publishing notes or remarks that might encourage local malicious gossip, to the detriment of those who, without knowing it, aided us in our enquiries.

Lastly, the reader will find two further appendices, one containing, by way of evidence, all articles and communiqués which appeared in the Press, and the other a statement setting out the principles of 'contemporary sociology', which dictated the methods adopted during our investigation. Thus the reader will progress from synthesis or summary to actual evidence, from a would-be objective report to its subjective adherences, in such a manner that he can himself reopen the dialectic between material information and the systematising mind which attempts to set that information in order. In other words, he too, in his turn, will be able to play a critical part in the process of investigation.

This rumour (which our somewhat tardy enquiries found still very much alive, and already transmogrified) shook every leaf and branch in the social tree of Orléans. Using this shock wave as our excuse and our test case, we could very easily have conducted another investigation, on Orléans itself: a town of opposites, so near, yet so remote, so individual yet so commonplace, an average, middle-of-the-road community that suddenly became strange beyond belief. Our actual enquiry led us in two directions: on the one hand towards the *polis*, with its individual psyche, its own social, political and economic framework; on the other, towards the composite mental infrastructure of a myth, the unexplored depths of the collective subconscious. Orléans' sole privilege was to be the point at which this subconscious surfaced, in a crisis which may well shed light on the entire fabric of society. We firmly resisted the temptation to pursue our enquiries into Orléans as such: the focal point for our research was not so much Orléans as the myth. We have done our best to discover what this archaic rumour can reveal about the modern world which gave birth to it, and, at a deeper level, to clarify the perennial and crucial problem of belief.[1]

---

[1] The report on the *Rumour in Orléans* was written by Edgar Morin. Bernard Paillard read and criticised the first draft, making various suggestions and corrections. Denise Barcilon revised the MS as a whole; final corrections were made by Evelyne Burguière.

ONE

THE HISTORY OF A RUMOUR

In May 1969 a report grew and spread through Orléans that first one, then two, and finally no less than six women's dress shops in the centre of town were running a white slave traffic. Young girls were said to be drugged (by injection) while in the fitting-rooms, and then carried down to the cellars, whence they were spirited away, after dark, to exotic centres of prostitution abroad. The shops in question were all owned by Jewish businessmen.

We are concerned here with what may be termed a rumour pure and absolute; a rumour that is pure on two counts: firstly, no woman disappeared in Orléans, and, more generally, nothing whatsoever took place which could either start or lend support to such a rumour; and secondly, the information circulated exclusively by word of mouth. It got no support from the Press, from posters or from pamphlets; it did not even give rise to graffiti.

BACKGROUND AND ORIGIN
A rapid survey shows that neither the fitting-room-white-slave-traffic theme nor the involvement of Jewish shopkeepers originated in Orléans.

The fitting-room as trap
The notion of the fitting-room as a trap, a clandestine

17

antechamber to mystery and danger, turns up in the lower reaches of mass culture; the world of pulp fiction provides examples of it, and so does sensational journalism.

In the former category we may cite *Un couvent dans le vent*, by 'Maz' (*Collection Mystère-Espionnage*, Presses de la Cité, Paris, 1968), which tells one of the adventures of Scheherazade, a magnificent redhead and British secret agent. Innocent women customers who visit the Boutique Véronique in Piccadilly are given an anaesthetic gas in the fitting-room. A wall slides open to reveal a secret laboratory, where the victims are stripped, at one and the same time, of their underclothes, their consciousness and their identity.

In the second category, it looks as though we can trace matters back to Press items concerning one, or several, cases of genuine white slaving which came to light, and which subsequently provided the model, or models, for fictitious incidents such as the Orléans one. I had no leisure to conduct a retrospective enquiry along these lines, but while correcting the present manuscript I happened to discuss the investigation with my friend Annette Roger, and she recalled an incident that had taken place some twelve years ago. In 1959 she was incarcerated in the women's prison at Marseilles for aiding and abetting the Algerian FLN. While there she made the acquaintance of another detainee who had been gaoled for complicity in a white slaving affair. A young girl had been drugged while trying on a corset in a boutique on the Rue Saint-Ferréol, run by two old ladies. Her fiancé, who was waiting outside, became impatient, went in, and, observing the consternation of the old ladies, made his way through to the back of the shop where he found the girl lying unconscious. The Marseilles white slave ring had begun to exploit this corset-makers' boutique only because they were unable to recruit enough women for the export trade by normal methods (i.e. straightforward seduction), and were hard-pressed by their clients' demands.

This affair must have created quite a stir in 1958. Was it, perhaps, the original incident which gave birth to a whole subsequent proliferation of mythical pseudo-information? At all events, we find the same theme cropping up again (with a different date and place, and a few other minor modifications) in a literary source which, though apparently factual, is not nearly so well authenticated. Early in 1969 there appeared a French translation of a book by an English journalist, Stephen Barlay. This work, entitled *Sex Slavery* (William Heinemann, London, 1968), was a wide-ranging compilation of erotico-sexual news items and anecdotes, including the following (p. 96):

> Yet a case in Grenoble, south-east France, only an hour's driving distance from the Italian border, could perhaps be regarded as equally typical. A man drove his wife to an expensive store for a dress fitting and, as he could not park the car, he kept driving round the block waiting for his wife. After about thirty minutes he became angry with her, but when another fifteen minutes passed without her returning, he got worried. So he stopped the car, risking a fine, and rushed into the store. Upstairs, at the made-to-measure counter he inquired about his wife. They said they never saw her. He became suspicious. But instinctively he had the presence of mind to admit that possibly he had made a mistake, perhaps she had an appointment somewhere else. They assured him it must be so.
>
> He left unhurriedly, but drove straight to the police. Detectives who had heard this store mentioned in several 'missing women' reports now put out an alert. Within minutes, police surrounded the block and a search began.
>
> In the basement, they found her. Guarded by a young man, she was asleep. On her arm, the detectives found the mark of an injection.

The magazine *Noir et Blanc*, in its issue for the week 6–14 May 1969, reproduced this item as it stood, without any indication of source; the words 'not long ago' implied

that the information was quite recent. The article, entitled 'White slavers' tricks', was illustrated with photographs which, in a different context, would be purely
erotic. It was this account, according to the police, that
provided a basis for the rumour which developed during
the week after the magazine reached the news stands,
about 10 May.

White slaving by the Jews
The Orléans rumour was not, however, the first one of its
kind. From 1959 onwards, and more particularly during
recent years—a point made both by the anti-racialist
organisations and by the police officer who handled the
Orléans affair—rumours involving local shops, and built
round precisely the same story, were reported from
Toulouse, Tours, Limoges, Douai, Rouen (*cf.* Supplementary Note, below, pp. 259ff.), Le Mans, Lille, Valenciennes,
and—at the same time as the Orléans incident—from
Poitiers and Châtellerault. They also sprang up in Paris
itself, where shops involved included the *Hit Parade*
boutique on the Rue Caumartin, and another similar
dress shop on the Boulevard Saint-Michel. (A snap
sociological survey in the urban area enabled us to find
evidence of fourteen or fifteen such incidents during the
last few years.) At Le Mans, in 1968, the Sarthe garment-
workers' *Chambre syndicale*, 'alarmed by slanderous and
defamatory allegations concerning the disappearance of
women and young girls, and the existence of a white slave
traffic, both supposedly connected with various local shops
in the garment industry', lodged an official complaint.
This information was reproduced as a news item by the
local press.

To the best of my knowledge none of these mini-rumours,
except for those in Rouen and Le Mans, got as far as the
newspapers: they were simply transmitted by word of
mouth. No journalistic, sociological or police investigations had been made into the rumours as such. In those

cases of which the police took cognisance, the most they did was to carry out a quick check on the shops themselves, to see whether by any chance they *were* spiriting young women away. We may assume, then, that at least the overwhelming majority of any provincial rumours known to us form no more than the thin visible layer of a myth which is neither local, nor isolated, nor haphazard, nor—strictly speaking—provincial, but to a great extent an urban overspill, with roots reaching deep into one part of society's subconscious being.

Now while these local rumours and the pseudo-information disseminated by the mass media all stem from one and the same original story—the disappearance of young women or girls while in the fitting-rooms of fashionable boutiques, drugging by injection, the white slave traffic—it is worth noting that the Jewish element is totally absent from the mass media, and perhaps does not necessarily emerge as part of the myth in Paris (I say 'perhaps': the paucity of our information precludes any more positive claim). *Yet almost all the rumours in the provinces concern Jewish shop-owners.*

Thus everything suggests that what we have here is a myth operating at two levels. The first is common to both the mass media and the rumours, though the bogus information put out by the former (e.g. the article in *Noir et Blanc*) and the pseudo-phenomena on which the latter depend do not always coincide either in place or time. The information peddled by the mass media derives from events which took place earlier, and somewhere else; that contained in the rumour is located *hic et nunc*, here and now. At the same time there undoubtedly exists an underground dialectic linking one group to the other, and fed by the same myth in each case.

The second level of this myth relates to the rumours alone. Even if it simply associates one or two Jews with a despicable activity—in this case white slavery—it forms a more or less anti-Semitic leitmotiv, which becomes open anti-Semitic propaganda if it leads to judgments or reactions which reflect unfavourably on Jews as a whole.

The source in Orléans

The publication of one article in *Noir et Blanc* is, by itself, not enough to account for the birth of the Orléans rumour. If such were the case, why did rumours of a similar type not gain ground in numbers of other towns at the same time? After all, this weekly enjoys a nation-wide circulation throughout France. We cannot, it is true, exclude the possibility that it *did* trigger off multiple fantasies, or even proto-rumours, which were extinguished before they so much as reached the surface, in a social sense. But even this would already suggest that the important problem in Orléans is not connected with the actual source of the fantasy, but rather with the development of the rumour as such. The most that seems possible is that the article in *Noir et Blanc* acted as a catalyst, which happened to find favourable conditions at Orléans during the May of 1969. The first of such conditions would be some other catalysing event, more specifically linked, in essence, with Orléans itself.

This second catalysing event might well have been provided by the opening of a new department in a central boutique on the Rue Royale, which took place on 10 May. The department was called *Aux Oubliettes* ('The Dungeon'), and specialised in ready-made dresses for girls and young women. Its backer, Cassegrain, a big businessman and local notable, had launched it as part of a drive against the competition provided by shops like *Dorphée* and *Sheila*, where dynamic Jewish owners were beginning to attract all the younger clientèle. The fitting-rooms were in a cellar, and there had been an attempt to produce a mysterious, attractive décor for them, reminiscent of medieval dungeons or oubliettes.

Thus *Noir et Blanc* provided the script, while *Les Oubliettes* added an appropriate stage-setting, right in the middle of town. The two events, happening at the same time, encouraged a similar mythological pattern, summoned up identical fantasies. They became mutual catalysing agents, promoting and energising one another in turn. Yet this still does not suffice to explain an extremely active enzymotic process which substituted Orléans for Grenoble, and, more important, *Dorphée* for *Les Oubliettes.* For the myth, though stimulated by the latter, obstinately refused to settle there. It tore itself away from its predestined site—the owner of which, unfortunately, was the very embodiment of Orléans' traditional bourgeoisie— and made straight for the rival Jewish establishment, as lightning is drawn by a diamond, taking *Les Oubliettes* with it.

Here we may stop to consider the problem of the initial enzymotic agent. Who invented or disseminated the *mythe orléanais*? How? Why? What originally lay behind it? A practical joke? Auto-suggestion? Deliberate malice, provocation of a specifically anti-Semitic nature?

The anti-racialist militants were naturally attracted by the last hypothesis, which derived both support and discouragement from other rumours prior to that in Orléans. They supported it in the sense that numerous outbreaks of fire encourage one to suspect a pyromaniac; they discouraged it insofar as this very multiplicity could well indicate the spontaneous and haphazard upsurge of a new myth, from the depths of some collective subconscious. Now there is no evidence from the police, or from political sources, to support the idea that this myth was launched by a group of right-wing extremists. Moreover, the first culture-broth in which the rumour took root and developed was provided by young or adolescent girls. Thirdly, the 'Jewish businessman' theme acquires an increasing element of anti-Semitic virulence as it develops: *crescit eundo.* All this very considerably lessens the plausibility of our 'anti-Semitic provocation' hypothesis.

Two other theories—malice on the part of a rival, or

(more likely) a practical joke played by some boys on a group of girls, perhaps even (why not?) by one group of girls on another—cannot be absolutely ruled out, though they possess a merely anecdotal interest. The important point is the force behind the propagation of the rumour itself, once the initial impetus had been given it. Now there is nothing to stop us assuming that this initial impetus was identical in nature with the spreading of the rumour as such, the latter being a continuous process of creation, hysterical in type, which developed from contact between two or more persons, at each repetition of which the myth acquired fresh energy, a new departure, a new lease of life.

At this point it becomes clear that the question '*How* did this rumour start in Orléans?' is only of interest if it can be detached from another question which is liable to swamp it, i.e. '*Why* did this rumour start in Orléans?' The latter, in the last resort, has no real meaning. For one thing, the same rumour had already been started, on numerous occasions, in many very different sorts of town (and will probably continue to recur in the future). For another, the problem of the rumour's genesis reduces the whole thing to a personal level, links it with the psychological pattern (anecdotal even if not hypothetical) of some original pyromaniac.

On the other hand, a very pertinent question would be: 'Why should one rumour, among so many other similar ones, develop to such an extent at Orléans in particular?' Which stimulatory mechanisms operated more strongly here than elsewhere, or (and) which inhibitory mechanisms operated *less* strongly than elsewhere? To answer such a question at a deeper level than that posited by the bi-catalytic action of *Noir et Blanc* and *Les Oubliettes* would call for an exhaustive multidimensional knowledge, not only of Orléans—of Orléans in May 1969—but of other towns in France as well. Clearly, my colleagues and I cannot meet such requirements. Though the question has often returned to our minds, and driven us to propose a number of hypotheses that will be found scattered through the present study, we have not really tackled it. Instead, we have concentrated on scrutinising a phenomenon to which Orléans forms the background.

MAY 1969: FROM INCUBATION TO METASTASIS
First stage: incubation
We regard it as virtually certain that the initial incubation took place among young or adolescent girls, and very quickly spread to every group in this category: students, schoolgirls, shop-assistants and other employees, secretaries, manual workers.

In Bernard Paillard's opinion, the myth first took shape in a lower-class context, permeated with pop-culture of the kind represented by *Confidences* or *Nous-Deux*, boasting a fairly wide range of stock romantic novelette situations, and still half a stranger to that new culture of which the dress shops under attack were the representatives in Orléans. I myself regard it as more likely that the incubatory process took place initially among classes of young schoolgirls (the Catholic colleges of Saint Paul and Saint Charles, or the Lycée Jeanne-d'Arc). Such a context is doubly propitious for the transmission and proliferation of fantasy. These closed societies act as perfect sounding-boards and amplifiers, in addition to which their adolescent population (average age fifteen to eighteen), hemmed in by the double cocoon of school and family, has no real experience of ordinary social life. It is here that the myth could have built up its credibility-impact, which enabled it to spread among young wage-earners. One (admittedly fragile) piece of evidence which favours this thesis is the fact that, to the best of my knowledge, the first adults who got to hear of the rumour learnt it—whether as parents or teachers—from girls in high-school.

During the first period of incubation, the rumour was, in all likelihood, only directed against one shop, *Dorphée*. It

is *Dorphée* that emerges as the first (often the only) target
in retrospective accounts of this affair, and it was on
Dorphée that the rumour especially concentrated. This
boutique, which deals in ready-made dresses for girls and
young women, is very modern, does a thriving business,
and enjoys a high reputation for selling quality goods at
competitive prices. It is owned by a Jewish couple aged
about thirty, with young salesgirls to assist them. There is
a fitting-room at the back of the shop and a work-room
down in the basement. The first rumour stated confidently
that there had been two cases of women disappearing
while at *Dorphée*. The victims had been given injections
(which rendered them unconscious) in the fitting-room,
and were then carried down to the cellars.

Already the fantasy had been authenticated. The disappearances had been located in such and such a place. The
police had found two drugged women in the *Dorphée*
cellars. They were taken to hospital and regained consciousness there. This, again, was certified as coming from
a reliable source of information: 'The wife of one of the
policemen told her neighbour, who's a friend of mine,
that . . .', or even: 'The night nurse who was called in by
the hospital to resuscitate the drugged women told my
aunt that . . .' Thus the myth acquired the reality of objective, factual information, stemming from the most
reliable source (policeman or nurse), and supported by the
threefold confidence one could have in one's relatives,
friends and neighbours.

The Press did not breathe one word of such an incident
and the supposedly 'unmasked' shop-owners remained at
liberty; yet the adolescent myth, far from being worred,
by this circumstance, derived extra vitality from it. The
traffic must continue in order to keep the rumour in
circulation. The adolescent myth made no effort to explain
the silence of the Press, let alone the inaction of a police
force which abstained from arresting the white slavers it
had unmasked. This is why we can speak of a 'continuous

process of creation' in the myth: it kept the white slaving which nourished it, and the arrests which authenticated it, running in parallel, as it were, in that illogical fashion so characteristic of the mythological process.

Second stage: propagation
It seems to have been about 20 May that the myth, while continuing to spread among teenage girls, also began to spill over into the adult world. Girl told boy, pupil passed it on to teacher, daughter to parents, one employee to another. The rumour spread, not only among groups of young people, but in families, offices, workshops and factories. It fermented wherever people could get together and gossip. The main market-place in the middle of town (which on 31 May figured as a formidable echo chamber and the scene of something approaching a general panic) now became an information centre from which gossip spread to every part of the social and economic horizon. Cleaning-women carried the rumour back to their wealthy middle-class mistresses, housewives spread it in the suburbs. Saturday 24 May was the day before Whitsun: all the shopping expeditions and encounters that went on at this point must undoubtedly have hastened the diffusion of the virus throughout every level of society.

The further it spread, the more the myth grew. The number of disappearances spiralled: sometimes the figure quoted was about sixty, of which no less than twenty-eight had vanished from *Dorphée* alone. By now it was not just one shop that dealt in the white slave traffic, but a network of half a dozen: the *Boutique de Sheila*, *Alexandrine*, *Félix Le Petit Bénéfice*, *D.D.*, and (of course) *Dorphée*. All the proprietors of these shops specialised in ready-made dresses for girls and young women, with the exception of *Félix*, a shoe shop: here the drug was administered by means of a hypodermic syringe concealed in the heel of a shoe. All of them were relatively young, modern and fashionable. All were Jewish, except for the owners of

Alexandrine, newcomers to Orléans who had taken over
from Jewish predecessors a few weeks previously. The
rumour, however, did not incriminate Orléans' other
Jewish shop-owners—notably those in the Rue de Bourgogne, who sell popular ready-made dresses in traditional
fashions. Similarly, the rumour took no account of elderly
Jewish immigrants who still had a foreign accent, nor of
recent arrivals from North Africa. It concentrated exclusively on a group of shop-owners who had nothing
exotic about them, who looked just like anyone else, but
through that very fact contrived to conceal the one
mysterious difference which the whole world knew: their
Jewishness.

At the schoolgirl or teenager level, the myth produced
a feeling of fascinated terror, an adventurous *frisson*; it
was only when it began to affect grown-up women that it
aroused indignation or stirred up the protective instinct.
A number of teachers (at least in the Collège Saint-Charles
and some of the non-religious establishments), including
one who was Jewish herself, issued warnings to their
pupils against these 'dangerous shops' and advised them to
beware of 'certain seductive advances'. Mothers forbade
their daughters to enter such boutiques: they were traps.
By taking these precautionary measures, the women
responsible lent their authority to the authentication of
the myth, and helped to spread the rumour further.

With the transition from teenagers to grown women,
and the addition of five other establishments (four Jewish)
to the original one, *Dorphée*, the myth's anti-Semitic
potential began to become a reality. 'Ah, these Jews . . .'
But at the same time, the myth also came up against
obstinate suspicion and plain incredulity: 'It's ridiculous . . .
it's not possible . . . there are salesgirls around . . .' Such
objections, however, did nothing to stop it.

It was only when it reached the male population that the
rumour encountered a clearly less favourable atmosphere
for development. The boys' schools, unlike the girls', had

not acted as a breeding-ground for the myth in any way. Those boy-friends, fathers, husbands and colleagues who heard about the rumour regarded it as semi-fictional, an old wives' tale, to be taken very much with a grain of salt. The amplification of the myth made many people conscious of its innate grossness; but while rejecting it as it stood they tended to take into account what they thought of as simple exaggeration, and thus often accepted the original version; a case of white slaving which had taken place (or was still going on) in a Jewish-owned shop. But even if they accepted the truth of this clandestine white slave racket, very few of the men felt that their daughter or their wife, let alone the young girls of the town as a whole, were directly threatened by it. The myth's interest for them lay in its impropriety; they regarded it as a dirty story, but refused to become seriously involved, personally, in its implications. Here the rumour was not so much rejected outright as strained off, defused. Hardly any man, it would seem, swallowed the rumour whole.

At the same time, none of them suspected either its nature or its importance. Before 20 May F——, a police inspector, was told of 'abductions' by his schoolgirl daughter. 'Impossible,' he said. 'I'd have known about it.' Nevertheless, he checked the report with his superiors. Their denial that anything of the sort had taken place removed his suspicions and his interest in the affair simultaneously. On 20 May the Public Prosecutor was questioned by his secretaries as to the measures he intended to take against white slaving. Flabbergasted, he got in touch with the Chief of Police. The latter admitted he had heard nothing, and made discreet enquiries—not into the rumour, however, but rather into the lives of the shop-owners against whom such accusations had been brought. Quickly realising that the whole thing was a false alarm, he dropped his investigation. A journalist whom he had tipped off about the affair, and who happened to be a friend of the suspected shop-owners, was far more con-

cerned to go bail for his friends than to investigate the
accusation itself: its anti-Semitic nature was no more
apparent to him than it had been to the Chief of Police.
Also on 20 May, certain Communist militants (and doubtless members of other political parties too) heard rumours
of vanishing girls and white slavery, but did not treat them
as anti-Semitic—or, indeed, as a phenomenon of any
political interest. On 23 May Licht, the owner of *Dorphée*,
learnt through a friend, whose daughter was in high-
school, that a slanderous report was going round about
him, but not that he was caught up in what had by now
become a positively gigantic myth.

Thus even before 24 May the police, the civic authorities,
the political parties and the principal victim were all
aware of the myth; but what they saw was its illogicality
rather than its offensive mythological character. Incredulity, lucidity and commonsense explanations, far
from acting as an obstacle to the rumour's further development, suddenly, without being aware of the fact, gave it
the green light. By tracing the myth back to its original
embodiment as fantasy (or perhaps as a practical joke)
serious-minded people at once lost interest in it. The
police check-up, far from provoking counter-measures,
meant that the whole thing was dropped.

Third stage: metastasis

From now on, in the absence of all repressive measures, an
incredible metastasis took place during the three days
29–31 May. The rumour proliferated wildly. Anything now
added fuel to the flames: even the jokes of unbelievers
were transformed into incriminating evidence. It was
claimed that the shops (some of which were several
hundred yards distant from one another) were all linked by
underground tunnels, and that these tunnels met in a main
sewer that had its outflow into the Loire, where a boat (or
even a submarine) would steal up under cover of dark to
take off its 'cargo'. (Lévy, President of the Jewish Com-

munity, swears that he launched the submarine rumour
on Friday, as a joke, and had it reported back to him
twenty-four hours later as sober truth.)

More and more girls were disappearing. Yet why was it
that the police, who were in the picture, somehow failed to
arrest these white slavers? Were they carrying on with
their enquiries in the hope of smashing the entire ring?
How explain the total silence of the newspapers? Could
they be keeping quiet to avoid prejudicing the success of
the police operation? Anxiety and hysteria, however, soon
sought, and found, an alternative explanation. Thus it
came about that a new rumour emerged and spread, like
wildfire, within the framework of the old one, a parasite
which soon began to look as though it might devour its
host. Everone had been bribed, bought—the police, the
Prefect, the Press—*by the Jews*. The authorities had sold
the pass, and were now acting as agents for these hidden
powers, operating from their underground hideout. . .

The rumour ran wild. On 30 May the shop-owners in
question were so directly threatened that they woke up to
the situation, and found themselves confronted by a
menacing Hydra in which they suddenly recognised the
spectre of anti-Semitism. Licht received anonymous phone-
calls from people wanting 'fresh meat' or addresses in
Tangier. The President of the *Communauté israélite* heard
about these rumours concerning the Jews from his Spanish
shop-assistant. The victims got together, and that afternoon Licht made an urgent appeal to the police. He was
told to wait until Monday—that is, until the day after the
first round in the presidential elections. On Saturday
morning, 31 May, the market-place was like a cyclone area.
Housewives who had come in from all the suburbs round
central Orléans were bursting with alarm and indignation.
Crowds gathered outside the more accessible shops—
Dorphée, *Félix* and *La Boutique de Sheila*. Though this was
the main shopping day, customers were few and far
between. Licht felt himself surrounded by hatred; he

became aware of hostile glances from people in the street, from car drivers who slowed down as they passed his shop-window. He heard, or thought he heard, insulting remarks, such as 'Don't go buying anything from the Jews!' In *La Boutique de Sheila*, Jeannette Buki, who since separating from her husband had run the business single-handed, felt as though she was under siege, and expected an angry mob to break in at any moment. The evening before, one of the assistants at *Alexandrine* had been dragged off by her husband, who burst in shouting: 'I'm not going to let you stay in this place a moment longer!'

Was the crowd, despite its intimidating behaviour, itself intimidated? Did it actively prevent customers from going into the shops, or were they too frightened to do so anyway? (There were a few women customers, but all had escorts.) Had Orléans been on the brink of an explosion, for which only the spark was lacking? At all events, *something* happened—though nothing came of it. In due course closing time arrived, and people went home to dinner. The buses carrying housewives back to the outskirts of town hummed with scandalised comment. In one, the Amrofels' daily woman was told: 'You work for the Jews—you must know all about it!' However, the weekend break was already under way: a doubly effective break, too, since it was also an occasion on which people would be busy voting.

We may profitably ask ourselves, at this point, whether there was any connection between the rumour and the presidential crisis of May 1969. The former developed during the intermediary period between the referendum of 27 April and the presidential elections. It looks as though the two phenomena coincided by accident. The rumour did not interest the *polis*[1] except *in extremis*, as a means of

---

[1] *Polis* here designates 'city' in the social and political sense of that term, rather than with any geographical implication (urban environment, economic agglomeration).

denouncing the treachery of a police force and Press that
had been bought by the Jews. Even then there was no
attempt to link it with the election, which consistently
ignored its very existence. This supports the theory that
there was no connection between the rumour and any kind
of organised political group, and, at a deeper level, confirms its 'primitive' nature. At the same time there may
have been a relation of a different sort between the rumour
and this intermediary or waiting period, supposing that the
latter corresponded to a phase of uncertainty and uneasiness which, firmly thrust down below the level of
conscious political awareness, thereupon retreated to the
depths of the subconscious.

According to this hypothesis, the waiting period, while
certainly not responsible for the rumour, could well have
lent extra impetus to a development which, in other
circumstances, would have remained atrophied—at least
as far as the adult world was concerned. This impetus will
have been produced by the creation of a kind of void, a
section-draught or vacuum into which the rumour was
tumultuously drawn, especially during the two cyclonic
days when last-minute suspense about the election was at
its height. Since the waiting period affected all France
without producing comparable disturbances, one of two
conclusions is inevitable. Either national anxiety was so
deeply repressed that only a really violent psychological
disturbance such as the Orléans incident could reach it
and force it out into the open; or else there was nothing
more involved than a vague, diffuse and not wholly con-
sistent feeling of unease, which the emotional upheaval at
Orléans managed to condense and to monopolise. In either
case, the interim anxiety that followed will have played no
more than a minor part in the proceedings, unimportant by
comparison with the already full-blown (and self-evolved)
rumour. On the other hand, we cannot exclude the possibility that it may have been the decisive factor which
finally triggered off the metastasis. Such a theory is,

B

clearly, almost impossible to prove or disprove, and I advance it here without any real confidence.

Be that as it may, the last days of the campaign meant that any official reaction on the part of the authorities was temporarily postponed; but at the same time Sunday's election put a brake (if only a partial and temporary one) on the impulse behind the rumour. On Monday the rumour broke loose once more, with undiminished energy and enthusiasm; but the new and enlarged dimensions which it had assumed during the period 30–31 May meant that now, at last, it ran into some direct opposition.

JUNE 1969: OPPOSITION, RESORPTION,
    RESIDUA, GERMS

On 30 May, after Licht's complaint and the intervention of the President of the Jewish Community both the Prefecture and City Hall were alerted, but at once translated the affair into political terms, and postponed action until the day after the elections.

On the 31st, the Amrofels' two daughters, one a student and the other a high-school teacher, were informed of the situation by their parents, and at once took action. The former was in Paris, where she knew a number of Jewish students in the *Cercle Bernard Lazare*. Her news at first met with some scepticism (the organisations she contacted treated the whole thing as a practical joke) but on 2 June two national anti-racialist groups, LICA (*Ligue internationale contre le racisme et l'antisémitisme*) and MRAP (*Mouvement contre le racisme et l'antisémitisme et pour la paix*) got wind of the affair. The other daughter, Mme Klein, sent a letter to the Paris papers. A journalist working for *La République du Centre* passed this information to the AFP (*Agence France-Presse*) on 2 June. Nobody published it.

Also on 2 June, Guy Brun, the local LICA representative, heard about the anti-Semitic rumour from a cleaning-woman or secretary in his office, and was subsequently alerted by Paris. On the same day Renée Cosson, a former member of the Resistance and an active Communist militant, who worked for a firm in the suburbs, was told the 'white slave' story by a twenty-two-year-old secretary. She was personally acquainted with some of the shop-owners involved, having protected their family during the Occupation. 'Do you know their names?' she asked the young secretary. 'No, but they're Jewish.' She at once assumed that this was a 'fascist' campaign ('I know all about *that* sort of thing') and warned the Party what was going on.

Last, but by no means least, 2 June saw two brief but virulent articles published in the two provincial dailies. That in the *Nouvelle République* (left-of-centre) was headed 'An Odious Calumny'; that in the *République du Centre* (right-of-centre) 'A Campaign of Defamation'. Both indicated that the victims had lodged an official complaint, but only the first observed that 'behind this cabal one catches a vague whiff of anti-Semitism'. Though these articles completed the dissemination of the rumour, by carrying it into any sector of the community which might still be unaware of it,[1] the Press had nevertheless struck a powerful initial blow against its further development. By the same token, what had hitherto been a clandestine, underground affair now came into the orbit of the *polis*, politics and the police.

A vigorous counter-offensive now developed, conducted at first by the provincial press, and subsequently, from 7 June onwards, by the national press in Paris. The first official statement appeared on 3 June and came from the

---

[1] We are unable to indicate here the percentage of the population which the rumour reached on 31 May and 2 June—or the percentage of these whom the virus actually contaminated. The important point to realise is that while the rumour had reached every sector of the population (both sociological and geographical) *before* the Press intervened, nevertheless it found some sectors that were 'good' conductors, some that were 'bad'. We shall return to this point later.

Parents' Association of pupils in the Lycée Jean-Zay and
the CES Jeanne-d'Arc. Its signatory, Rebaudet, had at
first been seriously worried by the rumour, and on Friday
30 May had gone round to the Central Police Station to
seek enlightenment on the matter. Here he had run into
Licht (*Dorphée*), who at once disabused him of his mis-
conception. Conscience-stricken, he moved swiftly into
the forefront of the counter-attack against the rumour.
Formal statements of protest and condemnation continued to appear from 3 to 9 June. They emanated from
local associations of former deportees and Resistance
workers, from political parties of the Left and Centre
(except for the *Ve Union Départementale*, which abstained),
from the *Fédération de l'Education Nationale*, and from
a high-school branch of the *Comité d'Action pour la
Liberté Scolaire*. Two members of the Parents' Association
of the Lycée Pothier published a statement on their own,
which shows that the Association itself had not been
willing to join in the fray.

The Bishop of Orléans wrote a letter in which he expressed the wish that 'a speedy end might be put to this
odious cabal'. The Châtelet Mixed Chamber of Commerce
and the Union of Orléanais Tradesmen and Manufacturers
published a statement denouncing the affair. Some attacked the slander, the 'odious cabal'. Others (e.g. the
Loiret Communist Party Association) chose rather to
emphasise 'this anti-Semitic campaign' which 'recalls the
mores of Hitler's Third Reich', and hinted that 'those
close to Tixier-Vignancourt and Xavier Vallet are doubtless no strangers to this odious cabal'. At national level,
Jewish and anti-racialist organisations issued statements,
badgered the authorities, and got in touch with various
well known figures in the *département*. On 4 June
the LICA held a branch meeting in the town hall of
Saint-Jean de la Ruelle. Numerous influential persons
attended, including representatives of the Centre Democrats, the Radicals, the Socialists and the Deportees'

Associations. It was decided to lodge an official complaint.

On Sunday 8 June, Louis Guilloux presided over a round-table conference in the Orléans *Maison de la Culture*, the topic being 'Slander, defamation and racism'. This was open to the general public, and brought together a wide range of people, representing various shades of opinion, among them some 'leftists'. An anti-defamation committee was set up, and a round robin sent out for the populace at large to sign (it only collected about a thousand names). Between 7 and 10 June the Paris press entered the lists, most notably with an article in *Le Monde* and news coverage by *L'Aurore*, *L'Express* and *Le Nouvel Observateur*.

Thus the period between 2 and 12 June saw a decisive battle fought out between the whisperers and the printed word, between myth and rebuttal, between the rumour and the *polis*. From now on the myth could only do one of two things: deflate itself, or expand still further, to bursting point; and it was becoming progressively more difficult to believe that a group of Jewish white slavers was in control of *everything*—public institutions, almost all the political parties, the national press. Although the official authorities—Prefect, Mayor, Public Prosecutor—avoided making any open statements on the matter, nevertheless all these interventions by various parties and organisations, coupled with official complaints and threats of legal action (not to mention words like 'slander', 'cabal', 'racism' and 'Hitlerism') had the effect of intimidating and discouraging the rumour-mongers—though at the same time triggering off a few minor boomerang-reactions. Then the tide began to turn ('least said about all *that* soonest mended') and there followed a growing inclination to forget the whole episode. ('Oh no, I never believed it,' said one person we interviewed, even while recalling various temporary doubts experienced at the time—doubts which came a good deal closer to suspicion than to scepticism.) By the end of the first week in June, the shop-owners who formed the target for the rumour had got all their old clientèle back.

After 15 June one or two further news items appeared concerning the judicial complaints and gestures of protest, but the only local event of any note was the MRAP's round-table conference of 26 June, on the theme 'Watch out for race-prejudice'. About two hundred people rallied round the movement's national leaders. They ranged from the widow of Jean Zay, a former local Deputy, to the Area Secretary of the FEN (*Fédération de l'Education Nationale*), from the Abbé Sejourné to Dumas, the Protestant minister. On 4 July Sidos, a leader of the extreme right wing, held a meeting (announced before the affair). Those present included about twenty ex-deportees and a similar number of representatives from the Jewish community. The hall was ringed with police cars, and the speaker never once referred either to the affair, or to the Jews.

The anti-myth campaign petered out by the beginning of July, and the authorities closed their file on the case. On the eve of 4 July, a national holiday, the entire affair seemed to have been wound up and forgotten. On 17 July, a police spokesman, talking over the telephone to Pierre Andrau, who was producing a television programme about the affair, on Channel Four, declared: 'It's a dead letter as far as we're concerned.'

The rumour could be regarded as effectively squashed by mid-June. Yet at the time of our own investigation (early July), numerous sub-rumours had been thrown up by its disintegrating fragments, and were in circulation everywhere. The myth had been smashed and broken up; yet it could still dissolve into a swarm of mini-myths.

We ascertained and established the following facts:

1. Even after the dismissal of the myth a vague substratum of fear remained. This affected elderly women, who had never been into this kind of shop ('From now on

we'll keep clear of these rather exclusive Jewish establishments'), and girls and young women, who during June
were prepared to patronise such boutiques, but almost
always under escort; their companion might be a girl-
friend, a man or even a dog. The shop-owners had been
exonerated, but people still felt vaguely uneasy about
them.

2. In certain under-informed and peripheral sectors of
the population the myth either lingered on, or actually
underwent (in attenuated, derivative or residual form) a
species of renaissance. During 4–5 June a circumstantial
mini-rumour began to circulate, to the effect that the
brother-in-law of one of the shop-owners had just been
arrested by the police as a white slaver. Early in July
another rumour asserted that two young girls, relatives
of a woman (de Saint-Marc) who ran a draper's shop, had
been abducted—though in what circumstances, and by
whom, was not made clear. On 7 July the (elderly) priest
of a parish only four kilometres out of town told a fellow-
cleric: 'It really does seem true that they give young girls
"contracts" at *Alexandrine*'s' (i.e. working contracts for
pseudo-careers in exotic countries). The priest was still
advising his flock to give this 'wicked place' a very wide
berth.

Very often the idea persisted that somewhere, somehow,
some person or persons *had* been trafficking in young girls,
or that at the very least some odd disappearances had
taken place. However, from now on no-one quite knew
where to locate this traffic. People believed it had been
wrongly attributed to the shop-owners incriminated by the
original rumour, perhaps to divert the suspicions which
the real traffickers must have aroused, or maybe out of
pure spite. According to other new reports, *something* very
shady had been going on, of which the shop-owners were
either the instigators or the victims, and the white slaving
story was made up as a cover for some quite different
operation.

In all these cases, the explanation of the myth took on a
mythological character, and the original rumour was
replaced by a multiplicity of smaller ones. One allegation
was that 'there's a German behind it all' (who as a German,
a fortiori a Nazi, had started the anti-Semitic rumour);
people would mention the name of the German chain-store
that had branches in the area. Another suggestion was
that 'it's all a capitalist plot'. Elderly members of the
working-class saw the whole affair as a by-product of that
eternal fight which the rich and powerful keep up on the
backs of 'ordinary folk'. Yet another idea was that trade
rivalry underlay the whole thing. The Jewish shop-owners'
chief competitors were suspected of having tried to discredit them; sometimes, indeed, the Jewish shop-owners
themselves were occasionally suspected of spreading the
report that they had been slandered in order to discredit
their rivals.

3.   Put very broadly, the rumour rested on a persistent
suspicion, which found expression in two aphoristic statements: 'Someone's hiding something from us', and—above
all—'There's no smoke without fire.'

The second of these assertions, 'no smoke without fire',
forms the central backbone of all theories, every alleged
piece of 'evidence', and each new resurgence of the myth.
It forms the point of departure for the secondary proliferation in May 1969, and for its ultimate residuum. It is
the alpha and the omega of mythology, the final stage
which precedes a regression to some new beginning. In
June and July, however, there was no longer one myth,
but a mishmash of mini-myths; and consequently, no
general consensus of opinion on the nature of the fire that
gave off so thick a smoke.

4.   Conjointly with, or alternatively to, the themes
already mentioned, there was a tendency to discredit the
anti-myth campaign on the following grounds: it was the
Communists, or the Left in general, that had organised
the entire affair in order to make trouble (or propaganda);

journalists, who were either 'short of copy' or 'sensation-mongering', had blown up the whole scandal artificially, on the basis of a few old wives' tales; the Jewish shop-owners had launched the affair themselves in order to get publicity.

Such explanations do not in fact reject the myth, but merely repress it to the point of total amnesia, and, at the same time, see the anti-myth as an extravagant invention. Here we have the rumour's ultimate, last ditch strategy and line of defence: to denounce the anti-myth as though it were the myth, demystification as though it were mystification, the antidote as though it were the poison.

The journalists, and those organisations which attacked the rumour, now become the new guilty parties; and in the third 'explanation' the Jewish shop-owners, though no longer guilty of white slaving, are made responsible for such a notion having gained ground in the first place. This final theory implicitly admits that the whole 'white slave rumour' was a colossal fraud; but it lumps myth and anti-myth together in the same process of deception. Both result from the Jewish businessman's unscrupulous passion for filthy lucre. It contrives, by a remarkable *tour de force*, to discard the myth in a Jewish rubbish bin, and by so doing to keep its anti-Semitic virus alive.

One striking formula, which linked this 'explanation' with the preceding one (sensation-mongering journalists), was picked up by TV reporters on 20 July, interviewing people as they came out from Mass. One woman declared that nothing had happened in Orléans, nothing at all. 'In that case,' she was asked, 'why all the fuss?' With a knowing smile she replied: 'Papers have to keep up their circulation, and shops need to boost their trade.'

Thus the anti-myth gained a victory on the field of battle, but, like an army in occupied territory, failed to make itself complete master of the terrain. The myth left residual fragments and germs behind it, which launched

a guerilla campaign of mini-rumours designed to drive out
the stranger in their midst. At the same time, the disintegration of the myth, the very dispersal of its fragments,
brought it into contact with themes endemic to the popular
conscience, and gave these a new lease of life: the struggle
between capitalist big-shots at the expense of the little
man, cut-throat competition between rival commercial
firms, a conspiracy of silence (or lies) on the part of the
Press, political quarrels and manoeuvres. At the same
time, such political upheavals awoke memories of the
Occupation and the Resistance, of pro- and anti-
Communist battles. Thus the month of June was not a
period of resorption pure and simple, but one during which
people's collective memory, after a severe shaking up,
forced itself (in diverse ways, and with a great feeling of
confusion) to swallow, digest, assimilate and reject both
myth and anti-myth. Resorption was also absorption, and
the rout of the enemy not only drove the affair *back*,
across an external frontier, but also thrust it *down*, into
the hidden depths; and the logical consequence of this
diversion to the deep hidden level of the psyche was,
inevitably, amnesia. Thus a strange concoction, containing
both germs and residuum, forcibly penetrated the town's
subconscious mind, feeding and colouring it, in ways one
can only guess at, perhaps for ever.

CONCLUSION

In two months, a rumour completed a full life-cycle at
Orléans. It sprang from the subterranean depths of the
unconscious, and in due course returned there. Proliferat-
ing from a germ—of which we can determine both the
double mythological origin and the actual fantasy-source
—it passed through a period of incubation (10–20 May),
entered its virulent and rapidly expanding phase (20–27
May), burst out in a tremendous metastasis (29–31 May)
disintegrated under the pressure of a counter-attack (2–10
June), regressed into fantasy and mini-rumours, and

finally blanketed itself in amnesia, leaving only germs and residual fragments behind.

During the course of this cycle, 'people say' became transformed first into certainty, then into actual accusation, after which it reverted to mere suspicion and uneasiness, or sank into total oblivion. Fantasy transformed itself first into a myth, then into sheer delirium, after which it once more became fantasy, while the myth left behind numerous mini-myths, by way of legacy. A purely fabulous tale turned into a historical pseudo-event, stirred up scandal, all but started a panic, then became a bizarre and rather shady enigma.

This fantasy or fabulous tale, with its leitmotiv of 'they say', germinated more or less simultaneously among two related groups: adolescent girls in high-school or college, and working teenagers in shops, offices and factories. It spread by way of hairdressing salons and other public meeting-places (e.g. the market-place); from these groups it reached parents, colleagues and fellow-employees, swarming out towards the suburbs and the countryside. From adolescents and teenage girls it spread to grown women. By the time it really exploded even the men were beginning, here and there, to be convinced by it. It penetrated all sectors of the town and, with varying degrees of success, every level of society. During this evolutionary process a myth developed and was transformed. Like a living entity, it threw out phagocytes, proliferated, struggled to survive; finally it disintegrated into fragments (which retained a life of their own) and died away. We must now attempt to elucidate this myth.

TWO
STRUCTURE OF A MYTH

NEW-LOOK WHITE SLAVERY : A NOVEL ARCHETYPE

The White Slave Traffic

The entire mythological pyramid that grew up in Orléans rests on a basis of white slavery. This is a perfectly genuine phenomenon, well known, often described, documented and guaranteed true by newspaper and other similar reports. The white slave traffic operates according to a familiar pattern. Naive or penniless young girls, after an initial process of seduction and/or mystification, are won over by promises of travel, or richly remunerative jobs abroad. They are then sent off to various exotic ports overseas, where they find themselves, in fact, forced to become prostitutes. The white slave trade is an underworld activity, run by crooks, pimps, racketeers and gangsters. Natives of Marseilles are particularly associated with it; so are Corsicans, North Africans and other similar 'foreigners'. In France, whatever the case may be elsewhere,[1] Jews are hardly ever connected with white slaving.

Since it first came into being, the white slave trade has always exercised a twofold fascination on people. It combines two potently attractive elements—sex and the

---

[1] In some other countries (e.g. Poland) the situation would appear to be rather different; here Jews are traditionally supposed to play an important part in the white slave traffic.

44

criminal underworld—at their single, subterranean source:
elementary drives, at once aggressive and sexual, of the
sort that our well policed society and the super-ego of the
moral conscience constantly repress, so that their only
outlet is through reading, entertainment or fantasy. At
this level the theme unites an imaginary male figure (with
a bent for violence, abduction and the possession of women)
and an imaginary female figure (obsessed by rape, the
idea of being carried off, and prostitution). This is why the
white slave traffic has always given rise to so vast a proliferation of novels, stories, newspaper articles, television
programmes and documentary reports—a flow which
shows no sign of abating, and which caters for every type
of public. In this field facts stimulate the imagination, and
the imagination then stimulates the facts; both tend to
contaminate each other, in a highly active amalgam of
fantasy and reality.

In its traditional form, the white slaving motif never
strayed beyond the 'low quarters' and 'shady bars'; in
small towns, it would attach itself to some particular
innkeeper. But if it is true that white slavers move with
the times, and adapt their methods to modern civilisation;
if they now entrap girls with the lure of modish boutiques,
and employ such technical devices as the hypodermic
syringe or the drugged chocolate; if, moreover, they set up
their snares in broad daylight, and on the busiest streets—
why, then the danger, hitherto limited and peripheral,
becomes omnipresent. Situated at the very heart of the
town it can, by the same token, become a permanent,
fundamental, feminine obsession.

Statistically, the risk is negligible. Psychologically, however, it has everywhere entered the realm of the possible.
It is not hard to see how the formidable fantasy-cum-erotic
potential attaching to the white slave trade motif could,
at the slightest disturbing stimulus, spill over wholesale
into everyday life. It is not hard to foresee an increasingly
active—and increasingly confused—blending of romantic

fiction and real life fact; from here it is only a short step
to the point at which reality presents the romantic
characteristics of fiction, and fiction borrows genuine
features from reality. The no-man's-land between truth
and fiction is already a broad enough fringe area in all the
mass media; it will inevitably expand still further in the
naive minds—let alone the souls—of young girls. Any
equivocal or ambiguous incident in real life—a prolonged
pressure of the hand in a fitting-room, a hard stare from a
shop-owner, the unexplained absence of the girl next
door—will suffice to remind one of the archetypal scenario.
Such a reminder (e.g. the article in *Noir et Blanc*) can
metamorphose some common feature of urban life—an
attractive shop-window, for instance—into an equivocal
and ambiguous symbol; and beyond a certain point the
symbol loses its ambiguity, becomes perfectly clear,
testifies to the realisation, *hic et nunc*, of the scenario
itself.

This script or scenario, as I pointed out earlier, has
figured very widely in pulp literature and the sensational
gutter-press since about 1960. Though such a new-look
version of the old white slave motif may have some
interest for men, clearly its main concern is with women,
above all with adolescents and young girls. We can see how
it corresponds with certain fantasies that assume a particularly virulent form during adolescence, a time when
sexual awareness is still mainly fantasy, an age at which
erotic longing, terror and anguish all blend and ferment
together. The emancipation of the modern girl, far from
putting a stop to such fantasies, actually encourages them.
It is not merely that the danger of white slavery now lurks
in the very heart of town, in broad daylight, looming over
each and every girl; it is also due to the fact that, with fewer
and fewer restrictions, these adolescents and teenagers can
now go to cafés, visit shops, try on dresses, go out in the evening, meet strangers. They do not, it is true, have that terror
of 'the big city' which formerly afflicted the young

provincial girl (whether from village or small town) who had never been let out on her own. Yet their continual exposure, day and night, to the hazards of city streets, the solicitations of desire, means that they are endlessly bombarded with countless tiny stimuli, which variously induce erotic longing, terror and fantasy.

Mothers and teachers regard such premature emancipation as a threat not only to their young girls, but also to their own authority as guardians. This, combined with the fermenting erotic fantasies that still afflict married women (and indeed mothers of families), explains the tendency they have to exaggerate the dangers which threaten the young: they are protecting, not only their adolescent girls, but also their own status. Hence, too, the habit of seeking out (and finding) specific fixed points round which their vague fears and resentments can crystallise. Thus for reasons which in ways are similar (but in another sense very different) the white slave motif can serve as a focal point for teenagers and grown women alike. Given propitious conditions, it is not at all hard to see how the 'white slave trade myth' could expand beyond its normal juvenile incubation area, and penetrate every sector of female society. Such a development would encourage a dialectic of contagion and confirmation, thus ensuring that the myth was propagated wholesale.

We see, then, that the modernisation of the white slave trade, the modernisation of the myth which it engenders, the modernisation of the teenage girl, the modernisation of life and the city are precisely the conditions which facilitated the emergence of a rumour which, on the face of it, was so retrograde as to seem positively medieval. At Orléans, as elsewhere, what we have to do with is not backward provincial tittle-tattle, but rumours that unfold in the heart of modern urban agglomerations, including the metropolis itself (and with an energy that gathers up provincial tittle-tattle as it goes); not old wives' tales, but conversations between trendy young girls: not the fan-

tasmagorias of a closed world, but fantasies disseminated
by the swinging generation, an integral product of the
Zeitgeist.

We must now analyse the succulent nourishment, the
hallucinogenic factors that fed this myth, and thus
enabled it to inebriate an entire town.

Anaesthetic injections, drugged sweets

With the introduction of sleep-inducing injections and
sweets, the drug, it might be said, replaces the drag. From
the viewpoint of fantasy, this element makes a welcome
and easy change from the subornation of naive young girls
by some louche seducer. The sophistication spread by
modern mores and a wider knowledge of the world meant,
in effect, that the old technique would now only work on
really stupid and ignorant girls. The devices employed
now—a sweet proffered by some respectable looking lady
or gentleman, the surreptitious insertion of a hypodermic
needle in the fitting-room of a shop-owner whose premises
stood on the main road—were such as might well deceive
girls who combined virtuousness and sophistication in
about equal quantities.

At the fantasy level, injection and drugged sweet have
a double and interdependent function to perform. The
first is that of esculpation. Even before, the act of seductive
beguilement had the effect—in fantasy—of removing all
blame from the girl herself, who could then dream of
being an *unwilling* prostitute. She bore no guilt, but was
rather a victim, and could thus enjoy the imaginary
benefits of moral compassion in addition to those provided
by physical pleasure. The sweet takes advantage of the
adolescent girl's natural sweet tooth (behind which lurk
the delicious mysteries of orality), while the injection
puts even a virtuous woman to sleep unawares; both
guarantee total exoneration. Their second function is as
an extra erotic stimulus. Though the drug is here reduced
to its anaesthetic aspect, it nevertheless preserves the aura

of its aphrodisiac associations. The syringe with which it is administered (and which is more popular in fantasy than a drugged sweet) performs an act of penetration: this penetration has actual erotic effects besides being sexually symbolic. It is, in every sense, the prick of love: not the spiritualised love of idyllic romances or marriage, but the love which starts deep in the vagina, and longs to fulfil itself (at least in fantasy) by plumbing the lowest depths of social degradation. By this injection a woman is transformed, not merely into a chattel, an object for sexual commerce, but also into woman-as-love-object, the cosmic whore, dedicated to deep and primal pleasures.

There is, I fancy, another element involved here, which lurks within the notion of a drug *per se*, rather like the contents of Pandora's box. It is a remarkable fact that the myth never specifies the actual substance employed. One might suppose it was afraid of lessening its own impact by naming some common or garden anaesthetic; it is as though it wished to maintain, within the aura created by the very word 'drug', all those associations it summons up, and all the commutations it could guarantee.

We may remind ourselves, at this point, that 'drugs' are no longer a mere abstraction for young people in cities—Orléans included. Introduced recently among certain groups of adolescents, the use of marijuana and of LSD is spreading rapidly. Young people talk and dream of 'acid' and 'turning on'; their fascination with the subject betrays a mixture of attraction and repulsion, fear and desire. Thus the presence of a 'drug' at one key point in this juvenile white slave fantasy must irradiate a whole sequence of ideas in the subconscious mind.

First we have the drug-travel association. The injection of this drug, in the fitting-room, forms the prelude to an exotic voyage, to 'going abroad'. Now the desire to travel is an almost obsessional passion among girls and young women. This became clear the moment we began our enquiries in Orléans ('Aren't you lucky, being able to

travel!'), just as it had done during previous interviews,
held when we were investigating another provincial town.[1]
Is it mere coincidence that the extraordinary sense of
escape which such drugs induce in those who use them
(Americans to begin with, then their French imitators)
should be known as *taking a trip*? Like a two-way turntable, linking intercontinental travel with that other
journey, to the interior of one's self, the drug motif opens
the gates of imaginary adventure still more widely. The
kind of adventure, I mean, that is to be found in television
serials or pulp fiction, and which sends its addicts travel-
ling, in fantasy, not only through the criminal underworld
of the big cities, but also into the mysteries of the In-
telligence Services, whose agents employ such drugs as a
weapon. Thus the drug motif, considered mythologically,
extends far beyond the idea of an anaesthetic endowed
with latent aphrodisiac qualities; it constitutes a mar-
vellous invitation to take a trip, any kind of trip—out of
town, through the wide world, in the parallel and multiple
universes of the imagination, into the cosmic depths of
the self.

We see, then, that the drug injection, by reason of all
the connotations and associations it stirs up, unconsciously
acquires a far wider field of application than its merely
functional role in a cleverly organised racket. From echo to
echo, from one analogy to another, from dream to dream
and myth to myth, from the cervical cortex to the depths
of the vagina and back again, it constitutes the key source
of erotic stimulus and fantasy—a fantasy which is encouraged and excited by the injection itself, in a hidden
summons to accursed passion, to the impossible journey,
the forbidden escape, the ecstasy of the abyss.

The fitting-room
Modern feminine dress-design has undeniable erotic im-

---

[1] *Plodemet: Report from a French Village*, Allen Lane the Penguin Press,
London, 1971; Fayard, Paris, 1967.

plications. The 'young miss' dress contrives to absorb and tone down the plunging neck-lines or midi-skirts of the emancipated avant-garde, and—as far as the provincial towns are concerned—to embody the virtues of elegance and seductiveness that one associates with Paris. It is in the boutiques devoted to fashions of this sort that the diffuse erotic powers latent in dress and skirt, outer garments and underwear, ribbons and frills tend to gather and spread themselves; but it is, above all, in the fitting-rooms of such places that they achieve maximum concentration and intensity. It was just such boutiques—and their fitting-rooms—that the white slave myth picked on as a location; and by bringing in the establishment known as *Félix*, it added the element of foot and shoe fetishism for good measure.

The fitting-room is a private place, and, like the toilet, somewhat taboo, the difference between them being that the fitting-room enjoys a less total degree of privacy. For the most part it is only shut off by a curtain; and the mirror which it invariably contains facilitates voyeurism and fantasy. Undressing in such circumstances is somewhere halfway between doing it in your own bedroom and performing a strip-tease act. You contemplate and rediscover your own person, under the intimate yet unfamiliar self-to-self gaze which the mirror reflects. It is by no means uncommon for a girl to be accompanied by her boy-friend, or to leave the curtain half open. Some wear no pants; is this their normal practice, or just for the occasion? Narcissism and exhibitionism flourish here with naive abandon. The setting both encourages and exonerates them. When you want to try on a dress, surely it is necessary, the normal thing, to undress, and move your hips and body about, and get other people in to look at you?

Trying on a dress legitimises what would otherwise be taboo, lifts a minor barrier of censorship, and thus becomes charged with a half-latent, half-open eroticism. If the salesgirl's hands linger a moment during the fitting, this is willingly construed as a lesbian caress or invitation. Every dress that is tried on provokes fresh mannequin-like poses, more attitudinising, a physical perfomance calculated to set off fantasy sequences in the mind. It is all a game, a dream, a metamorphosis.

You came here to choose a dress; but you would like to try on other dresses, the most attractive and expensive ones. You want a whole mass of dresses—not to mention all those other nice things, so strange and so seductive, which are apparently being offered you. But one thing holds you back: money. You feel, at some deep level, that the fitting-room is a place of temptations—temptations to which you can only succumb in your dreams.

Thus the fitting-room is, at one and the same time, the erogenic setting in which a young girl transforms herself into a source of seduction and an object of desire; the dream-palace in which her physical nakedness, and her metamorphoses, give rise to a thousand fantasies; and a place of temptation which sets her desires aflutter. It is, in fact, a hothouse, where the fantastic, the seductive and the erotic mingle and stimulate one another; and is it not also, in one sense, a secret chapel of love, in which, all unknowing, one worships Eros as a devotee, unconsciously invoking the act of transubstantiation?

It should by now be clear how the myth contrived to attach itself to such a place, to settle in it, and by so doing to install the fitting-room as a central element of its own structure. It is an ordinary place, visited by adolescents, teenagers and young women in ever increasing numbers; yet it is also a *different* place, which suddenly lifts them out of their everyday lives. It is a functional place, specially designed for trying on dresses, and at the same time a place of magic, the scene of something resembling that performance or mime associated with an act of initiation in the mysteries by which a woman is fulfilled as a being made for love. It is a place of reassurance, where every kind of deceit is permitted; but also the alarming place in which you are liable to be jabbed by a hypodermic. Once it establishes itself in that fitting-room, the myth is going to squeeze every last heady drop out of the latent eroticism inherent in undressing and trying on new dresses—and then, suddenly, inject this mixture straight into one's flesh with a hypodermic syringe. The injection both induces oblivion, and facilitates the accomplishment of a too-bold fantasy which otherwise would overstep the limits permitted by censorship. It is like a trap-door suddenly opening under sin, to swallow it up in the dark night of the senses, and bring it to fulfilment *down there*, far away, somewhere different. . .

Thus the fitting-room forms an ideal substitute for the louche inn or the shady bar, in the sense that now *every* girl and young woman can feel herself personally concerned, worried, threatened even, by the white slave trade. But there is more to it than this; it is also the perfect setting for a girl or young woman to have around her when she is catapulted into that mysterious fantasy-ridden no-man's-land between the act of undressing and making oneself desirable, and the act of prostitution. It does not merely incarnate a fantasy-myth in the midst of one's daily life, at the very heart of the city; it also skims off all the dream-vapours and virulent erotic fancies which city-centre and daily life produce. If the injection constitutes the mythological instrument by which sin and innocence are conjoined, the seeds of such a conjunction already exist in the actual dress (which serves not only as clothing but also to make the wearer desirable), and in the fitting-room, which enables a girl both to change her dress and exhibit herself narcissistically.

So we see that it is the administration of an injection (involving marked overtones of both fantasy and the erotic) which provides this myth with its centre of gravity. It is the juxtaposition of these two elements which forms the shackle necessary to link two chains together: one

based on everyday life, on the idea of the pure young girl
or virtuous woman, and leading to the little changing-
room; the other starting from the lower depths of prostitution, and prowling round the streets of the city by night.
This operation makes it possible to divert all 'badness'
onto the injection, while canalising any sin towards the
shop-owner-cum-white-slaver. By the same token it permits the unification of two states—sin and innocence—
which the super-ego (both society's and that of the individual) keeps firmly apart.

By so doing, the white slave myth goes to the very heart
of all myth, which rejoins what society separates, performs
what it treats as taboo, and unifies what is contradictory.
It comes in at the tail-end of a great mythological *Arkhe*,[1]
which was responsible, during the nineteenth century, for
the widespread popularity of that romantic legend in
which a virgin became a prostitute, yet remained pure.
The white slave trade—a social phenomenon rooted in the
underworld—has given this legend genuine, modern and
non-fictional support. The new 'white slave motif' was
born of the modernisation this racket underwent; it dwells
on the fact of its modernity, adapts it to the New
Modernity in general, and (better still) not only owes its
mythic genesis to this modernity, but sets itself up at the
very heart of it, amid our new urban agglomerations.

Once again, we find a close conjunction between *Arkhe*
and New Modernity. This is no chance encounter; as I
pointed out above, it is the New Modernity itself which
engenders the return of the *Arkhe*. Yet this *Arkhe* is all
cluttered about with the realities of news items, bulletins,
daily life, shops, the city; and in this amalgam of the real,
the plausible and the fabulous, *it has made itself an astonishing and explosive mixture of dream and reality*. This
transfigures places that are quite genuine (if full of fictional

---

[1] *Arkhe*: a principle at once fundamental, primitive and ideal, which
modern mythologies either rediscover unconsciously or else are deliberately searching for.

touches) by making them the scene of a white slave traffic well enough attested elsewhere, but here a mere product of the imagination. Or rather, by fictitiously juxtaposing certain places and a racket, which though authentic *per se* have been torn from their proper social context, it succeeds in mythologising them both.

By leaning on these two pillars of reality, the fantasy is able, in an hysterical fashion, to secrete a reality of its own, and thus to become myth. How did the young rumour-mongers of Orléans react to those who showed incredulity, even in the face of personal testimony that was guaranteed from a reliable source? 'Don't you read the papers?' (which describe such things as abductions, and drugging, and the white slave traffic). Or, again, 'How naive can you get?' (to assume that such a thing is impossible), or alternatively 'You're too old' (i.e. 'You're not in the groove', or 'You don't know what's going on'), which comes to the same thing. In this way a complete reversal was achieved between the believable and the unbelievable, between credibility and credulity. Thus what we have to deal with is a real myth, in the archaic sense of the word (and not in that attenuated sense according to which a myth can be *experienced* without inducing *belief*); that is, an imaginary narrative, organised consistently within the framework of its own psycho-affective logic, which claims to be rooted in reality and truth.

A sporadic, intermittent, epidemic type of myth, to be sure; it somewhat resembles those complex amino-structured viruses, with a biological nature which remains latent for a long period, until, suddenly, they begin to live and proliferate. What factor was lacking to give this myth an all-consuming life of its own? The Jew, perhaps?

THE JEW

The Jew is wholly absent from all news items, reports and fictional accounts put out by the mass media concerning the white slave trade: and his appearance in provincial

rumours seems, on the face of it, both surprising and
preposterous.

The myth, which starts from a fitting-room and leads
to white slavery, is to all appearances complete, and in its
narrative form seems wholly self-sufficient. Yet when one
sets it against the traditional white slavery motif, one
realises there is a blank space to be filled, one previously
taken up by the shady tavern-keeper, the criminal seducer,
the Marseillais, Corsican or generally 'foreign' crook. Up
to a point, of course, the place is occupied by a shop-owner,
and any shop-owner could, *prima facie*, be cast in this
Jekyll-and-Hyde role. Yet from the mythological viewpoint such an arrangement clearly fails to fill the bill. The
shop-owner must not be a mere faceless cypher; he must,
like the crook, be *the one who*. If the new white slave myth
is to regain its fundamental archaism, it will be highly
desirable, if not essential, for it to find an archetypally
two-faced figure to play the central role, that of the shop-
owner-cum-white-slaver.

Just who *is* this mysterious person? Who is this seemingly honest tradesman who owns a modern boutique, and
would be well content with what he has were it not for the
strange rapacity that consumes him? Who is this being,
on the face of it like any other shop-owner, like anybody
else, period, who nevertheless belongs in secret to a mysterious alien world? Who is this two-faced monster of
duplicity, living at the heart of our cities and yet alien to
them, behind whose blandly reassuring front lurks a
menacing personality?

Enter the Jew.

To begin with, it is statistically plausible that, if a white
slave traffic *is* being organised through the agency of
ready-made dress shops, especially in the provinces, the
shop-owner concerned should be Jewish. We should have
to ascertain the proportion of Jews to non-Jews in the
garment industry for girls and young women in order to
estimate the statistical probability of a myth which, the

moment it took root in the provinces, seems to have concentrated one hundred per cent on the Jew. As we saw
when discussing Cassegrain's *Les Oubliettes*, the myth
carefully avoids the *non*-Jewish. It does not, statistically
speaking, pick any fashion-boutique proprietor at random.
It goes straight for a Jewish one. On the other hand it is
able to make such a choice because the large number of
Jews in the ready-made dress business permits it.

The choice itself is, on the face of it, absurd, to the extent
that nothing hitherto had suggested the least connection
between Jews and white slaving. But it begins to make
much more sense when we consider how exactly the Jew
fits that Jekyll-and-Hyde role which the myth needs if it
is to take on a life of its own. His connection with the town
is slight, or of recent origin, and his line of business a
comparatively new one. He is, more often than not, a
young man, not at all like the old Jews with funny
accents, who are quite obviously not 'one of us'. He is
just like anyone else; he doesn't even possess the famous
hook-nose which enables us to recognise 'them'. Herein,
precisely, lies his two-faced quality: he is exactly like
everybody else yet he is different, *Jewish*. That is to say,
he *conceals* the difference, which is so mysterious and so
disturbing. Furthermore, he is already somewhat suspect.
What we have here is not the general vague suspicion
which hovers round Jews as such, but a more specific,
indeed a local anxiety. These boutiques started from
nothing, and in a few years became extremely prosperous,
especially *Dorphée*.

'He arrived here with his hands in his pockets' (the implication being that his pockets were empty). 'How did
he make such a profit so fast when he sells at the prices he
does?' The myth—on the side, as it were—provides a
solution to this economic puzzle: the dresses sell cheap,
but the women whom they entice fetch a very good price
indeed. Thus the Jew enables the fantasy to acquire life
hic et nunc. In the earlier myth, located elsewhere, there is

no Jew. Had he already appeared in the great capital, that quasi-abstract milieu?

Are we to assume that he emerges sometimes, often? . . . The paucity of our information precludes any answer to this question. In any case, when we turn to the concrete myth, the one that exists on our own doorstep, in our town, here and now, yes, there are one or two Jews. The Jew allows the myth to take on a life of its own in the city because he achieves its physical embodiment. He steps into the empty place, becomes the guilty two-faced villain whom this myth demands. His outward appearance, that of a perfectly respectable shop-owner, completely exonerates the young victim from any suspicion of wrong-doing. As a Jew he is naturally suspect, and thus the obvious person to shoulder the blame.

At the same time the rumour is totally unaware that it has picked a suitable candidate (or candidates) from its reserve pool of suitable scapegoats—nor even that such a pool exists for its benefit. During the initial phase there is no reference to 'the Jew' or 'the Jews'; instead we hear of 'a Jewish shop-owner', 'some Jewish shop-owners'. The fact of their Jewishness seems to be a minor, contingential attribute. At this stage, the 'he's-a-Jew' line comes as an afterthought: 'Oh, I heard it from my daughter in high-school—she absolutely believed it. So did I at first. They're Jews, you know.' (This woman was a member of *Action Catholique*.) 'There's white slaving going on from *Dorphée* and some of the other boutiques.' 'Do you know their names?' 'No, but I do know they're Jews' (conversation between Renée Causson and a young stenographer in her firm).

Thus the mythological sequence does not begin with an 'It's-the-Jews-who' line, nor does it offer a 'Because-they're-Jews' explanation for itself. At this level there is no conscious awareness of anti-Semitism, and those few people who already detect its presence, and say so, get the obvious answer: 'Why not? You get Bretons in the white slave trade, and people from Auvergne, so I suppose there are a few Jews, too.' Moreover, this non-awareness of anti-Semitism encouraged the propagation of the myth, and it was not until the feverish metastasis got under way that anyone picked up the 'anti-Semitism' alarm-signal.

Jew underground, Jewish phantom, Jewish fantasy
To begin with, then, the myth was not utilised against the Jews; rather it utilised a Jew to plug the hole in its mythology. But this hole was concerned with malice and culpability, and the plug already carried within it the virus of both vices. It follows that a *de facto* case of anti-Semitism can be made out from the very beginning of the rumour.

Firstly, on the face of it the shop-owner victimised by the rumour did not conform to the stock anti-Semitic image, a fact which helped to conceal the anti-Semitic side of the rumour from those who spread it. He emerged neither as the rapacious usurer, nor as the grasping businessman, nor yet as the sworn foe of all Gentiles. Yet did he not act like the usurer, going so far beyond the decent limits of commerce as to traffic in human flesh? Was he not a businessman first and foremost, in the very marrow of his bones, to the point where he converted his customer into merchandise? Did not the corruption, dishonour and misery he brought on his victims' families make him a civic enemy?

There was, indeed, a new factor here as far as the French tradition of anti-Semitism was concerned, which—as we shall see—had some trouble in recognising the Jew with which it was familiar. The point was that it associated the Jew with a sexual threat. But are we not dealing here with a latent feature of racialism? The 'Negro menace' in the USA, like the 'Jewish threat' in Nazi Germany, contains a superabundant sexual element, the peril of blood contamination. Here, it is true, the contamination is liable to come from Arabs and dark-skinned Brazilians and all those multi-coloured aliens who throng the North African brothels, and the superabundance will be that of all the sperm poured forth in houses of prostitution; but the shop-owner's injection symbolises an initial defloration, and suggests the basic idea of contamination, defilement. Furthermore, if the myth associates the Jewish shop-owner with a sexual threat, while limiting the realisation of that threat to other races, it thereby brings out a more obscure and archaic motif. The trafficker in pure flesh, who by his infamous practices not merely reduces an innocent virgin to so much merchandise, but renders her a sacrificial object, to be immolated on the altar of some shadowy sexual power, evokes a faint, attenuated echo of the old medieval belief—that the Jewish Passover was not complete without the ritual sacrifice of a Christian child. In this sense the Orléans rumour—itself a vague echo of those vast panics which sprang up from time to time during the Middle Ages—was to resuscitate the same anti-Jewish fantasy, though in a disguised, attenuated, modernised form.

If we can evoke such parallels, even hypothetically, it is because the Jewish shop-owner finds himself assigned a specific mission by the myth—that of pinpointing, and purging, the guilt attendent on a genuine libidinous fantasy and a fictitious white slave traffic. This guilty responsibility, a product of our society's cultural heritage, cannot but conjure up the spectre of congenital guilt, enrooted deep in two millennia of Western Christendom. The reappearance of this spectre (which operates with the implacable logic of subconscious impulse) also takes place in the obscure depths of the unconscious mind. The shop-owner is not guilty *because* he is a Jew—at least, not on the conscious and rational level. Yet that *because* still lurks below the surface, and conveys its meaning to the subconscious mind in clear mythological terms. It is embodied in the phantom of the Jew as traditionally pictured, a phantom that looks back further, to the phantom of the medieval Jew, which contains within itself the phantom of Judas and of the Tempter. And all these phantoms stir into gesticulating life behind the smiling shop-owner, who sells such attractive dresses, at such competitive prices, just so that he may put innocent girls to sleep and ravish them of their most cherished possession.

Secondly the spectre of the 'guilty Jew' only acquired a lease of life with respect to first one, then six shop-owners. It did not affect the rest of the Jewish community. Nevertheless, for most Jews the rumour came as a reminder of that mysterious, disturbing, fascinating, obsessive, repugnant difference. Our enquiry revealed a somewhat disturbing fact which goes to confirm this assumption. Though the rumour had been circulating through the town for about a fortnight, no one thought of warning the other Jews until 29–30 May. The Jewish families of Orléans, to the number of several hundred, were kept in ignorance of the affair. Jewish girls, whether at school or at work, were told not a thing by their friends. The rumour only reached a few Jewish ears (including those of a woman teacher) when the actual word 'Jew' filtered through to them, though even then it was mostly forgotten or ignored. M. Lévy, President of the *Communauté israélite*, a man long established in Orléans, who every day, in his shop or at the café, met countless customers and friends, did not hear the news until 30 May, and then from his Spanish shop-assistant.

It is true that 'people' did not regard the rumour as anti-Semitic, and one must also take into consideration, not only the self-consciousness and embarrassment characteristic of a provincial town, but also the *de facto* segregation that already existed there (I shall return to this point later). Nevertheless, we regard this fact as significant: it suggests that, as far as the rumour was concerned, *all* the Jews were accessories to the affair, even if only in an indirect or latent manner. It suggests, too, that the rumour already contained a tendency to move on from individuals

to a whole group, from 'some Jews' to 'Jews'—as we can
see from that remark: 'Don't go buying anything from the
Jews', made during the metastasis, which expresses it
clearly enough.

Prodromic symptoms, but no pogrom

The two themes of 'Jewish otherness' and 'Jewish guilt'
fermented and developed as the rumour grew, spreading
from the adolescent world to adult society, and the myth
swelled concomitantly, until it reached the metastasis of
29–31 May.

During its triumphant phase the rumour did not trigger
off any direct political anti-Semitism, but it did succeed
in touching various residual anti-Semitic feelings at different levels of society; above all, it brought out those
pejorative true attitudes dormant within the notion of
'Jewish otherness'. One woman, a militant Catholic, said,
during the session held on 18 June: 'You have to admit it,
the people who don't stick up for them have got their
heads screwed on,' and again—surmounting the barriers
maintained by clear-headed self-censorship: 'Well, I'm
not anti-Semitic, but I did go as far as to say, oh well,
these Jews, you know. . .' (*ibid.*) But it was the metastasis
which, in a sense, brought about the transition from the
singular to the generic, from a few Jewish shop-owners in
particular to Jews in general. It was, first and foremost,
the metastatic development *per se* which dug and linked up
those Jewish tunnels beneath Joan of Arc's city, which
conjured up and inflated the theme of Jewish power over
press and police (their silence and inaction being due to
bribery by 'the Jews').

So we have a gigantic fantasy, played out in Orléans,
which by its own unaided efforts repeated the archetypal
idea embodied in the *Protocols of the Elders of Zion*: the
idea, that is, of a hidden underground power eroding the
world at large and establishing its domination by bribery
and corruption. And furthermore, just as happened a cen-

tury ago with the *Protocols of the Elders of Zion*, the modern
fulfilment of the anti-Semitic myth is, at one and the same
time, the fulfilment of the archaic and medieval myth,
which at a deeper level equates this subterranean Jewish
power with the Infernal Powers themselves.

Thus these metastatic developments tended to bring
the 'Jewish bogey' into greater prominence, to make it the
central feature of the myth. There was even a possibility
that it would engulf the white slave motif which had produced and nourished it. Under it, ever more dizzily, terror
and hysteria gnawed at people's minds: above it there
descended an increasingly unreal sense of guilt. It was now,
perhaps, that the notion of an expiatory act of sacrifice
flitted through people's minds, the feeling that only thus
could the town be purged of the sudden evil in its midst.
When the crowds gathered outside *Dorphée*, was this not
the first phase, so to speak, of a potential pogrom?

But this potential pogrom was, in fact, an impossibility.
Even at the rumour's delirious climax, the transition from
individual instance to generic statement did not imply
totality in the concrete sense, did not embrace all Jews
physically. As I said earlier, from its outset the rumour
treated all Jews as latent accessories; but this complicity
remained latent throughout. The maleficent zone never
spread beyond the six shop-owners actually incriminated;
it left the boutiques on the Rue de Bourgogne severely
alone. In principle, all Jews were affected, but in practice
only *some* Jews stood to suffer. Furthermore, though
pejorative comments were made with regard to the Jews,
the anti-Semitic motif still remained closely dependent on
that of the white slave traffic. Even during the metastasis
it did not acquire an independent status; it never discarded
the white slave motif altogether, as a space-rocket, once
on course, will jettison the first-stage propellent that got
it off the ground.

We may also note that the major fantasy of a plot
against the town was a gigantic bubble, which quickly set

off the counter-offensive of 3 June, and indeed provoked
it in the first place. Anti-Semitism, as such, was rejected
during June, the moment it stood revealed for what it was
by the ugly mirror of Nazi persecution which the anti-myth
held up to the public. The fantasy dissolved, dispersed,
shrivelled into nothing. On the other hand, it should be
noted that all its germs survived. People in general were
left with a sharp awareness of the difference between Jews
and other folk. They were astonished and dismayed to
learn of all the upheavals—pro- and anti-Jewish, racialist
and anti-racialist, polemical and political—that were
liable to be provoked by putting that one phrase, 'the
Jews', into public circulation.

It follows that though the rumour, when it got really
out of hand, may have had the notion of a pogrom lurking
somewhere on its psychological horizon, this never figured
on the sociological horizon of the *polis*. The very development of anti-Semitism as such itself set in motion an
effective counter-attack, launched by repressors and antibodies at both national and local levels.

Unrealised and renascent anti-Semitism
Like a ghost, the Jew emerged from those subterranean
haunts—deep, archaic, medieval—to which he had returned at the close of the Second World War. He became
incarnate in a few shop-owners selling mini-skirts and
mini-dresses. Vampire-like, he brought about a reign of
terror. Then he was exorcised, withdrew to his underground retreat, rejoined the world of shadows.

As should by now be apparent, throughout this affair
the Jewish motif forms a non-constant factor, susceptible
alike to inflation and attenuation, in an ambivalent, symbiotic, evolutive myth from which it never completely
breaks loose. To begin with, this element is grafted on. It
becomes in turn secondary, unifactory and dominant.
Then it more or less suffers expulsion. Its role and its importance undergo ceaseless modification, but it is never

STRUCTURE OF A MYTH

neutral or inoffensive, just as it never succeeds in maturing
a firm, self-assured myth. It escapes the normal definition
of political anti-Semitism, but at another level comes
within that of a matrix-archetype. Almost invulnerable
as germs or residuum, it is highly vulnerable to those
antidotes secreted by the *polis*.

Why was it so difficult to answer the apparently simple
question of whether this Orléans rumour was, or was not,
anti-Semitic? Furthermore, one difficulty led on to another: how were the frontiers of anti-Semitism to be defined?
Had we to do with some doctrine or ideology explaining
the generic attitude of hostility towards Jews? If so, it
was clear that in Orléans neither doctrine nor ideology
existed except by implication. Can what is anti-Semitic
by implication be regarded as genuine anti-Semitism? If
so, all neutral remarks about Jews are virtually anti-
Semitic, since they indicate, and emphasise, that mysterious otherness which, in our society, is still liable to
conjure up the underground Jew, the Jewish phantom or
fantasy. Thus for us the real problem is not to determine
whether or not the Orléans phenomenon should be labelled
'anti-Semitic'. It is rather that of a social body in which
there persist, or recur, ferments capable, granted certain
conditions, of bringing about a recrudescence of anti-
Semitism.

Now this social body is in the process of losing the
immunity which it had acquired by 1945. A new incubation area has developed, centred on the white slave myth,
fostered by the innocent, fantasy-ridden minds of countless budding adolescent girls. This new incubation area,
besides modifying an important element in the genetic
code of the traditional Jewish myth, also adapts it to
modern society. The Jew now under fire is neither the
typical old inhabitant of the ghetto, nor the big financier,
but the young, modern, bourgeois Jew, without any outward distinguishing marks. Yet, I would repeat, this
young, modern Jew, like his mythological ancestors,

C

reveals himself as an unscrupulous businessman, ready to trade in any commodity; and—again like them—he carries within himself, in embryo, the archaic characteristics of Judas, for Western Christendom the focal point of all suffering and guilt.

Yet even here we find no stability; all remains ambivalent. We have seen how the germ was incubated in a modern culture; yet we have also seen the singularly modest part played by traditional strongholds of anti-Semitism, which did not so much as recognise 'the Jew' when they saw him. We have seen how strong an anti-Jewish atmosphere can be generated by modern and archaic elements in resonant conjunction; we have also seen the way this atmosphere collapses at the first hint of an external counter-attack.

To sum up, then, Orléans offered us an example of anti-Semitism that, while not yet fully realised, had advanced beyond the stage of mere *de facto* implication. It was, in fact, at a transitional point between the two, but regressed before achieving complete realisation. We might term it an unrealised and renascent case of anti-Semitism. Those who carried it, in germinal form, were unaware that they did so; *but analysis revealed the existence of the germ, with its familiar genetic code and the new, unfamiliar element it now also contained.*

FEMININE EMANCIPATION AND THE
MODERN CITY

The entire affair stemmed from an up-dated archetype of the white slave myth; it simmered, stew-like, among modern schoolgirls and teenagers, and concentrated on shops which acted as distribution-centres for modern fashions in dress. Modernity not merely supported the myth, but formed one of its basic themes. To begin with, modern fashion is not something that can be kept separate from a woman's mores and life in general. These mini-skirts and seductive undies and trendy party dresses symbolise not merely the desire to please, but also the cult of novelty, the triumphant self-assertion of youth or the wish to remain young, the aspiration to live in the Parisian manner (that is—or so people believe—freely and happily), the emancipation of the adolescent from her family and the slightly older girl from tradition, a special type of personality, an individual life-style.

Orléans is a city which has undergone rapid change, accelerated by the solar proximity of the capital. In this metamorphosis it is the girls and young women who form the advance guard of the new modernity when it comes to transforming manners and morals. The *Dorphée* boutique, right in the heart of town, was a part of this metamorphosis; it still remains a fascinating and active centre for the new feminine modernity. It is not only a place where novelties are sold, but one from which novelty radiates. It is a place of initiation in modern femininity, not only for the girl or young woman who wants to keep abreast of the times, but for an adolescent taking her first header into the erotic potentialities of dressing up. It is a, perhaps the, symbolic centre of feminine emancipation.

This emancipation, which has developed faster as regards outward appearances than it has in people's hearts, stands in a cultural no-man's-land, between the abandonment of, or the wish to reject, an old way of life, and the aspiration to, or the search for, a new life-style. From the adolescent to the fully-fledged young woman, every girl is busy conquering, absorbing or enlarging her own area of independence; but each would like to go further, longs to travel (a reasonable substitute for adventure), dreams of adventures. The satisfactions gained are still inadequate, ambitions remain unfulfilled, and yet already latent fears have begun to multiply. For the adolescent, these fears centre on initiation; the rest are made anxious by the thought of breaking with traditional norms. Both find uneasiness in what most attracts them.

Their erotic impulses, still half-attached to traditional

morality, now aspire to such pleasures as would result from
a general enhancement of the erotic principle in life. Dress
constitutes the simulacrum of such a change rather than
any guarantee that it will happen. They feel, confusedly,
that it symptomises both danger and sinfulness; they are
aware, that is, of its more unpleasant side. This produces a
climate favourable to fantasy, in which there would be, at
one and the same time, total emancipation and total
freedom from guilt. Here we see what the Orléans myth
had to offer those adolescents and teenagers who formed
its chief breeding-ground. The gates it opened led not
only to the fatal world of drugs and prostitution, but also,
in secret, to the joys of travel, adventure and ecstasy.
However, this escape-myth should not blind us to the
problems which the new feminine modernity, with all its
handicaps and aspirations, continues to thrash out, alone
and in private. And if the *Maison Dorphée* provided the
myth with its first gravitational centre, that was—among
other appropriate characteristics, including the fact of
its Jewishness—because this boutique for young girls
symbolically summed up the young girl's problems.

Long before the rumour got under way, both the girls'
mothers and the conservative, traditionally orientated
women of Orléans—the former with uneasy concern, the
latter with active repugnance and hostility—had come to
the conclusion that new shops such as *Dorphée* were, in
effect, propagation-centres for the new virus of modernity,
and that their with-it dresses symbolised the danger-
fraught emancipation of the young.

During the sixties, in Orléans as elsewhere, the *yéyé*[1]
had formed the central bone of contention, not only between different generations, but also between two con-

---

[1] It is curious that the English language has no *generic* equivalent of the
French term *yéyé*: Teddy Boys, Beats, Mods and Rockers, Hippies and
Flower Children, the Swinging Generation—all these are restricted to
the specific phenomenon they describe. I have therefore retained the
French term in translation.—Trs.

trasting ways of life, two opposed moralities. From then
on mothers and women teachers, though they could not
stem the tide, did everything in their power to slow it down
or canalise it. When the May '69 rumour reached grown-up
society, mothers of families, and some schoolmistresses,
saw these fitting-room abductions as a fatal but inevitable consequence of the *yéyé*, a concrete embodiment
of the threat he represented. They never tired of denouncing this peril in detail; the dissipation, the frivolity, the
premature (and dangerous) sexual licence, the plain
degradation or immorality. Now they had proof positive
of its harmful nature. In more general terms, and at a
deeper, less coherent level, they felt that the myth merely
encouraged fantasies of rape, abduction and whoredom.
In the monstrous form of drugging and prostitution it did
no more than develop what female emancipation already
implied: sexual licence and moral anarchy. The proliferation of the myth simply confirmed what anxious con-
servatives had already inferred by the light of reason:
that the mini-skirt led directly to prostitution.

Yet while the mini-skirt deepened the generation-gap,
fear of prostitution tended to close it. For teachers and
mothers alike, here was a chance to renew contact with
these scared adolescents, and to win back some authority
over them. The myth—a licentious and problematical
topic when discussed *by* the young—was taken over by
mothers and teachers and turned into a morally edifying
sermon for delivery *to* them. In a wider sense, this fantasy-
myth, the product of adolescent culture, gave the traditional forces of provincial female society an excuse for
launching a counter-offensive against the *yéyé*. The
Jewish shop-owner rendered involuntary support to the
forces of tradition, not only by seeding the Jewish threat
into that of the *yéyé*, but by providing the latter with a
vertiginous metaphysical basis in the shape of evil and
disintegration.

The turbulent interplay between the young girls' secret

attraction to the myth and their mothers' distaste for the *yéyé*, between the girls' fear of white slaving and their mothers' private weakness for a myth which came in so handy (and was also, perhaps, rather disturbing on occasion)—all this helped to create the positively cyclonic movement of the rumour as it spread through town. In this cyclone, two separate movements, those of the older and younger generations, which had clashed violently at the time of the row over the *yéyé*, and had been in opposition ever since, found themselves temporarily united by the conjunction of two different anxieties. It is this reunion which may provide one explanation for the remarkable powers of persuasion which the rumour possessed, where the fair sex was concerned, during the period 20–31 May.

Their alliance, however, lasted no longer than the rumour itself: the shattering of the myth at once restored the *status quo ante*. A week later the accused shop-owners had picked up their clientèle again; in other shops of the same type trade had not even slackened. The new adolescent culture, the new feminine modernity, were both too solidly established already. But as we have seen, their key problem was one which a whole town experienced, by way of a fable, for the duration of a rumour. The Orléans myth is also, at bottom, a myth of female emancipation and—more broadly speaking—of the new modern way of life.

The town
Modern life also implies the modern town. The town of Orléans did not function as mere background décor for a myth. It found itself directly implicated in the action. As we have seen, modern changes in the white slave myth widened the range of its menace. Previously it had been restricted to the periphery, to shady districts and the criminal underworld, to night and darkness. Now, however, this menace walked in broad daylight, and haunted the very heart of the city.

In such circumstances, the town-centre ceased to be that civic (and civilised) hub of rules and regulations whence emanated the protective, paternal authority of the *polis*. It remained a lively focal point, but now only as regards the social and economic side of the town's activities. Henceforward it was not only a case of the town-centre having seemingly lost its controlling brain: the entire town seemed psychologically and ethically enucleated. It was no longer a city, but a mere shapeless and disorganised agglomeration, without either head or heart. Now this vision imposed by the myth corresponds—in a manner at once schematic, exaggerated and fantastic—to that real life evolutionary process which transforms provincial cities into mere modern agglomerations, and has seriously affected Orléans during the last decade. We begin to see how the degradation of a *polis*-type culture, and the related development of a shapeless conurbation, might well produce some sort of malaise: a sense of vague, nagging emptiness that would descend on the city-centre when people suddenly realised that the tutelary protection extended by the *polis* was no longer available, and to the general atmosphere of unhappy anxiety would add a specifically urban concern.

During its metastasis the myth returned to the assault of Orléans, but this time it set about undermining the town's very foundations. Rumour suddenly resuscitated a motif common to every ancient city, the subterranean network of tunnels. During the nineteenth century, when capital cities were being pulled down and rebuilt, to emerge, transformed, as vast conurbations, popular fiction gave this motif a new lease of life. It was the 'big city' which, beneath its bustling inhabitants and display of civic authority, concealed a subterranean labyrinth where some occult power held sway.

In Orléans, the myth conjured up childhood memories of mysterious underground passages. 'Everyone knows about them, they go back to Joan of Arc's day.' Suddenly people became aware that the town was honeycombed with tunnels. 'Orléans? Like a Gruyère cheese.' Ancient galleries or catacombs once more figured as those secret passages of medieval times, which the occult power used both as a residence and for purposes of communication.

Thus anxiety about white slaving, combined with anxiety about the Jews, threw up a third anxiety which was rather more than the sum of the other two, and which, starting from the centre, went underground, spread out through the town's subterranean levels, to attack it at its foundations.

How are we to interpret these two anxieties—one lurking in what should have been the reassuring heart of the city, the other undermining the very foundations on which it rested? On our assumption, they were both latent, though not in the same way. The first came into being after recent urban developments—was, indeed, brought about by the actual process of modernisation. Orléans has come very much within the Parisian orbit; and ten years ago the population not only underwent a marked increase, but became, on average, a good deal younger. For the roots of the second we must look to the *Arkhe* of childhood stories, and of the town itself. It was resuscitated not only by the development of archaic features in the Judaicised white slave myth, but also by the town's contemporary anxieties. Thus here, too, we find modern anxiety resuscitating its ancient counterpart. Here, too, counterpointed against the dynamic energy of the Orléans myth as such—and under the impulse of new modern developments—we find those same modern developments triggering off, and then combining with, a resurgence of pure archaism.

Furthermore, as in the problem of women's emancipation, we see how the conjunction of two latent concerns from opposed and contrasting sources can fuse to produce a new and virulent sort of anxiety. On the one hand we have the city of tradition, with its provincial bourgeois

STRUCTURE OF A MYTH

society: now very much under pressure, in retreat, figuring less and less as the central element in civic life, failing conspicuously to impose the sovereign will of its super-ego. On the other, we have the modern agglomeration of the new immigrants, from the *département* and elsewhere, forming completely new juvenile strata in the town's society.

The first Orléans regards the city, now, as to all intents and purposes devoid of inner substance, a vacuum, tending more and more to become a mere shapeless mass, and increasingly threatened by corruption and breakdown, twin legacies of the new modernity.

The second Orléans, in particular its female element, sees the city as a mysterious, chaotic, anonymous urban fabric. No one quite knows if the place is a small backwater town or a vast Parisian suburb that has somehow broken loose from the capital; very often it feels like both at once. The *polis*, and the structural notions it embodies, stand far above most people's heads, far above the pattern of their daily lives. There is no true urban civilisation peculiar to Orléans, which would let each person feel himself a responsible citizen. Over and above the sense of provincial emptiness which permeates modern thinking we have a further void, something vaguer and more confused.

It is the young people who feel this emptiness most clearly, and with the greatest force. The specific boredom attaching to a provincial town (which strikes them as dull and flat in comparison with the capital) is powerfully boosted by the general boredom characteristic of modern youth as such. Those who suffer from this blanketing *ennui* without being aware of its true nature will often blame its genesis, and its prevalence, on the cramped provincialism of Orléans. In this state of boredom all the trips and parties and minor illicit experiences do not really satisfy the crying need of young people for poetry, adventure and excitement; they merely exacerbate it.

Already certain groups are experimenting with marijuana: perhaps, in isolated instances, with heroin injections.

Thus for everyone—though the manner of experiencing it may differ—there is an emptiness at the very heart of the town. Different kinds of emptiness—ethical, political, affective, existential—combine to form one great void: and in everyone such a void will inevitably produce a sense of malaise.

Teenagers and young girls stand, as it were, at the intersection of all these voids, in the hollow centre of a vast communal emptiness. They feel this condition as one of boredom no less than anxiety; or rather, in them the various anxieties linked with sex, entry into adult life, and the new modernity become indistinguishably mixed up with the special urban anxiety we have been discussing. It is they who feed most avidly on those poetic fancies disseminated by magazines, especially women's magazines. They are hedged about with boredom, anxiety and uneasiness. Perhaps that is why they picked on a shop in the town-centre, and at one stroke turned it into something out of fable, depositing there a Pandora's box from which all else would spring—the drug element, the Jekyll-and-Hyde Jew, the descent into the depths, the voyage overseas, prostitution.

At this level, the fitting-room injection is also a shot of transfiguring poetry injected into the town's general ennui. But by injecting this shot of poetry, the young girls of Orléans aroused anxiety all round—in themselves as much as anyone. As long as the rumour lasted, all the inhabitants of Orléans found themselves in the same communal void, which was both source and focal point of this anxiety. The uneasiness experienced by both sides blended into one, and found a symbolic vehicle which, by exacerbating and exaggerating what they were feeling, contrived to give it expression. Orléans the provincial town and Orléans the urban agglomeration found themselves attuned to one another. The rumour put about in the modern agglomeration by schoolgirls, typists and shop-assistants triggered off a wave of malicious tittle-tattle among the provincial gossips of an older generation.

Here we can glimpse one of the factors that enabled the myth to reach fruition in Orléans: that is, the coincidence of provincialism and modernity. While this is doubtless a characteristic of most towns in the country—thus rendering them potentially receptive to rumours generally—in Orléans both provincialism and modernity are, so to speak, exacerbated by the proximity of Paris, and become what might be termed exemplary instances of the phenomenon, so much so that opinion polls use Orléans as an 'average town'. Average, that is, because of its double status. Here the uneasiness of an already defeated provincial city contrived to profit from a myth thrown up by anxieties peculiar to the modern agglomeration, while at the same time pouring their own contribution into the mixture—and forming the kind of resonance-box that only a provincial centre, as hollow as it was Paris-influenced, could hope to provide.

Here was a town, then, in which old structural patterns (supremacy of the bourgeoisie, whether traditionalist or liberal; rigid social stratification; manners largely dictated by strict old-fashioned morality) were breaking up on all sides, without any new ones having developed to take their place. A town in which the provincial ideal was dead, but metropolitanism still non-existent. A town in which, under the symbolic guise of fable, the problem of generalised structural breakdown (affecting not merely the town itself, but also the society within it) effectively emerged to confront both sides alike.

A POLYMORPHOUS MYTH

The Orléans myth is not a political invention of anti-Semitic origin. Nor, on the other hand, is it a mere school-girl fantasy, fuelled by perversely erotic imaginings, and freeing itself from guilt through the use of a Jewish

scapegoat. Nor, again, is it a straightforward patching up
of some worn-out traditional theme, which (like a retread)
takes off once more, effectively enough, under a slick
top-dressing of modernity. In Orléans, sex is more than a
game, it is a worrying concern; while modernity is not any
kind of top-dressing, but the core and heart of the matter.

Our enquiry has laid bare the history of this myth, and
attempted to isolate and fit together the various different
elements which went to form it—elements not only in
constant flux themselves, but also constantly modifying
the structure and nature of the myth as a whole. How can
one hope to render justice, in the broad sense, to so
evolutive, symbiotic, complex and ambivalent a phenomenon ?

A real life event in 1958 (but who is to say that the idea
for it did not derive from a crime novel ?) undoubtedly was
the catalyst leading to a total revision of the traditional
white slave motif. The new mythological construct, which
modernised the archetype by a process of modification,
in due course transformed an erotic fantasy into a myth
intimately bound up with young girls' problems—and
one that brought these problems into the closest juxta-
position with one another. From the very outset, the
modernisation of this erotic myth was in fact no more than
the crystallisation of a modern myth with erotic overtones.
It was quintessentially modern, not only in its background,
which was that of contemporary daily life; not only
because it implied the (equally modern) problem of
emancipation for young girls—a two-headed proposition
here, involving the emancipation of women on the one
hand, and that of youth generally on the other—but
also because, being located at the heart of the modern
town, it thereby came to affect all real life problems in this
new urban environment, and all problems posed by the
metamorphosis of provincial towns as such.

From the very first, again, this myth established a
connection between the secret lairs of the *Arkhe*—where

desire and anxiety reign in their primal form—and such things as dresses, mini-skirts, shop-windows, city streets: that is, with the trivial *ad hoc* phenomena of the young girl's world, which, on a broader level, is that experienced by each and every one of us. Lastly, from the very outset the myth carried an aura of poetry and romance about it, with its drugs and hypodermics, its theme of abduction (followed by an exotic voyage to foreign parts), its prostitution. At the same time it gave this atmosphere the circumstantial plausibility of a news item, the kind of reliance one would place on an eyewitness account or article that appeared in the press.

From the word go, then, the myth was quite extraordinarily rich by sociological standards, and already contained in embryo—with the single exception of the Jewish element—the whole mythical constellation that would afterwards emerge full-blown at Orléans. Right from the start it revealed this interesting blend of profound fantasy and profound realism. That is why everything combined *ab initio* to encourage its genesis. It was not merely that it had such a very everyday background, or the kind of apparent veracity that gets constant confirmation from the mass media; more positively, it was the mass media and the everyday background which encouraged its development in the first place. It did not merely enjoy the advantages of modernity; it was modernity that fed and activated it. It did not merely dispose of the magic inherent in all myth; the unconscious logic of desire and anxiety gave it life. Fact and myth, the probable and the fabulous, archaic instinct and modern self-awareness were all, in the first instance, conjointly enlisted by a story about white slaving—which they then turned round and enlisted themselves, in such a way as to let it acquire instant reality, *hic et nunc*.

But to achieve this *hic et nunc* incarnation called for a two-faced tempter. The accident of Jewish shop-owners being concentrated, socially and geographically, in just

the right sector (that of girls' and young women's dresses)
meant that such a tempter was ready to hand. This is the
point at which a wholly unforeseen element intruded upon
the endogenous logic of the myth: the presence, within
its sphere of action, of so ideal a scapegoat. In a flash, the
mythical star cluster labelled 'white slavery', by hooking
out the satellite of which it had need, attracted another
constellation, that of the 'Jewish menace'. On the face of
it the latter should have dissolved into pure airy fantasy.
It did not. Such a process of attraction was made possible
by the weakening—especially among the younger feminine
generation, always a largely apolitical group—of those
repressions and inhibitions which, ever since 1945, have
served to protect the Jew. From this point on the two
myths were in progressive symbiosis: the Jew became
responsible for a new chapter of the myth, which he duly
brought to fruition. At the same time this fructifying
process triggered off a naive, infra-political (and hence by
definition archaic) case of anti-Semitism.

What was the motive force that broke through the dyke
and transformed a spurious local news item—the drugging
of two girls at the *Maison Dorphée*—into a full-scale
epidemic of disappearances, one after another? At all
events, from that moment on, schoolgirls and teenagers
not only lifted the barrier which keeps the adolescent
world separate from that of the grown-ups, but themselves
sought out their elders, and begged protection from them.
The dissemination of the myth amongst adult women
aroused them to fresh anxiety about the *yéyé* and the new
emancipation of young girls; and this in turn made them
more ready to believe the myth itself. Through girls and
grown women alike, all the ills—both social and civic—
that had resulted from the new juvenile modernity
rushed headlong into this growing cyclonic depression. The
common mood of anxiety merely served to enhance all
similarities between individual anxieties of any sort,
whether archaic, traditional or modern; while the factors

that tended to isolate them from one another remained very much in abeyance. In this extraordinary encounter— still for the most part between the distaff element in society, whether girls or grown women—old and new Orléanais met and shared the same hallucinatory experience. This was what occasioned so great an expansion of the mythic star cluster.

Nevertheless, this mood of generalised harmony, this moment of flowering and expansion, could not but be ephemeral. If the myth swelled up too far it was bound to burst, partly because its credibility would be spun out bubble-thin, and partly because its very inflation, by unleashing a preliminary wave of panic, alerted the *polis*. Now the *polis*, as the myth saw very clearly, with the special lucidity of delirium, was, affectively speaking, absent from that concrete universe in which the rumour had gained ground. What happened next was that the myth, in an attempt to assault a town, came into collision with the *polis*.

THREE

THE ANTI-MYTHS

THE SPONTANEOUS ANTI-MYTH: INCREDULITY

The rumour did not gain universal credence; it ran into a
number of disbelievers, though just how many it is hard
to calculate now that the anti-myth has created a widespread mood of non-acceptance. However, these original
pockets of incredulity, though they resisted the rumour,
did not put any effective obstacle in its path: it simply by-
passed them and went on its way regardless. It seems
likely that the areas of disbelief included not only a good
proportion of the male population, where the ground was
unreceptive for propagation, but quite a few women and
girls as well. I must repeat that we have no idea of the
percentage of disbelievers amongst those who were exposed
to the rumour.

Incredulity assumed three forms:

The disbelief which (like its opposite) rested on some
personal assurance (through a relative or friend); but
which, in contradistinction to credulity, depended not on
some imaginary witness, but on the accused shop-owners
themselves: 'I know them, they're my friends, they could
never do a thing like that.' What is rejected here is not so
much the myth *per se*, as the likelihood of relatives or
friends committing so heinous a crime. This area of disbelief was comparatively limited.

80

Careful checking up. This is not disbelief in the strict sense, since there is no immediate rejection of the myth. What we have is rather a blend of credulity and incredulity, which sets a checking-up process in motion. Such a process must have been more or less automatic for the police, who were bound to check on whether or not anyone had, in fact, vanished from the area within their jurisdiction. But a private citizen like M. Rebaudet, who checked his information back to source with the police, was a comparative rarity. *Rarer still, it would appear, were those for whom the non-arrest of those shop-owners on whose premises (according to rumour) the police had found the drugged women, taken in conjunction with the silence of the press, constituted proof positive that the rumour was false.*

Critical scrutiny, not of the myth's veracity *qua* gossip, but rather of its intrinsic characteristics. This is the disbelief that is rooted in the myth's fundamental incredibility. Sceptical analysis (to begin with) could isolate a weak point in the plot sequence: 'After all, there *are* girl-assistants around, aren't there?' said one incredulous young hairdresser, whose critical acuity was based on personal experience. (Yet her reaction, surprisingly, was by no means general among shop employees.) There was also commonsense incredulity, stimulated by the sheer enormity of the myth: 'I mean, it's just ridiculous,' said one woman customer at *La Ripaille*. This commonsense incredulity may go with a tendency to distinguish between the plausible and the more unlikely elements in the myth: 'Sure, white slavery exists. Maybe there *are* disappearances. But it's out of the question to think of anything like that going on *chez Dorphée*.'

All these sceptics want to reduce the rumour to mere gossip and tittle-tattle, old wives' tales—but without perceiving that it carries (and is carried by) a most potent myth, just as they fail to appreciate its anti-Semitic aspect. Thus incredulity provided individual resistance to the myth, but without ever being able to create a

collective anti-mythic force. It produced personal im-
munisation, but bred no active antibodies.

THE ANTI-MYTH OF DISSUASION

The anti-myth of dissuasion was produced by a combination of legal action, the intervention of VIPs, associations
and officials, and articles in the press. The parts that went
to make up its whole were varied, and up to a point, as we
shall see, heterogeneous where not positively contradictory. Nevertheless, this whole did contain a minimal
degree of unity at the initiatory source, or *de facto* headquarters, and on target, where the articles, official statements, etc., had a cumulative effect on the population of
Orléans.

Hence the need for a preliminary general survey, before
the detailed analysis, which, in turn, will be followed by a
final summing-up. The first point to emphasise is that the
anti-myth is a dissuasive *force*. The arguments and explanations it advances both support, and are supported by,
action undertaken at the instance of individuals, groups
or parties, and aim to get action, not merely from various
sectors of society, but from the authorities of the *polis,*
starting with the police. To refute, however, is not an
all-sufficient end; this objective is closely linked to another,
that of securing condemnation—not only at a moral and
political level, but also on legal grounds.

Thus the refutation of the charges embodied in the
rumour did not attempt to conduct an enquiry such as
would prove that there were no disappearances, no subterranean tunnels, and so on. Instead, it tried to investigate the accusers. It did not aim at obtaining rebuttals
per se, but rather sought to predicate them through
denunciation and condemnation. It started from the
proposition 'It is blameworthy, therefore false' rather than
from its opposite, 'It is false, therefore blameworthy'.
What the anti-myth movement wanted from the civic
authorities was a condemnation; and it was only very

grudgingly, when faced with the reluctance of City Hall
and the Prefecture to become involved in the affair, that
it compounded for a refutation pure and simple. It all
looked very much as though the anti-myth movement was
aware that a plain rebuttal, applied to so virulent a myth,
would simply strengthen it still further—according to that
inverted Aristotelian syllogism: 'People deny it, *therefore*
it is true'—a proposition now and then borne out by the
facts. Thus the rebuttal never emerged *as such*, directly,
but was vigorously implied in the dissuasive counter-
attack, with its 'lies and calumny' motif.

Similarly, the proposed explanation of the affair was
inseparable from a denunciation. At the same time the
anti-myth went beyond mere straightforward denunciation of calumny as such. It advanced, or rather tried to
impose, a coherent overall explanation which took both
myth and rumour into account.

It was fighting a *shapeless* rumour, something as elusive
as air, disseminated by everybody and nobody, without
posters, pamphlets, graffiti or signatures. Thus the anti-
mythic technique was to endow this rumour with form and
substance, to give it a face, an author, an objective. The
rumour was not merely slanderous, but a 'campaign of
slander'. It was a 'campaign of slander', an 'odious cabal',
that sprang from fascism and led to more fascism. This
slander had a face; and the features were those of anti-
Semitism.

The 'anti-Semitic plot'
The explanatory development of the anti-myth followed
two basic lines. Firstly, there was the establishment of a pattern relating the *new* phenomenon in
Orléans with a *familiar* phenomenon that was both
out of date and out of favour. Here the anti-myth
at once picked out two models. The first was that of
'medievalism', that is to say, a mentally retrograde world
of witch hunts, superstitions and ridiculous waves of panic.

However, this model served mainly as a makeweight to another still more barbarous and alien one, of which people had had direct personal experience. This was the Nazi or Hitlerian model. As an explanation the Nazi motif might be lightweight, but its powers of dissuasion were considerable. It enabled those who used it to hit hard, and also to divert their fire on to a target outside Orléans itself. They could denounce this myth as something alien to the indigenous community, a foreign body that had infiltrated Orléans unbeknown to the town's inhabitants. What they did, in fact, was to identify the myth with the enemy who had occupied Orléans and France, who was responsible for the horrors of the concentration camps— *and with whom no-one could identify himself.*

Secondly, there was a tendency to localise the cause and origin of the phenomenon in the conscious will, and actions, of malicious individual agents.

It was, clearly, the idea of a plot ('odious cabal', 'campaign of slander') which made it possible to resolve two problems simultaneously—what caused the rumour, and who was responsible for it. Such a thesis allowed for its occult, obscure nature, got round the difficult problem of pinpointing its beginning and end, and at the same time accounted for the successful way in which it contrived to dupe the innocent masses. A 'plot theory' made it possible to utilise the same mental constructs as the myth did; they merely had to be turned back to front. There was, indeed, a plot, not on the part of (shop-owning) Jews, but *against* (shop-owning) Jews. The idea of a plot came naturally enough to the Jewish shop-owners themselves, who tended to imagine that they were being victimised anyway, either by some concrete machination on the part of their rivals, or else by an anti-Semitic conspiracy. In similar manner, the anti-racialist or anti-fascist extremists scented a plot the moment they heard about the affair. Renée Cosson's reaction (2 June) was instantaneous: 'It's an anti-Semitic plot . . . it must have been started by

political fascists, only fascists would do such a thing.'
Katian, at the *Maison de la Culture*, warned the Abbé
Sejourné that it was 'an anti-Jewish affair', and talked
darkly of *L'Action française*. This 'fascist' theme united
the left wing of the anti-myth, its most active and com-
mitted section; yet in the event it dispersed.

Where people looked for culprits depended on the way
they interpreted the term 'fascism'. Those who took it in a
narrow sense concentrated on the right-wing *ultras*, while
those who used it more broadly had an eye to the Govern-
mental party. Some even saw the affair as proof of a
hidden connection between the Fifth Union Départemental and the fascist groups, and held CDR or SAC
agents responsible for carrying out the plot. Some restricted themselves to the idea of a local conspiracy, which
they tried to tie up with the actions of a 'fascist commando'
during May and June 1968 (in which a Minister's son was
supposedly involved), while others saw the affair as a
ballon d'essai for some much vaster plot at national level:
'It's a top-level job and we haven't heard the last of it'
(Renée Cosson). The police themselves became implicated
in the conspiracy. If they failed to lay hands on the culprits, that was because they had made no effort to find
them: 'The police know what they're doing, all right' (a
leftist platform speaker in the *Maison de la culture*). The
anti-myth picked up the theme of some hidden power
controlling the town; this time, however, the Mayor and
the police and justice generally were corrupted not by the
Jews, but by secret fascism, lurking behind the national
and (or) local civic authorities.

As regards the plot's motivation, the anti-myth fell
into various opinions, some contradictory. Yet whatever
form it took—and versions ranged from the machinations
of an anti-Semitic competitor (who was said to ask his
employees for certificates of baptism, and to have sacked
a man who scrubbed the floors because he also worked for

rival Jewish firms) to a huge nation-wide conspiracy that
aimed to set up a fascist state in France; from a strictly
anti-Semitic plot to one which simply used anti-Semitism
as an anti-Communist or anti-popular weapon[1]—the plot,
as such, remained the basic ingredient of the anti-
myth, though, it must be said, wholly mythological
itself.

WEAKNESS AND STRENGTH OF THE ANTI-MYTH

The strength and weakness of the anti-myth are closely
linked. Its main dissuasive instrument—intimidation—
was bound up with its feeble powers of elucidation. It did,
certainly, shed a crude light on the myth's hidden face,
its anti-Semitic character; yet this light was not only
blinding, but contained its own blind spot. It confused the
virtual and the actual; what might conceivably take
place in the future became here-and-now reality. The
other facet of the myth, the white slave trade, it plunged
abruptly into darkness, regarding it, at best, as a mere
launching-pad. It also failed to perceive the new form
which this anti-Semitic motif assumed.

The anti-myth contained the seeds of a correct explanation for the rumour, as we can see from its reference
to the latter's 'quasi-medieval' character. But the phenomenon of the rumour as such it tended to brush aside,
as though any recognition of the spontaneous, semi-
conscious method by which it was spread would risk
weakening the condemnatory force against it. In point of
fact, anyone who admitted or emphasised the fact that
the rumour was based on 'gossip' and 'tittle-tattle' thereby
weakened the theory of a concerted campaign or cabal,
which was what gave the anti-myth its violent impact.
The hint of truth which the moderates touched on very

---

[1] Not to mention the plot of Arab origin. In Paris certain members of the
Jewish organisations speculated as to whether the whole thing might not
have been started by Arab students on the Source campus (University of
Orléans).

nearly dissolved the whole thesis; it brought people back
to airy impalpabilities, to the everybody-and-nobody
pattern, the nameless, invisible enemy.

Here we come up against the anti-myth's second area of
weakness and strength. It needed a mythological structure,
homologous, if antagonistic, to that of the myth it was
opposing. The plot did not serve merely to localise, identify
and denounce the Enemy—and by so doing to exculpate
the population *en masse*, leaving them mystified and, in a
sense, victims. It became an instrument of communication
with those mental constructs that had fed the myth; one
effect of the anti-myth was to displace the plot's epicentre, to shift it away from the Jewish shop-owners to
other shop-owners, to the Germans, to the fascists even.
If, as seems likely, the 'fascists' in fact played no direct
part in the myth's origin and propagation, they were
introduced instead of the Jews, to serve as alternative
scapegoats—no longer for the white slave trade, to be
sure, but for the criminal rumour that was circulating, for
all the anxiety, scandal and anger it had aroused. The one
important difference was that while anti-Semitic activities
could reasonably be attributed to anti-Semites, making
the Jews responsible for the white slave trade was pure
lunacy.

Thus in some respects the anti-myth was itself a myth.
Would another anti-myth have been possible? Would
elucidation have had a dissuasive effect? This question is
a fundamentally tragic one.

VARIANTS ON THE ANTI-MYTH

In its most resolute and aggressive form, the anti-myth
tended to embody all those elements isolated by our
analysis. It could be expressed thus: 'What we have here
is an anti-Semitic cabal. It shows certain medieval features, but is primarily of the Nazi type; and it has triggered
off a slanderous campaign for which those responsible
deserve prosecution.' This statement was not, however,

fully endorsed by all those who opposed the rumour.
Other fragmentary versions of the anti-myth existed, and
the more fragmentary they were, the closer they corresponded to a moderate attitude.

Thus the anti-myth, while restraining and denouncing
the 'odious cabal' or 'campaign of slander', left the source
and origin of this campaign discreetly vague; anti-Semitism was seldom, if ever, referred to in this connection, and
if it was, figured as a mere unpleasant smell rather than as
an active fermenting agent.

In its minimal form the anti-myth eliminated the cabal
and the slander campaign altogether. What it retained,
basically, was gossip and tittle-tattle, the notion of people's
'stupidity', reinforced by healthy scepticism, a spontaneously critical and rational approach that regarded
both myth and rumour (the latter especially) with
deep suspicion—but was totally lacking in offensive
power.

Each of these variants contained a policy-by-implicat-
ion. If there was a plot, it must be suppressed. If a
campaign existed, it must be exposed. If the whole thing
was a mere tissue of old wives' tales, one merely shrugged
one's shoulders, or, at the most, issued a rebuttal.

Clearly, then, it was the idea of a plot which gave the
anti-mythic movement its unity. But at the same time it
made for division. There were those who, while denouncing
the cabal, refrained from identifying it: their caution may
have been due either to critical or to political considerations.
Those who wanted to moderate the political aspects of the
affair were, by and large, themselves political moderates.
Some located the plot outside politics altogether in the
strict sense of that term, tying it up with bitter professional rivalries (though this theory was seldom referred
to by the press, and then only as a hypothesis, it nevertheless, as we shall see, gained ground in several quarters).
Others wanted to keep it as purely political issue. Here
again we find variants. One group tried to pin it on the

extreme Right[1] (*Action française, Occident*), another on the traditional Right; it all depended on how far those involved meant to use the plot, *per se*, as an instrument for branding the party in power as fascist.

But here already the affair was deeply involved in the cleavages and canalisation of local and national politics. The anti-myth found itself, inevitably, drawn more and more towards the Left (which then rejected it), while the party in power from now on set about minimising, if not actively suppressing, the anti-myth, being criticised by it on two alternative counts, those of complicity and inaction.

THE EFFECTS OF THE ANTI-MYTH

We have already diagnosed the effects of the anti-myth. The rumour was squashed, but gave birth to a clutch of sub-rumours, which were still circulating in mid-July. The myth was broken up, but a swarm of mini-myths arose to take its place. The anti-myth, then, was generally effective: what is important at this stage is to find out the limits of its efficacy.

Residual fragments

Though essentially geared to anti-Semitism, the anti-myth did succeed in shaking the credence which the rumour had acquired. On the other hand it did not strike it a really mortal blow. It drove a wedge between the 'here' and 'now' of the rumour's dissemination; yet a form of 'here' and 'now' clung on with some tenacity, despite the fact of their separation. Not only did people still say things like 'Well, the white slave trade's a fact', but some even stuck to the idea that there *had* been a white slave scandal—distorted perhaps by rumour, but in any case hushed up

---

[1] Far from being taken out of politics, of course, the plot was given extra political significance by the anti-fascist anti-myth's refusal to allow fascism the dignity of political standing (treating it instead as a mere criminal aberration).

as a result of the anti-myth. At a deeper level, then, far
from discrediting the notion that something shady was
afoot in town, the anti-myth more or less confirmed it.

Secondary boomerang effects

On the other hand, the projectiles fired off by the anti-
myth came back and hit it with a kind of return shock,
not exactly like a boomerang (where the return is envisaged in the very act of dispatch) but rather sent back
on the rebound, with a diminished impact, by the myth
itself.

Thus the publicity which the affair received had a
boomerang effect. If the press picked it up, that was because the papers always loved a sensation, and journalists
were hard up for copy. This publicity was even seen as a
clever piece of self-advertisement on the part of the
supposedly victimised shop-owners. Hence that knowing
remark made to the television interviewers: 'Papers have
to keep up their circulation, and shops need to boost their
trade.'

Another point was that the publicity given the Jews, by
drawing attention to them, inevitably reminded Orléans of
that mysterious difference between Jews and other
people—including the Jews' talent for attracting calumny.
The idea that 'they're not like us' gained ground steadily.
This was what worried Félix, the shoe shop proprietor, who
had adopted the chameleon's trick of camouflaging itself
against its background, and now feared that the anti-
mythic movement was liable to backfire rather badly.

Just as the rebuttal provoked a secondary feeling that
it might conceal a confirmation, so—by virtue of the
cardinal principle dominating the Orléans affair throughout, that of no smoke without fire—the sheer strength,
importance and virulence of the anti-mythic counter-force
suggested that there must have been something very
important and mysterious behind the rumour in the first
place.

Finally, fear—provoked by threats of legal action and the anti-myth's dissuasive powers—produced a vague feeling of hostility. The anti-myth aroused a fresh enemy, that formed by the silent majority: a vast coalition including all those who wanted to forget the affair—and to have it forgotten. By the same token it brought into being an anti-anti-myth.

THE ANTI-ANTI-MYTH

The anti-anti-myth was not merely, or solely, a defensive reaction on the part of the myth when hard hit by the anti-myth. It sprang from numerous factors in conjunction: residual fragments, boomerang effects, the silent majority, political forces. In June rather than May, these combined to shift the affair's centre of interest from the myth to the anti-myth. Here there once more appear those rationalising processes which tend to interpret (denounce) a phenomenon in conspiratorial terms. The anti-myth became a subversive political device, with a whole gamut of possibilities, ranging from large-scale subversion (the political Left) to limited subversion (the Communists, or more rarely Leftists generally, the latter being equated with Communists in the lower depths of people's political consciousness). Here, too, we see the possibility of bracketing all these opposition elements together—i.e. of using the anti-myth itself as proof that all one's opponents are in some way connected.

Secretly linked with this we find the idea that the Jews themselves either took advantage of the situation to pose as martyrs, and to make a diversionary rumpus—in their usual manner—as a way of escaping richly deserved criticism; or else that they personally organised the entire affair. Thus the Jews could be made the instigators, at one and the same time, of rumour and counter-rumour alike. Here we reach the final step in anti-Semitic rationalisation. The Jew becomes responsible for every scandal, anti-Semitism included. Not merely is anti-

Semitism thought to be occasioned by Jewish malice and
intransigence; it is the Jew himself, deliberately and
wantonly, who stirs up anti-Semitism—and afterwards
blames the Gentiles for it.

THE SYNCRETIST MISHMASH

Mini-myths, anti-myths, boomerang reactions, anti-anti-
myth—all these blended turbulently amid a swarm of
mini-rumours during June and July 1969. The one solid
element was that provided by the plot-motif, which sus-
tained at least two hostile systems, so that waverers could
pass from one plot to the other, and syncretise features of
both. A plot, it was felt, had undoubtedly existed—though
just who or what were involved in it, no one knew.

This syncretist hotchpotch resulted from people's attempts to clarify the situation by making an eclectic
combination of myth, anti-myth, and anti-anti-myth. For
one group, the whole thing could be explained as a
struggle between two rival clans or competitors, which
would account for the two-stage machinations—the first
being the rumour started by one side, the second the
campaign whipped up by the other. One housewife
(appealing to the traditional common sense of 'ordinary
folk') saw 'all that business' as 'a battle between the
tycoons' who had manipulated 'the little man'—like
those national wars engineered by armaments manufacturers.

The already syncretic theory which attempted to explain the rumour in terms of a manoeuvre by the German
firm with branches in the area swelled and grew until it
implicated both the Communists and De Gaulle. There
was a vague attempt to resuscitate the old Resistance
pattern, with Communists fighting Germans; but by now
no one felt at all sure where the Gaullists stood in this
picture. By the beginning of July Orléans was aswarm
with a mishmash of incoherent, larval rumours, parasitic
on (or copulating with) one another. People began to

doubt whether the process of elucidation was in fact
getting anywhere.

Their doubts were well founded. There remained a
residue which neither the anti-myth nor the anti-anti-myth
could explain, and this residue no doubt constituted the
heart of the matter. There was now an urgent, pressing,
unanimous need to lay bare the intelligible cause, not
merely, of the rumour alone, but of all that followed
it. There was a need to identify the fire that had thrown
off so much smoke, the fire that continued to smoulder
somewhere—while people asked themselves whether the
magic efforts to discover its cause might not have helped
thicken the smokescreen. There *had* to be a culprit; and
this need (whether it pursued a scapegoat-turned-wan-
derer, or kept the ancient scapegoat, merely modifying his
crime) meant that a suitable victim had to be chosen from
among the bric-à-brac of the mini-myths.

Thus the anti-myth, despite its immediate efficacy, left
vast areas of the myth unilluminated, darkened counsel at
the same time as it shed light, provoked boomerang
reactions and even an anti-anti-myth. What would it have
taken, what would it take to produce an anti-anti-anti-
myth, or, in other words, a permanent critical elucidation?

FOUR

CONDUCTORS AND ANTIBODIES

CONDUCTOR AREAS

It was a rumour that crossed the barriers of age, social class and, partly, of sex. Some areas, however, acted as better conductors than others.

First in order of conductibility we have young girls. Is it possible to differentiate within the limits of this general category for example between adolescents (average age seventeen) and young women (average age twenty-two)? Were high-school girls (mostly middle-class) better conductors than shop-girls, secretaries and manual workers (mostly lower-class)? Schools and colleges, in my opinion, formed the best—and earliest—incubation-areas; but on what grounds? The age or social breakdown of their population? Or perhaps the closed society—an ideal breeding-ground—which they constitute both at work and at play? I would be chary here of formulating even a hypothetical preference.

Secondly we have specifically feminine (as opposed to specifically masculine) areas. Does this mean that feminine areas are markedly more liable to generate gossip and rumour than their masculine equivalents? It does seem to be true that masculine centres of conversation (cafés, offices) tend to swell on public events, while places where women get together incline rather towards private affairs. A more important suggestion, I feel, is that which sees

94

masculine incredulity as closely linked to a wider experience of the *polis*; the masculine tendency to check on
facts is due, in that case, not so much to a sharper critical
mind as to a greater ease of movement amid the complex
machinery of the *polis*[1] (e.g. going round to the police-
station to verify a rumour). *In my opinion, however, the
key point here is the realisation that the white slave fantasy
is a fantasy precisely because of its intimate connection
with the feminine sex.*

Next we have the young rather than the adult or aged,
with these two caveats: there is no sharp break between
youth and maturity—i.e. the latter does not, in this case
certainly, show any decisive gain of experience; and there
may be a renewal of credulity among old folk, whose
ignorance concerning the conditions of modern life could
form a propitious breeding-ground for myth.

And lastly there are the urban middle and lower classes,
and the semi-rural strata from the outer suburban
fringes, who were probably more affected than the intelligentsia or the upper middle classes. The latter, being
comparatively isolated, can have heard little of the rumour
save through their maids or typists and were thus, as
always, ready to treat such popular gossip with conde-
scending irony.

Where must we lay the emphasis? On the middle classes?
On the semi-rural strata? On the working-girl? At all
events, it does not look as though the middle classes found
anything in their urban bourgeois culture to distinguish
them, as far as insight went, from the under-educated
masses. Nor would the working class appear to have
benefited, as a result of its class-consciousness, by the
acquisition of a built-in radar that could unravel this
mystery. Certainly none of these strata or classes offered
any notable resistance to the rumour during the myth's
sub-political period (May 1969).

---

[1] The regular soldier, living in barracks on the periphery of the *polis*,
would seem to have been more credulous than most.

It was only during the second phase (June-July), when
the epicentre of the affair shifted from the white slave
myth towards the sphere of political conflict and ideology,
that we find cleavages beginning to develop. The upper
middle and part at least of the middle classes showed some
inclination to suppress the anti-myth, which (we assume,
though without any supporting evidence) would be more
widely accepted in lower-class areas where the influence
of the Left was strongest.

In fact the myth found its best conductors, broadly
speaking, in politically under-developed areas. I am using
the term 'political' not in its narrow sense, but rather in
that which approaches the matrix-concept of the *polis*,
and includes knowledge of how the city and urban
district's administrative, economic, social and political
machinery functions.

These politically under-developed areas will, obviously,
be found on the sociological periphery of the *polis*, among
the very young, the very old, and women; but they also
exist on the *geographical* periphery (suburbanites, semi-
rural fringe-dwellers), among the lower classes (manual
labourers, junior employees), in closed communities (workshops, high-schools), and in those levels of society nurtured
more or less exclusively on mass culture (middle to lower
classes): *in other words, they are represented almost everywhere.* We may presume, then, that an area where several
of these determining factors exist will have acted as a
particularly favourable conductor. Such an area *par
excellence* is that occupied by girls and young women. As
a group they are sociologically peripheral on two counts:
they are young and they are female. They live in closed
communities, such as schools or other similar groups; and
(or) they are particularly receptive to mass culture (this
applies above all to wage-earning working-class girls).
Such a picture fits in well with our original observations;
it also lays fresh emphasis on two kinds of cleavage,

between teenagers and adults, and feminine as opposed to masculine.

At the outset the teenager-adult cleavage was a radical one, since the rumour incubated in a juvenile context without the adult world knowing a thing about it; but from 20 May onwards it disappeared. The temporary bridge that was established between the age-groups is perhaps one of the most remarkable elements in the whole Orléans phenomenon. Yet even during this period different groups reacted differently to the myth, and their various fantasies continued to develop in isolation.

The masculine-feminine split was visible right from the outset of the rumour, in the juvenile sector (though here it also circulated among boys without encountering much opposition). It is only at adult level that it emerges as the true major dividing-line of the entire affair. Not (let me repeat) that the men were altogether incredulous. But they watered the rumour down, and in the last resort did no more than flirt with it; they seized on its anecdotal, libidinous, even its Jewish aspects, without ever accepting it as a real inner experience. Throughout our investigation we were made aware of this obvious banal split between the sexes, but on a level that most often tends to be ignored or forgotten; it was their dreams that stood a world apart.

Is it possible, then, that this major split was primarily a psycho-oneiric one? I think not. *Rather it brings us back to certain irreducible, fundamental experiences, in which various factors—biological, economic, sociological, psychological—meet, intermingle and modify one another, and which add up to conditions: the condition of being a woman, the condition of youth.*

Since the problems stemming from such conditions apply to all social classes (though to varying degrees, and in different social terms); and as, furthermore, the myth covertly posed general problems concerning not merely the city, but the whole modern world, one can understand

D

its quasi-classless character, and the way it cut across a variety of heterogeneous social categories. This is not to say that its purpose and direction escaped profound modification according to their context. When the myth got into the hands of grown women, it became a weapon against the excessive or premature emancipation of young girls. When it reached traditionalist circles it became a sermon on conservatism. However, all these differentiations started out from an initial state of non-differentiation, and in a highly confused atmosphere, which explains how the virus caught on so widely.

Can we perhaps account for this inter-class confusion by the reasons advanced above? It seems to me that there is something more involved. What we can detect here is one of the symptoms of modern society's homogenisation: the widespread development of an immense middle-class agglomerate, under the umbrella of mass culture (which, let us not forget, was what first activated the Orléans rumour). In such conditions the weakening of certain major class-barriers now permits mythic or ideological elements of a highly generalised or ambivalent nature to circulate unimpeded.

We can also see here the psycho-social symptoms of a confused situation parallel, in some respects, to those which facilitated the modern development of Fascism in the West. In both cases we find wildly disparate layers of the population being united by some profoundly ambivalent speech or message, in which each person believes he recognises his own aspirations; in both there is the same mixture of violent, frustrated revolutionary tendencies (here feminine emancipation, and, more generally, a secret urge to change one's way of life), fears and spurts of pure fantasy, which the forces of conservatism sometimes hold in check, and sometimes unleash.

The Orléans myth emanated from sectors that were, at one and the same time, very modern in outlook, politically immature, and by no means wholly free of the fears generated by a dependence on millennial beliefs. It is very striking that such a myth could, on the one hand, trigger off a wave of collective hysteria, complete with Jewish scapegoat, and on the other become a platform for conservative propaganda. It is also striking that, right from the beginning, certain basic features of the 'modernist line' were borrowed from the same archaic mythology that had served to support reactionary ideologies in the past. It is striking, lastly, that the sheer audacity of the project should also, *ab initio*, have aroused atavistic terror.

In this sense the anti-myth was both very clear-sighted and very blind as regards its handling of fascism. Blind, in that it envisaged a political phenomenon, whereas the Orléans rumour was infra-political, in all the main senses covered by the term *polis*. Could one talk of extra-lucid feminine fascism? At the same time there did exist in Orléans, if only in larval form, certain developments, and a state of mythological confusion, analogous to parallel phenomena that had either nourished the growth of fascism, or at least been attracted by it.

Though they set out from basically different standpoints, there is nothing to stop us introducing, at this point, the hypothesis which regards any new homogenising developments in modern society as analogous to those phenomena that formed a breeding-ground for fascism. Homogenisation, far from opposing psycho-social ferment of every sort, actively encourages it. Such upheavals, at present still submerged beneath *polis* level, could, granted favourable socio-political conditions, develop into—*what*? We cannot as yet tell; but the problem is one that must claim our attention.

At all events, one fact emerges from the various sidelights we have shed on the rumour's tendency to jump class barriers: the sheer extent of cultural ignorance involved. This is not, we believe, to be regarded as the mere residue of an uninformed state now rapidly in process of abolition; if it were so, it would be restricted to the less urbanised or socially under-developed areas. In fact it has grown up in modern living and working conditions, among the middle no less than the lower classes, in the tertiary no less than the productive sectors. Modern means of communication may have made it easier to fight the Orléans rumour; but the sluggish tide of mass culture they poured out contained germs of its own—which took root.

THE ANTIBODIES

These consisted of the following, in order of their appearance and their importance:

The victims themselves.

The Jewish community.

Militant anti-racialist groups.

The (or some) political militants of the Left (in the loose sense of that term, which includes leftists, Communists, the *Parti Socialiste Unitaire* [PSU], socialists, left-wing Christians, and any other radical groups).

Simultaneously with the last group, a proportion of the intelligentsia.

THE AMBIGUOUS INTELLIGENTSIA

What struck us most was the failure of teachers to take a responsible line with their pupils and the population at large during the period of the rumour's incubation and subsequent outbreak. Some women (we are here concerned with girls' schools) not only swallowed the rumour but gave it active encouragement. During the LICA meeting one militant anti-racialist declared: 'It is much to be regretted that certain members of the teaching profession warned their pupils against patronising the shops in question.' It is true, of course, that during the incubatory period the anti-Semitic aspect of the affair had not yet become apparent; even when the rumour was assuming epic proportions we find a *Jewish* teacher issuing the same sort of warning to her class. On the other hand, the lunatic nature of the myth should surely have put people on their guard.

CONDUCTORS AND ANTIBODIES

When the anti-mythic counter-offensive got under way, a number of teachers—but by no means the majority—joined it as militants. The FEN made a denunciatory statement which differed in no specially remarkable way from any other communiqué issued at the time. The faculty at the Université de la Source remained more or less detached from the whole affair. It is true that La Source lies geographically, and to some extent socially, outside Orléans; a large number of its teachers are Parisians, and live in the metropolis. But the mere fact that it stood aside is a sign of inertia.

Let us leave higher education on one side, and concentrate here on the teaching in girls' secondary schools, where there was a clear lack of responsibility among the staff. Our explanation for this lack rests on three interlinked causes in conjunction:

Women teachers—especially the numerous young girls, spinsters and old ladies who fall in this category—are, by reason of their sex and age, good natural myth-conductors. Yet why, in so many cases, should this characteristic completely eclipse the fact that they also belonged to the cultivated class?

Here there intervenes an allergic reaction peculiar to the teaching profession. For these educators, these standard-bearers of the classical humanities, modern adolescent culture—referred to by them as *yéyé*[1]—is the very distillation of teenage frivolity and self-debasement. *Yéyé* is a case of bad culture driving out good; it is the cultural enemy that substitutes Sylvie Vartan for Racine and square roots, that makes students gawp at the ceiling and yawn at Corneille, and prefer Pascal (Jean-Claude) to Pascal (Blaise).[2] Did not these teachers see their chance to strike a double blow, at *yéyé* and mini-skirt, by

---

[1] See above, p. 68.

[2] The French for a square root is *une racine carrée*; to gawp at the ceiling is *bayer aux corneilles*. M. Morin's puns are highly ingenious, but untranslatable into English.—Trs.

denouncing the shops which purveyed such frivolities, and
in which perdition and perversion lay concealed? Did
they not see a golden chance to regain the authority they
had lost—now suddenly offered back to them by the
teenagers themselves, who had been scared silly by their
own fantasies? Was it not, at the very least, an opportunity
to get some sort of discussion going at last? As one
militant woman Catholic said, 'The positive result of all
this is that we've been able to broach a number of topics
with our younger generation.'

All this must be seen as part of a deep, widespread,
general crisis which the teaching profession is at present
going through. Under the constant assault of mass culture,
amid the general crisis in the humanities, a growing inclination to give up adds its weight to the development of
a mentality more suitable for civil servant or petit-
bourgeois. Teaching is becoming increasingly a career, less
and less a vocation of the Enlightenment (*Aufklärung*).[1]
What is more, education as such is rapidly losing touch with
the cultural problems of the modern world. If it hopes to
achieve some understanding of daily life and concrete
social phenomena, it is hardly likely to do so through the
ideologies at its disposal, or by means of opinion polls and
sociological enquiries (whether independent or official).
The white slave trade is just as mysterious and mythological
a phenomenon for the schoolmistress as it is for her pupil;
what little knowledge she may have of it derives from the
same sources. What is more, her knowledge of the *yéyé* is
based purely on fantasy, and the mores of the young
people she meets every day are less familiar to her than
those of Amazonian tribesmen—for information about

---

[1] *Aufklärung*: the equivalent, in the history of German thought, of what
France termed the Enlightenment (*l'époque des lumières*). The German
expressions *Aufklärung* and *Aufklärer* (the bearer of enlightenment) are
preferable to the French terms, because they express, in a richer and
more condensed manner, the quasi-sacerdotal function of one who introduces the light of reason and awakens the mind—a task long associated
with the teacher.

whom she at least has the findings of ethnography at her disposal.

If teaching, the ancient stronghold of the intelligentsia, showed up as a weak element in the affair, the *Maison de la Culture*, by way of contrast, was its strongest point. The fact is that the *Maison de la Culture* constitutes a politico-cultural centre, strongly militant in character, a focal point for cultural activists from various different strata of the intelligentsia (including students and high-school pupils), where leftism is not only present, but pre-dominant. The *Maison de la Culture* also acted as a spear-head of the anti-myth movement by initiating a public petition (though this seems to have collected only about a thousand signatures), and by organising the mass meeting of 8 June presided over by Louis Guilloux. But here, too, the dissuasive force was in inverse proportion to the degree of elucidation.

A final note, for the record, on the subject of students, concerning whom our information is minimal. Those resident at La Source are virtually outside the Orléans orbit; the myth began to circulate there about 20 May, though it does not seem to have assumed epidemic pro-portions. The same applies to the anti-myth. One theory, suggested by Léon Poliakov, was that the pro-Arab line taken by left-wing students might well have inhibited the normal process leading to a rejection of anti-Semitism; but we have not been able to verify this hypothesis one way or the other. What we did find abundantly clear was that not only at the *Maison de la Culture*, but also at the two high-school branches of the *Comité d'Action pour la Liberté Scolaire* (CALS), the Left was very much to the fore in combating the rumour, with simultaneous attacks on Fascism, the Government, and the police. Broadly speaking, it does not look as though that anti-Zionism which has become fashionable among left-wing intelli-gentsia was either directly or indirectly responsible for the passive role assumed by so large a proportion of the

Orléans intelligentsia. However, we have not investigated this side of the problem at all, and therefore must restrict ourselves to scrutinising the hypothesis in the light of such meagre evidence as we happen to have available.

But nevertheless, whichever way we look at it, the intelligentsia presents two different faces, according to which of two contrasting spheres of influence we choose to scrutinise: on the one hand the teaching profession, and on the other the *Maison de la Culture*. On the one hand ineffectuality and weakness, no compensating insights, and, moreover, some serious failings on the part of certain women teachers; on the other, militant energy, though unaccompanied by what should be the hallmark and function of the intelligentsia—clarification.

FIVE

STRESS AND DISTRESS AMONG THE JEWS

The Jewish community of Orléans numbered about thirty families before the war. As a result of the Nazi persecution this figure was decimated. Today there are roughly a hundred families, half of them repatriated from North Africa. These are mostly clerks and low-grade civil servants. As we have already noted, the rumour did not strike at the highest category of Jew, those of French extraction and old family who had been long settled in the town. It attacked neither the 'old-style' shopkeepers on the Rue de Bourgogne (who specialise in cheap ready-made dresses, and whose accent is still sometimes noticeable), nor the Mediterranean newcomers. Instead it concentrated on the commercial *nouvelle vague*—all young, go-ahead, modern types, born in France. Some might be outsiders in relation to Orléans, but on account of their Parisian background, not as foreigners.

The community lived in the town in what might be termed a state of cordial immersion—though doubtless also in a state of peaceful, and invisible, segregation. Amiable relations were maintained with neighbours; friendships, both casual and intimate, developed between Jews and non-Jews, especially at high-school. Yet in the main, social relations were limited to the group—not so much within the community, in any overall sense, as between people of the same age and background. All this seemed quite normal to the parties concerned; it was not thought to suggest any kind of segregation, either externally imposed, or desired by the group itself.

The Six Day War of 1967 did not create any split between the Jews and the rest of the population. When the President of the community organised a collection for Israel, he was greeted with sympathy rather than distrust. The Jews themselves, on the other hand, felt greater self-assurance; it was as though some of the prestige won by the Israeli army's lightning victory had rubbed off on them. It was only among left-wing students that an abrupt break became visible, a sudden feeling of rejection. 'For the first time,' Monique Amrofel—then a student of literature—told us, 'I heard the phrase "You only say that because you're Jewish".'

The really virulent centres of anti-Semitism had been swept away and dispersed along with the war-time 'Kollaboration'. Yet though it now seemed accepted that Jews were as other men, the feeling of their difference remained widespread. After the war people talked about 'buying from the Jews', a term which here implied both 'price-cutters' and those 'who are not like the rest of us'. The rapid success of the new boutique for young ladies showed that the Jews were 'sharp', that they always 'knew how to get by'. They were 'regular thieves' to sell at such cut-throat prices, but it all turned out to the customer's advantage. Such reactions were very far from crossing that invisible danger line beyond which the normal pejorative sentiments expressed by one group towards another turn into smouldering hostility.

Thus the invisible and peaceful segregation was unconscious on both sides. However, one factor that would clearly seem, in our opinion, to confirm it is the fact that the rumour abruptly went silent when it got anywhere near Jews—or, in those rare cases when it *did* reach a Jew's ears, omitted the word 'Jew'. We regard it as

significant rather than accidental that the President of
the community was only tipped off when the scandal was
at its height, and even then through a member of his own
staff. His father-in-law had lived in Orléans since 1880.
He himself had been an Orléanais since 1932. He is an
affable person, in close daily contact with dozens of
customers in his shop (which sells electrical equipment),
and with numerous café acquaintances. Yet it was not
until 30 May, at midday, that a shop-assistant of Spanish
origin, whom he had taken on after the Civil War, warned
him that hostile rumours about the Jews were circulating
in his own office.

On 30–31 May the explosive development of the rumour
put the Jewish shop-owners themselves in the picture,
with brutal suddenness. What got through to them was
not only the accusation of white slaving, but a real anti-
Semitic threat. During the next few days it was this threat
that became the prime or even the unique aspect of the
slander as far as they were concerned. We have no record
of the immediate emotional reactions which the metastasis
of 30–31 May provoked in the other categories of Jew in
Orléans, and here we shall simply follow the reactions of
those persons directly concerned.

It was a genuine stress reaction, an extraordinarily
violent and deep-reaching emotional upheaval which far
outweighed the mere emotional anxiety provoked by
falling receipts (in fact the actual losses appear to have
been minimal). However, it was by taking this economic
anxiety into account, and exaggerating it, that the shop-
owners attempted to translate an unspeakable injury into
generally comprehensible terms.

What rose up in them was a feeling of solitude, distress
and fear. On the morning of 31 May crowds gathered
outside the three shops, staring. Others drove slowly past
in their cars, also staring. 'People looked me straight in
the eye,' Jeannette Buki told us. Were these glances
hostile, inquisitorial, intrigued or due to mere idle curi-

osity? Who can tell? But one thing both Jeannette Buki
and the Lichts saw very clearly. This was the look that
isolated, stigmatised, labelled one with a yellow star; this
look spoke of Drancy and Auschwitz and the crematoria.
The fear did not last long; but it was still there at the
beginning of July, and the sense of solitude must have
persisted a great deal longer. A young high-school girl, the
daughter of one of the shop-owners, realised (thought?
knew?) that she had been abandoned and betrayed by a
very close friend. 'She'd been saying things behind my
back for ages . . . she was anti-Semitic.'

Anti-Semitism. Though it was still half-imaginary, not yet
detached from the white slave myth, and directed merely
against *some* Jews (rather than against all Jews as such),
the victims reacted allergically. A small dose of anti-
Semitism had had the terrifying effect of strong poison.
A germ, an egg, abruptly hatched out in the minds of the
victims, and reconstituted an entire persecution-cycle.
At the same time as the circumstances of persecution were
forced upon the victims, making the shop a ghetto and the
street scene the prelude to a pogrom, so was the conviction that a plot existed. The whole thing had been 'planned
and organised'. But by whom? By business rivals? This
original idea was far from having completely faded out by
the beginning of July. During June, however, the political
and anti-racialist organisations had overlaid it with the
notion that if a plot existed, hidden political forces were
responsible for it.

During the first ten days of June, it is true, support
arrived; various expressions of sympathy reached the
victims, from local businessmen and their own guild; the
customers drifted back. But—as the victims were not
slow to notice—they did not return alone. Behind neigh-
bourly cordiality, they felt, lurked indifference, while
silence was a token of overt hostility.

The town had become stifling. Members of the group
wanted to get out. 'We can't stay here any longer,' said

one. 'What's left for us in Orléans?' said another. The owners of *Alexandrine*—Jews despite themselves—also talked about leaving. Leaving for Paris, the great metropolis from where most of them had come; but in any case going somewhere else.

In this mood of distress, Israel was seen as the refuge, the lifebuoy. There were no schemes for emigration; but one family cancelled its reservations in Spain and went to Israel for its holidays instead. Another derived some comfort from the arrival of Israeli television . . .

Though all of them took this attack very hard indeed, the reflex instinct for a counter-offensive was by no means unanimously shared. While the younger businessmen mostly had a typical *sabra* reaction—hit back hard—their elderly parents (and even one of their own number) were afraid that hitting back hard would simply make matters worse. The two with shops opposite one another, *Dorphée* and *Félix*, represent the two contrasting faces of Judaism. Licht *(Dorphée)* fought back, brought charges, gave interviews to journalists and was prominent in the anti-myth movement. Félix brought no charges, never talked to journalists, went to ground, faded into the landscape.

But among the victims Félix's attitude stood out as exceptional, whereas that of *Dorphée*, the principal victim, was very much to the point, and swung most of the rest into line behind him. However, this majority was now faced with the increasingly political atmosphere of the affair. For the most part, they allowed themselves to be drawn into the anti-myth movement launched by the LICA and MRAP, without making any great effort to find out what difference there might be between them. Still, the near-Communist characteristics of the MRAP caused hesitation in some; while for others the LICA could seem either too far right or too far left, according to conviction. In the latter case, the moderates feared that either one of these associations might prejudice contact with the official

authorities, whose protection they hoped to obtain. It was
the President of the Jewish Community who found himself
at the point where these lines of force intersected. He
encouraged the victims to bring suit. He approved the
decision of the anti-racialist associations to enter the fray,
and had no wish to discriminate between them. An old
radical socialist himself, he maintained friendly contacts
with the Left, up to and including the Communists, but
was also on good terms with the Right. He did his utmost
to ensure that the community he represented should not
be crushed, sandwich-like, as a result of the political clash
which now developed between the opposition and officialdom. He sought some support—even moderate or implied
—from the authorities.

Thus the President reflected and embodied those multiple
tendencies and facets which—under the stress of shock—
came to light in the Community, and which provoked
different reactions according to age, profession, opinions
and origins. But at the same time he also reflected that
cumulative feeling of communal solidarity which was set
in motion by the shock itself.

Then, with time, the effect of the shock wore off, and
things began to move back to the old state of peaceful and
invisible segregation.

SIX

THE POLITICAL
BACKWASH

From the moment the rumour erupted into the *polis*, it became, inevitably, a political issue. On 30 May Licht was at the central police station. The superintendent told him: 'Hold on for forty-eight hours, and then raise hell.' His point was to avoid disturbing the last two days before the elections. From the beginning of the week of 2 June, the parties on the Left endorsed the anti-myth and gave it their active support. Henceforth active involvement and a wait-and-see attitude were no longer merely individual attitudes, or strategic options adopted for combating the rumour, but became ways of behaviour liable to produce certain political effects. The politicalisation of the affair was probably stimulated, during the first fortnight in June, by the interim period between the two stages of the Presidential election. But this national event (which, in any case, the left wing of the anti-myth pointedly ignored) made no difference at all to the nature of the affair, or indeed to its development. Already, moreover, three separate policies had evolved, in embryo, among the victims: violent denunciation, middle-of-the-road tactics, and prudent silence. Each was to be picked up and fostered by local political forces. From the beginning three contrasting political lines emerged, based respectively on scandal, discretion and silence.

POLITICAL TECHNIQUES

Scandal

The anti-myth, the 'anti-Semitic plot' born of the victims'
own reactions, was fated to become a political weapon from
the moment the opposition claimed to reveal its 'fascist'
nature. For the Communist Party, and indeed for the Left
generally, the rumour was a pointer to secret collusion
between the Government party and right-wing extremists,
with the State's more or less passive connivance. In addition to this, the Communist Party was perhaps concerned to show that it did not confuse anti-Zionism with
anti-Semitism, the former being a good progressive attitude,
but the latter beneath contempt. Perhaps, too, the MRAP
was eager to make some indirect rejoinder to the anxiety
felt by its supporters: recent news about events in both the
USSR and Poland might well have given them grounds
to fear that beneath the red star a yellow one lay hidden.
Alternatively, perhaps both the Communist Party and
the MRAP were anxious to dissociate themselves, indirectly, from the stand taken by the People's Democracies
on the Jewish question.

By a natural process of evolution, the eruption of politics
into the anti-Semitic scandal made it a fascist scandal—
which many people hoped to use as a means of embarrassing
the governing party, especially since in Orléans this party
also controlled City Hall.

Discretion

Like the scandal technique, this too existed embryonically
in a Jewish reaction, and can be summed up by the attitude of the President of the Community, who played a
'scandal line' without ever overstepping the mark in a way
that would alienate official authority. The technique of
discretion is, by its very nature, a compromise attitude
between opposing forces, a middle-of-the-road policy.
Thus it could equally well, in this case, have been based on
prudence, moderation or opportunism—or simply have

resulted from the pressure of the anti-myth on those who were forced to shed ballast but had no wish to be swamped. The technique of discretion denounced the rumour as a plot or cabal, but was very careful not to put the finger on any individual. It went out of its way to contain or limit the politically corrosive tendencies of the anti-myth. The technique of discretion was practised by a wide-ranging variety of people—the moderate Jews, the bishopric, those professional organisations to which the victims appealed; for a certain time, and in a certain sense, it was also adopted by the Préfecture—or rather, was embodied in the compromise bargain struck between the Préfecture and the Jewish community.

The technique of discretion found its perfect illustration at the time of the Sidos meeting. Neither the Préfecture nor the President of the Community (who doubtless largely reflected the opinion of those he represented) had any intention of allowing the anti-myth movement to become identified with the political opposition. The difference between them was that the Community insisted on at least a token show of intervention as the price of their discretion, whereas the Préfecture had no wish to intervene except in a virtually invisible fashion.

As was mentioned earlier, a Sidos meeting had been booked well in advance for the beginning of July in Orléans. The Préfecture could either ban it, which would mean taking a *de facto* anti-fascist line—something the authorities steadfastly refused to do—or else authorise it, and thus risk being credited with fascist leanings. The Prefect, it would seem, took the initiative in a way that enabled him not only to avoid running on either reef, but also to take positive action on the victim's behalf without prejudicing the Government party. He authorised the meeting, but suggested to both the Jewish Community and the FNDIR (Federation of non-Communist Deportees) that they should each send a delegation of about forty members to intimidate the speaker and prevent his taking

an anti-Jewish line. At the same time, the presence in the
hall of police inspectors would put a stop to any im-
moderate tirades against the Government. The ostenta-
tious presence of numerous police cars in the area was
calculated to make this operation a complete success.
Sidos in fact attacked neither the Jews nor *Gaullisme*.
The Prefect had made a gesture on behalf of the community,
and the Community one on behalf of the Préfecture. That
evening the division lay between the moderates and the
extreme right, not between the anti-myth and the
moderates.

Silence

The technique of silence, again, corresponded, at the
beginning, with a Jewish standpoint: that disillusioned
and fatalistic attitude which regards fire-fighting activities,
of any sort, as merely liable to stir up the blaze still further.
But—also from the beginning—it was the line adopted by
the municipal authorities (i.e. by the Government party)
and, for most of the time, by the Préfecture. The Mayor
found it comparatively easy to avoid committing himself,
since during the crucial period in late May and early June
he was on holiday, and only made one quick trip back into
town for election-day. The Fifth Union Départemental was
the only group that failed to answer the LICA's letter. The
Prefect, when approached by the SCRIF (in a letter from
Dr Modiano), wavered between silence and discretion. He
refused to make a public declaration—at the same time
explaining, unofficially, that his position precluded any
such activities on his part, and assuring the victims that
he was watching the situation closely.

The technique of silence justified itself by the assertion
that the rumours were private, not political, and that
gossip, or even slander, did not necessarily add up to
anti-Semitism. Unofficially, the advocates of silence
presented themselves as the advocates of discretion; that
is, they claimed that the best way of combating the rumour

was to avoid attacking it head-on. In fact it looks rather as though the official party went out of its way, *ab initio*, to avoid affronting the general public, and above all, in June, not to get forced into alignment with a movement that would bring it into opposition with its own declared position. The official party feared precisely what the left wing of the anti-myth movement hoped for—i.e. that any denunciation of anti-Semitism would bring about a revival of that anti-fascist line which was especially associated with the Left. It was scared, not only of letting itself be lured on to its adversaries' ground, but also of creating divisions within the heterogeneous electoral coalition that had supported it, the most obvious potential split being between former Resistance workers and former Vichy men.

In its second phase, the party of silence became the party of suppression. This time it was concerned, not with the rumour, but with the anti-myth. The anti-myth was an instrument of war, directed against the official party. It had to be smashed. But here, again, this could not be done by a direct show-down, for fear of seeming sympathetic to anti-Semitism; the line would be to denounce its political supporters as Machiavellian schemers. Once again the plot motif reappeared. The Communists, it was said, had thought up the whole affair. They had taken some idle rumours and turned them into a pin-prick campaign. It was hinted that they had even put these rumours into circulation themselves. Thus the entire affair shifted its centre of gravity, became a conflict between Right and Left—and, in more acute fashion, between moderates and Communists. As a result, the moderates decided to suppress the whole pestilential story; it was now that the Préfecture stopped fence-sitting and adopted a policy of suppression. On 17 July 1969, the police informed the producer of a projected television programme on the affair that it was a 'dead letter'. Next day the divisional police superintendent dismissed a group of journalists from

his office with the words: 'The affair is over. Gentlemen,
with the greatest possible politeness, I must ask you all
to leave.'

THE EBBING OF THE TIDE
This coincided with a desire to forget the whole thing,
which privately affected a large part of the population:
all those, at least, who had believed the rumour and now
found themselves the target for attacks by outsiders,
who not only condemned their behaviour, but also exposed
them to ridicule. Thus this unprecedented event, which
had blown up during the last days in May, was simultaneously driven back and given a fresh lease of life. On
the one hand it retreated into the sub-political depths
whence it had emerged, fostering larval rumours; on the
other, it was recharged by traditional political antagonisms,
and dissolved in them.

SEVEN

THE INTERROGATIONS

THE ORLEANS INCIDENT

What in fact took place at Orléans? A rumour, a wind of
fantasy which, assuming the form of a cyclonic depression,
met with a somewhat disorganised reaction on the part
of the *polis*. The Orléans incident was just that: the
turbulent encounter between a fully-fledged rumour and
the various repressive elements which it set in motion, a
maelstrom which, by a series of chain-reactions (and
counter-reactions) shook every filament in that mysterious
entity which constitutes a town. Orléans, in fact,
went through a genuine crisis, which we may analyse
as follows: the sudden opening of a breach in the
social fabric, and the eruption into this breach of
a hidden, subterranean reality, as new as it was unfamiliar; the triggering off of a destructive chain-reaction;
the triggering off, as a counter-move, of a reconstructive
process, i.e. the entry into action of the *polis*, which
exacerbated those local political conflicts through which
the crisis simultaneously prolonged itself, became side-
tracked, and (after one or two final spasms) ceased to
exist; the triggering off of psychological repressors which
provoked—either conjointly or in a differentiated fashion
—first, rationalisation (explanation of this new element
by reducing it to ancient behavioural patterns), second,
containment (of the new elements, or of the phenomenon

117

itself), and, finally, an amnesia similar to that which, after waking, disperses one's recollections of a nightmare.

Thus the Orléans incident involved something more than the appearance of a myth (the structure, and the very virulence of which contained within themselves a species of somnambulistic truth); it was also, in a sense, a mini-crisis. Now a crisis of this sort, a situation which brings hidden elements to light and upsets the whole corpus of society, is not only *ipso facto* of considerable sociological interest, but also—in the original and more than ever valuable sense of that term—something which facilitates a *diagnosis*.

Let us attempt a preliminary survey of the valuable facts which emerge from the Orléans incident. Firstly, we have been able to observe, without interruption, the genesis, spread, metamorphosis and metastasis of a rumour which —attacked at this point by various repressors—underwent fresh metamorphoses in its dissolution and death agony. And this phenomenon embodies, at one and the same time, the eruption, incarnation and efflorescence of a myth. The latter catalysed certain floating anxieties, some of which lurked unsuspected, like gases, and—had it not been for this crisis—would have remained invisible, or have been blown away by any passing wind. Endowed with surprising phagocytic and metamorphic powers, it very soon attracted to itself a whole swarm of mythological fancies. Could it be that the period covered by the myth has acquainted us with certain myths of the period? Thirdly, this myth, the product of young girls' fantasies, rapidly spread throughout the subsoil of an entire town, and by so doing revealed to us the civically immature[1] depths of a particular society—depths that were linked with those of mass culture. Fourthly, belief in the reality

---

[1] 'Civically immature': the terms 'under-cultivated' or 'politically un-developed' would be either inadequate or too specific. Civic maturity implies a conscious self-alignment with the *polis* as such in one's day-to-day life.

of the myth reveals a flaw in the filtering system between the real and the imaginary as commonly conceived; this flaw, itself produced by joint pressure from the myth and some catalyst (*Noir et Blanc, Les Oubliettes*, plus an x-factor) was what provoked the initial phase of the crisis. And finally, the second phase was marked by the late arrival on the scene—as active participants—of elements of warning and repression. This delay was partly due to the absence of radar stations covering those civically immature zones from which no trouble was expected; and partly to the absence of a code suitable for correctly interpreting such information as spontaneously emerged from the area in question.

Thus what we have is a crisis operative not merely at the lower, civically immature levels of the *polis*, but in its higher echelons as well. The crisis was, it is true, met and surmounted; but it left its germs and residual fragments behind.

In its double character—accidental inflation of lower-depth myth, failures in the system of warning and repression—this crisis was strictly localised and limited to Orléans. Yet even if such an inflation of lower-depth myth occurred in Orléans and nowhere else, we have discovered, in retrospect, that there had been anterior symptoms occurring sporadically throughout France. This both raises the problem of possible renewal and reactivation in these underground mythological forces, and leaves one speculating on the likelihood of fresh outbreaks.

The fact that no such cases of inflation took place elsewhere may lead one to suppose that the inflation itself was caused by specific failures in the Orléans system of warning and repression. Now nothing has given us reason to suppose that there existed, in Orléans, some atypical feature (whether as regards the population generally, the teaching profession, the political parties, the local press, or the powers of the Préfecture and the municipal authorities) which would mark Orléans off as an aberrant exception

among the other towns of France. On the contrary:
Orléans is an average town, a test example very popular
with opinion-poll institutes. Thus the failures which revealed themselves in the social system as an overspill from
the lower depths have a more general significance and
compass. In what specific sense? This is what we must
attempt to discover. First, however, we must try to
establish a bridge by discussing, not only what the
Orléans incident can teach us about contemporary French
society, but also what society can teach us concerning the
incident at Orléans.

THE MIDDLE AGES TODAY

What Orléans really brings home to me personally is my
ignorance concerning the fantasies of the other sex—
whom we men love so much and in whose company we
spend so much of our time. It is the discovery of new
blank areas in that still little known continent of feminine
adolescence (which I previously flattered myself I had
explored). It is, too, the realisation that the dark corners
of that mass culture and modern mythology I had been
studying for over a decade were swarming with unsuspected motifs (e.g. the white slave myth, which I had
never stumbled on). Lastly, it is the revelation of a newly
fermenting anti-Semitism which, as a Jew myself, a *néo-
marrane*, balanced between two worlds, I should certainly
have been able to sense in advance.

By way of compensation I propose to set these new
discoveries in the context of their society and their time,
that is, in a general evolutionary sequence.

We know that the economic boom which got going
about 1950 modified—and continues to modify—the
entire body of society, by a series of chain-reactions;
according to which aspect of the process one chooses to
dwell on, one talks of the development of industrial society,
or of urban society, or of neo-capitalist society, or of the
consumer society, or of the bourgeoisie. I have attempted

elsewhere to study this question in general terms, and do not intend to reopen the discussion here.

What we should note, very briefly, is the multi-dimensional modification of our society. This modification becomes increasingly accentuated as the after-effects—not only economic ones—of the war become steadily more remote, and the searing experience of the war generations fades out, to be replaced by new generations, with new experiences of their own.

It seems to me that the sixties constitute a kind of watershed, a turning-point during which the last of the post-war era (or perhaps the beginning of a new *pre*war era?) merged into the new society whose lineaments were just beginning to emerge. This was the beginning of a new phase, in which trends hitherto vague and embryonic took on firm shape, and the pattern of society was in many respects broken down and rebuilt.

This was the context—with women being less and less suppressed, no longer automatically relegated to the home, and playing an increasingly prominent part both at work and in social life—in which adolescence and youth began to emerge as a separate age-group. The sixties also witnessed the emergence of the *yéyé*, and—by no fortuitous coincidence—the appearance of rumours among young girls about the new white slave trade.

This new age-group not only exerted pressure on adult society to modify the authoritarian relationship in which one class stood to the other; it also radiated a specific influence. In their own different ways, both May 1968 and May 1969 demonstrated this.

During the latter period, in fact, Orléans showed us a myth which, having originated among young girls, then spread to adult women, exerted an influence over a section of masculine society, and provoked a considerable disturbance in the overall structure of local society. But at the same time, Orléans also showed us that even after their absorption into the *polis*, young people, and the fair sex,

remained quasi-foreign bodies, bringing their own areas of
darkness with them; that by traditional *polis* standards
they were, in some respects, both semi-barbarian and
only semi-acclimatised to the idea of the *polis* as
such.

Are we to stop there? In my opinion the perspective
must be drawn wider still. During the last decade urban
society has witnessed not merely the eruption of new
factors (demographic upsurge and growth of juvenile
influence; emergence of women in all sectors of social life;
cityward drift from the country), but also, correlatively, a
breakdown in the old provincial hierarchy and the re-
structuring of traditional manners and morals. The provincial town is tending to become a modern agglomeration.
In this agglomerate, the various forms of traditional
authority, as vested in the upper classes, the *polis* authorities, the political parties, or even the provincial press,
tend to be a little fossilised at the roots. Round these
roots, on the other hand, there circulate the cultural
influences of the mass media, and those undercurrents of
mass culture which have not got to the point of making
contact with established forces, or of expressing themselves in terms of their ideology. These can nurture fantasies or anxieties of a sort that the *polis* authorities know
little about, and are ill-equipped to exorcise. Which
brings us back to the failure of the *polis*'s warning-
system, and the late intervention of the repressors in
Orléans.

To continue: these new developments encourage an
individualistic attitude to one's private life, and the
specialised sub-division of labour. They have been marked
by an increase of knowledge, both at a specialised level
and in a more generally informative way. Yet neither
allows one to attain an overall, systematic, concrete
understanding of the society in which one lives. The former
offers limited if coherent knowledge, which does not extend

beyond the bounds of professional competence; while the latter provides a smattering of information about everything, but in an incoherent manner.

Thus what we have seen to be true for youth, women, the town and daily life in general suggests not merely that the ancient hierarchical checks and balances have been destroyed by a normal process of transformation, but also that the spread of non-cultured and non-civilised zones goes hand in hand with the spread of civilisation and culture; that the progressive features of change are at the same time regressive. This sub-culture is in no way the result of a so-called retreat from humanist culture. On the contrary: the latter continues to spread *pari passu* with secondary education. The void is not caused by the disappearance of such regional cultures (terribly impoverished for all their incidental richnesses); here mass culture comes in as a substitute. It is also bound up with the fundamental inability of both humanist and mass culture to understand this new world, or to supply norms of life suitable for it. As a result both cultures become elements in the new non-culture.

In this society, moreover (which to superficial observers seemed obsessed with the achievement of well-being and the conquest of happiness), the springs of anxiety, far from drying up, appear to be entering on a new lease of life. What produces these worries? External threats looming over the world? Uprootings for which the new roots that are put down cannot compensate? That tight network of micro-repressions which constitutes the price paid for the advantages and securities of urban life? The new failings and new problems produced by the advance of bourgeois individualism? Here, again, I do not intend to extend my investigation too far, in any direction, beyond the scope of the rumour itself. We may note briefly, however, that the latter was nurtured and accompanied by sexual anxieties, modernist and anti-modernist anxieties, a collective civic anxiety; while underneath all this there perhaps lurked something else, something altogether deeper and more obscure.

Now the natural tendency of anxiety is to secrete fantasies, to seek some archaic refuge, and by that very fact to activate the mechanisms of expulsion and purification: the sacrifice of a scapegoat.

Among the crucial functions of mass culture is that of both feeding, and feeding on, these anxieties. It provides emotional nourishment. A centre of mythological ferment. It resuscitates archaic myths by giving them a modern form. It tends towards fiction, the mythological consummation, and in this sphere it constantly fabricates guilty or expiatory victims—which it then immolates. Or, again, when these mythological situations occur in real life, it pounces on them and turns them into news items. Now since the 'turning-point decade' of the sixties, we have seen a vast increase of fantasy in fiction; and the general image—notably since the spread of television—is that of a cumulative holocaust; endless deaths, i.e. immolations. Also, in certain magazines which now make it their speciality, there has grown up a confused fringe area of pseudo-information, where the process that formerly distinguished the imaginary from the real has ceased to operate. This constitutes one of mass culture's main functions after it has succeeded in giving life to what is imaginary as though it were real (fiction), and making the real live as though it were a product of the imagination (news reporting).

Let us not forget that it was in the *Noir et Blanc* article that there took place the first disruptive step in that dissociation of reality and imagination which produced the entire Orléans mythological chain-sequence. It was the undercurrents of mass culture which (starting from a genuine episode, itself perhaps based on some novel or film) picked up the old white slave motif, gave it a modern form, infused a new charge of fantasy into it, and endowed the full-blown myth with factual rather than fictional status. The rumour, in a hysterical fashion, picked up and embodied this pseudo-information, giving it the semblance of on-the-spot reality. It is true that the well policed zone of the mass media, by virtue of its controlling position, was able to repulse and shatter the rumour (thus re-establishing its own supremacy); but only after some delay, and then not with complete effectiveness.

In this way one can 'frame' the double myth of Orléans, a myth at once highly modern and highly archaic, the origins of which go back to the watershed of the fifties and sixties. It was only under the conditions I have set forth, and attempted to correlate, that the fantasy dreamed up by a group of adolescent girls could spread through an entire town, provoking no more than a feeble defence from adult/masculine/urban society at large; that a localised sexual anxiety could spread and deepen into anxiety of the most general and far-reaching sort; that the obscure and archaic need for a scapegoat should swim up to the surface of people's consciousness, together with the medi-eval spectre of the Jewish Tempter—disguised as a bourgeois and offering mini-skirts.

Doubtless it was necessary to wait for the post-post-war period, when the exorcism of the Nazis had lost much of its force, and the experience—or inexperience—of new generations could blend with the larval reminiscences of their elders, before the Jewish phantom could re-emerge from his subterranean hiding-place. There had to be new sources of anxiety—plus the devitalisation of those two ancient scapegoats maintained by the *polis*: the 'Communist' and the 'Fascist'. Of these the former was by now half-assimilated to civic life, and the latter half-forgotten; nor was it, I am convinced, accidental that the anti-myth resurrected the 'Fascist' and the anti-anti-myth the 'Communist' in order to drive the Jewish phantom back into the dark hole whence he had sprung.

One can think of the Orléans affair as an accident. It *was* an accident—but a highly revealing one. One can think of it as the product of something left over from the past. Yes—if one concedes that a germ, too, is 'something left over'. Personally, I regard our contemporary society—the way it is developing—not so much as a society which still embodies traces of archaism, but rather as one which is actively promoting archaism of a new kind. As I see it, far from driving out myth in the name of reason, it stimulates new myths and fresh instances of irrationality; instead of overcoming the problems and crises of humanity in a decisive manner, it provokes new problems and crises itself. The Orléans affair should not be treated as a sequel (or throw-back) to the Middle Ages in the modern world; it is, rather, *one symptom of our own modern Middle Ages*.

A word of warning here. The formula I have advanced is one I found particularly satisfying because of the seemingly paradoxical truth it contained. At the same time there is a risk of its foundering beneath the portentous concept of 'medievalism'. What I want to emphasise is the archaic element which features in the new modernity, and is likely to do so more and more as time goes on, assuming many diverse forms. Equally, I would like in this context to scotch that over-popular notion (produced by the use—and abuse—of the concept of industrial society) according to which we are heading back, at one and the same time, to rationalism and stability. On the other hand I am *not* in any way suggesting that our present new society is liable to stabilise itself over a long period by establishing some sort of equilibrium between modernity and medievalism.

It is in this process of becoming that we must place the Orléans outbreak, together with the phenomena that brought it to birth. Are these phenomena temporary ones, leading to the establishment of a new set of rules? It is not legitimate to suppose that eventually women and young people will be better integrated into the *polis*, that the modern city will acquire a new overall structure, and cease to be the agglomerate of a transitional period? Or is this rather one of the early abscesses heralding a general crisis in the *polis*? What do such phenomena portend? Is it impossible for our society, in its present state, to cross the threshold beyond which real civilisation begins? Or do we have here, on the contrary, that mortal sickness of civilisation foretold by Freud in his *Civilisation and its Discontents*? Are these its early premonitory symptoms?

In any case, we have reached a point at which one cannot foretell the future development of our society. It will experience a mass of corrective and modificatory feedback, together with the effect of powerful counter-currents determined by dominant trends, in addition to such counter-attacks as are liable to be decisive—or fatal—for the future of a crisis-ridden planet. Thus the predictive function of sociology must do something more than merely extend today's technical-cum-economic graph lines into the future, and credit them with a hypothetical growth rate. It must also give advance warning of cyclonic depressions, of shifting sands, of new growths (mythological ones included); it must pinpoint the sources of all new potential problems, troubles and conflicts.

PANDORA

Here, it goes without saying, the question of the future of anti-Semitism poses itself. We have already seen that, from the viewpoint of the Jewish theme, the Orléans rumour could not be regarded as a temporary aberration on the part of a myth which originated elsewhere and had a different destination. On the other hand it involved no anti-Semitic machinations either. Without any conspiracy, advance preparation, or political propaganda, there emerged a spontaneous propensity, in one section of the social organism, to contract the virus, not indeed, as yet, of pox proper, but at least that of smallpox.

It is true that all this was an ephemeral phenomenon, that it was driven back into the lower depths, and that from thenceforth the *polis* was alerted. But it had by no

means been blotted out of existence, and people's suspicions concerning the Jews were stronger after the rumour
than before it. The rumour's source turned out to lie in an
unexpected quarter, among those areas of non-culture
which at present seem to be extending rather than expanding, and are—as we have seen—perfectly compatible
with the culture of schools or, indeed, of universities.
Here we have the young and beautiful Pandora with her
box.

Furthermore, we may ask ourselves whether the factors
acting to repress all potential anti-Jewish manifestations,
so vigorous after the Second World War, are not now
losing a good deal of their effectiveness. We may ask
ourselves whether the political parties and intelligentsia
of the Left—amongst whom were numbered a fair proportion of the victimised Jews' guardian angels—are not now
being transformed into militant archangels, suspicious of
(or indeed actively threatening) the Jewish Zionist. In the
USSR and the People's Democracies, we find increasing
emphasis on that policy which, while seemingly dis-
sociating the Jew-as-victim from the Jewish Zionist, in
actual fact treats them as one and the same person. It
follows that any presumption of sympathy for this new
Jew, or even an absence of hostility towards Israel, can
incur an *a priori* suspicion of Zionism. Thus the Jew
resumes his old double-faced personality.

One other important factor has helped to further such a
correlation. The changes brought about by the Arab-
Israeli war all accentuate this duality, in the eyes not only
of the Communists, but also of all leftist revolutionary
movements, and above all of the left-wing intellectuals,
who constitute the Jews' principal mainstay. The Jew
himself will be sentimentally inclined to regard Israel as
his second country, and to credit himself, by a process of
identification, with all those military, agrarian and productive virtues which the anti-Semitic tradition has consistently denied him. For an ever-increasing proportion of

the left-wing intelligentsia, then, he will become less and less the martyred victim of Hitler, and more and more a 'bulwark of imperialism'. This state of affairs could only be changed by two things: a settlement in the Middle East (which at present looks highly improbable), or, at some time in the future, a massacre of the Israelis. Neither eventuality would gain for the Jew that immunity which the holocaust of five million souls won him twenty years ago.

Nevertheless, none of this gives one grounds for predicting a dangerous and virulent resurgence of anti-Semitism in France. It simply means that the days of the privileged enclave are over, and that henceforth there is liable to be a greater larval ferment of anti-Semitic activity, based on the bacteria and residual detritus of the past—though this will not sensibly modify the present state of affairs. At the same time it should not be forgotten that we are living through a period of history in which crises within the fabric of society are regularly forecast, in which religious and racial wars are once more flaring up, and in which neither nations nor groups have advanced one iota as regards mutual understanding.

The Jews' only chance would be to get themselves forgotten amid other ethnic conflicts—a catastrophic turn of events for humanity at large. This also makes it clear that the suffering undergone by the Jew is only one aspect—though one rendered perennially appalling by his perennial minority position—of a more general, widespread ill, and one which gives no grounds for anticipating its progressive extinction.

THE CONSCIENCE OF THIS WORLD

The Orléans incident, finally, leaves us with a strong impression that the intelligentsia, far from being an enlightened caste capable of elucidating the problems of these modern Middle Ages, was, on the contrary, afflicted by them itself, in its own way.

E

As was stated earlier, a society's culture and lack of culture develop *pari passu*. This applies even at the highest intellectual level. The intelligentsia (educationalists included) are extremely ignorant concerning the bottom of the pyramid which they inhabit. They condemn and exorcise the jets of steam blown off by these lower strata, but without understanding either their nature or their origin. There is a genuine case of communication blockage between the educated and the lower classes. Hence the range of credulity in this affair, extending from teachers who themselves believed in the existence of a white slave traffic, conducted by shop-owners in the very centre of town, to those who instantly interpreted the whole thing as a 'Fascist plot'.

The intelligentsia, too, are influenced by the non-culture of their age. What resources have they? Either classical studies, the humanities, which offer nothing to equip one with awareness of social problems and the modern world; or specialised areas of learning, which even if tacked together would not provide an overall picture of our society; or a chaotic mass of informative snippets, even less capable of being run together to form a whole: or ideologies and myths sold in the political market-place; or, more often than not, a confused jumble of all these simultaneously.

They cannot use sociology as a key to the society in which they live. For one thing, sociology is, in the last resort, a mere aggregate of specialised and fragmentary pieces of knowledge. For another, its dominant tendency is against analysing modern society except in terms of industrial or technological trends, new professional alignments, demographic modifications, and opinion-polls— things which merely skim off the surface foam from conscious and unconscious mind alike.

By constructing a mechanical model concerned with no more than one dimension of reality, such sociological studies have evoked the image of a predominantly rational society. This veneer laid over hard facts not only camou-

flages the neo-medieval aspect of reality, but also provides
a vehicle for neo-medieval scholastic thought—while at
the same time constituting a rationalistic, euphoria-laden
myth for the sustenance of intellectual technocrats. One
part of the intelligentsia, alive to the ills inherent in this
world, will have no truck with such a myth. Instead they
plump for the concept of the 'necessary revolution'—but
then make a myth of that too, finding it incarnated here,
there and everywhere, and searching the schemes of some
ideological vulgate for an explanation of all phenomena,
every disturbance in the here-and-now.

If we find the intelligentsia more prone to believe in
myths than elucidate them, this may, *inter alia*, be due to
the fact that, far from being immune to those anxieties
which secretly trouble society, they experience them in a
specially privileged manner. Such a state of affairs will
hardly enhance their aptitude for acting as the conscience
of society.

Hence the striking failures and inadequacies displayed
by the Orléans intelligentsia. One group allowed itself to
be persuaded by the rumour. Another remained more or
less indifferent to the whole affair. A third actively opposed
the process of demythification. What prevailed was not
elucidation but intimidation. It was not demythification
that operated against the rumour, but a mythologically
potent anti-myth. The spectres conjured up were the
increasingly remote ones of the Second World War, rather
than those which may conceivably presage the third.

One could stop at this point, on the problem of the vital
need for awareness and knowledge of the contemporary
world. But this would mean stopping without even touching on one problem which turns out to have been very
much at issue in Orléans: that of belief.

BELIEF

Let us scrutinise the rumour once more, for the last time.
How did the myth it embodied get to the point of actually

commanding belief? Here, right at the outset, we have to do with clear symptoms of hysteria. Not in the sense that there was a case of direct hallucination, i.e. that some person who transmitted the rumour actually *saw* a drugged woman, or a white slaver in action, or even claimed to have knowledge of such a 'disappearance' *de visu*. What I mean, rather, is that the fantasy gave rise to observation at one remove, on the part of some 'irrefutable' witness.

The corroborative strength of such testimony depended on its source being extremely close either to the person who actually found the vanished girl (the wife of the police-man who searched the cellar of the shop, the nurse who brought the drugged victim round), or else to the vanished girl herself (a relative or neighbour). It was, at the same time, closely linked with the person actually relating the information: she (he) would have had it from a relative, friend or neighbour who was *also* a relative, friend or neighbour of the corroborating witness. Thus the strength of the myth lay in the fact that it seemingly depended on the most rigorous verification anyone could want, that of direct testimony passed on and vouched for by a trust-worthy acquaintance.

Thus the myth spread, with the backing, now, of sys-tematic 'proof', specially designed to convince sceptics. But even at this stage it still presented certain constant features of a hysterical nature.

Thus even when it had spread far beyond its original source, the rumour continued to rely on first-hand quasi-direct testimony: that is, each fresh carrier knew some relation or neighbour or friend who was in direct and intimate contact with the nurse, or the policeman's wife, or some relative of the vanished girl. In other words, the hysterical process by which the myth took shape was repeated at each stage of the transmission. Every new carrier, in fact, suppressed the new link in the chain, and reforged it two or three links back.

This testimony at two or three removes, though still

extremely close, was always distant enough to avoid any direct contact between the myth-bearer in person and, not merely the vanished/drugged girl, but even the police-man's wife, nurse or vanished girl's relative. In other words, every myth-bearer unconsciously arranged matters in such a way that no *direct* verification of the facts could be called for.

In this connection we should also note a quite remarkable disinclination to check the facts further, either with the police or with any other authoritative source.

The non-arrest of the guilty parties (though caught *in flagrante delicto*) caused no worry at all during the initial phases of the rumour. It was only when the latter had spread fairly widely in adult circles that we find, not any sort of check-up, but merely an addendum (of the lunatic rationalising sort) to explain why the shop-owners were not only at liberty, but free to carry on with their nefarious business: it was then asserted that they had bought off the police. From this moment the myth became at once more frenetic and more fragile.

Lastly, one cannot but feel surprise at the very slight degree of alarm provoked, prior to 30–31 May, by so radical and so (one might have thought) repugnant a threat. Far from urging the police to do their duty, or even alerting the competent authorities, these auto-mythified young girls simply said 'I'm not going *there* any more'— or else continued to do so, but in couples.

Thus the rumour went *pari passu* with a developing pattern of hysteria, which formed it and gave it constant reinforcement, blocking off any potential verification of a decisive nature—*and, indeed, anything that might discredit the white slavery notion, i.e. anything liable to explode the rumour as such.*

This indicates that the alarmist rumour hid, or enveloped, some more delectable quality. So much is clear enough. What I want to emphasise here, however, is not this aspect, but the presence of a conscious-unconscious element (these two terms, on the face of it opposites, can never really be separated) which mystified itself no less than the world at large, which was at once coarse and subtle, innocent and diabolical. Driven by this need or desire to believe, it always served up the myth with a verificatory top-dressing—that is, ready for circulation in the domain of empirical certainty.

And not empirical merely, but rational as well; for the normal *démarche* of rational thought, the detection of a cause which bestows coherence upon a series of interrelated facts, here became that of plain lunatic rationalisation.

Such rationalisation was never developed explicitly through the rumour, but found its causal-latent foundation in the person of the mythological Jew. It was his insatiable thirst for lucre, his duplicity and unscrupulousness which explained how a respectable shop-owner in the centre of town could stoop to so vile a traffic. At the metastatic stage, the 'Jewish plot', with its wholesale suborning of the police and other authorities, became an instrument for rationalisation.

When the myth finally blew apart, numerous attempts at rationalisation took place. Some reassembled its shattered fragments, but attached them to new elements introduced by the anti-myth campaign. Others tried to work out an explanation that involved denunciation of the myth itself. Others, again, made great efforts to give an explanation which denounced the *anti*-myth. All of them, however, came back to the notion of some occult causality. The common denominator of this occult causality, which attempted to reduce an unconscious, diffuse, obscure and contradictory phenomenon to manageable proportions, was the 'No smoke without fire' slogan. And everywhere, to a greater or lesser extent, we find the idea of a plot, some deliberate operation, cloaked and perverse, transforming the vague anonymous drift of events into a single, conscious sequence of events, giving coherence and form to what had been mistily diffuse,

explaining obscurities, and, finally, pinning the guilt on a
specific culprit. For the myth, this culprit was the Jew;
for the anti-myth, it was fascism; for the anti-anti-myth
it was communism. When we analyse the mythological
mish mash, the endless fantasies we find there all bear
witness to intense intellectual activity aimed at detecting
the guilty ones: candidates include the Germans, rival
businessmen, the Jewish shop-owners themselves (publicity at all costs), the Press (shortage of copy), and so on.

The plot motif, that last resort of lunatic causality, is at
the same time a first step in the magical process of cathar-
sis. Once the responsibility has been pinned on certain
individuals, all the rest are thereby exonerated. What is
more, the real problem—that of a social group's aptitude
for secreting myths—is neatly shelved. Both magical
thought and political demagoguery find this highly convenient. The time is now ripe for the second stage in the
process, the immolation of the guilty. However, the mutual
antagonism of the various 'plots' prevents the purificatory
mechanism from concentrating on a single culprit, as was
possible in former times; the only recourse left to any of
them is that secularised form of malediction, the curse.

We have reached the end of our investigation. The time
has come to reconsign the Orléans myth to those depths
whence it sprang, and to dismiss, with proper contempt,
a mythological aberration which strikes us as alien to the
point of sheer insanity.

Let us, however, pause one moment longer. Insanity?
Or a barely exaggerated caricature of our own thoughts?

The search for a hidden cause capable of explaining the
various characteristics which go to make up a given phenomenon is the very essence of scientific investigation.
Intense intellectual activity embroidering innumerable
fantasies around the theme of 'No smoke without fire' is
the process of thought itself—though the latter remains
well aware that such fantasies are hypothetical merely.
To trust reliable witnesses is our common daily practice.

The double-level game involving both rationalism and rationalisation is one we play—and one that 'plays' us—throughout our lives. In the subtle balance between empiricism and reason on the one hand, and magic and myth on the other, all our beliefs are contained. Lastly, even in an Academy of Sciences there is little *pure* intellectual argument; it is always blended with authoritarianism or intimidation, with various affective pressures and resistances.

Thus the problem of elucidation goes far deeper than merely recognising, and denouncing, the myth-in-the-street. It extends even further than the problem of the intelligentsia, whose rationalisations and ventures into myth-making are little subtler than those of the common man. It is the problem of us all—not merely the moralising Everyman who speaks to the world at large (and thus to no one in particular), but our own personal Everyman, specially associated with the work we have done on the Orléans myth. From now on we ourselves are involved in the affair.

Have we managed to avoid injecting our own fantasies into our research in some hysterical fashion or other ? Have we avoided giving special weight to this or that piece of testimony which happened to suit us ? Have we, perhaps, followed the contour line of some rationalisation in the mistaken belief that it was founded on true reason ? Best, at this point, to abandon all certainty. Is it the truth we have sought—or our own version of it ?

EXTRACTS FROM RESEARCHERS' DIARIES

EDGAR MORIN

FRIDAY, 4 JULY 1969

On 7 June there appeared in *Le Monde*, under the 'Miscellaneous News' heading, a boxed item entitled 'Disappearance of women in Orléans', with the sub-heading 'Practical joke or plot?' On 9 June two reports on Orléans were published, one in *Le Nouvel Observateur*, the other (if I recall rightly) in *L'Express*.

I found these articles very arresting. Why? Looking back, I am convinced that my reaction was due to the following factors. Firstly, the strange nature (as I saw it) of the rumour, which bracketed the 'white slave trade' with Jewish shop-keepers (whereas it seemed to me that this motif should rather be associated with the Corsican or Marseillais pimp). Secondly, the *virulence* of the rumour as such, which survived denials by the official authorities, and by the provincial press and the bulk of the mass media. And thirdly, the resurgence, in a modified form, of popular anti-Semitic motifs.

Here, I said to myself, is the type of incident on which I ought to carry out an on-the-spot enquiry. It would, in fact, make ideal material for a 'contemporary sociology' project, a phenomenon where one could not merely observe, but also intervene, in a quasi-experimental manner. It is the kind of happening which sheds light in a number of directions, and by its very nature poses certain fundamental problems, notably with regard to the hostile re-

139

lationship between word of mouth rumours and information culled from the mass media.

But I know I shall never have the necessary funds for
such investigations (it being impossible to conduct enquiries on events which cannot, by definition, be pro-
grammed in advance). Besides, I haven't got the time.

A few days ago I got a phone-call from Gérard
Rosenthal. He had got wind of the affair in his capacity
as a lawyer: the LICA had brought suit against X for
'common slander, racial defamation and spreading false
rumours'. Apart from this, the Jewish Social Foundation
would like to see a sociological enquiry carried out on the
incident. G.R. approached me on their behalf. I raised my
various objections ('No time . . . too much work involved . . . the job should have been done right away. . .');
but already I was envisaging a descent on Orléans, with
Paillard, Johanne and a small team. Even if it *was* late
in the day, I told myself, it would still be possible to find
out what stage the rumour had reached, whether the myth
had collapsed and broken up or not, and if so, in what
way. . . In short, after we had talked a little longer, I found
myself saying I was ready to leave at once. Naturally, the
final decision would depend on the agreement of 'my
collaborators'.

Gérard asked me what sort of budget I had in mind. But
with this type of enquiry you can never tell in advance
what's liable to turn up: it's not until your investigation
is well launched that you begin to get some idea of the
scope and importance of the undertaking. 'Just name a
figure,' Gérard insisted. I was scared of asking either too
much or too little. Finally I blurted out: 'Somewhere
between five and ten thousand.' 'Just about what I
thought,' he said.

Two days later he rang up to let me know that the
Jewish Foundation had agreed to advance us five thousand.
Paillard was willing to join me. I now recruited Julia and

Capulier. We would have a team of five. We can leave on Monday 7 July and stay for three days. After that—who knows?

SATURDAY, 5 JULY

The Wednesday meeting. Wednesday 2 July, meeting at Rosenthal's. Bernard and myself; Rosenthal, Poliakov, and Kaufmann (a senior official of the United Jewish Social Foundation). Poliakov is a small man, the Gurvich or Lukacs type, one of these highly intense, highly poetical little Slavic Jews who can be terribly aggressive or (and) so amiable it almost overwhelms one. I hold his work in high regard, and he made a very favourable impression on me. Kaufmann is a tallish person, very correct and serious in demeanour: typical PDG character.

During our conversation we had a preliminary look at the press file (cuttings from Paris papers, and a few extracts from the provincial dailies). Photostats of this file are to be made and sent to me tomorrow.

Snippets suggesting a possible 'historical background' to the affair: Similar rumours reported from Lille and Valenciennes, but more limited in scope, well short of the public scandal stage. Extracts from *Noir et Blanc* about a (supposed) abduction at Grenoble, in the fitting-room of a ready-made dress boutique (but without any indication whatsoever that might lead one to suspect the 'ravisher' was Jewish).

Bernard reminds us of the latent myth existing in the provinces concerning the white slave trade and the disappearance of young girls.

First contacts established. Phone-call put through arranging an appointment on Monday morning with Lévy, President of the Jewish Community [*Communauté israélite*]. Attempts made to get in touch with Guy Brun, the Orléans representative of LICA and a leading figure in the resistance to the myth, all prove abortive. Could he be on holiday? It suddenly occurs to me that schools, colleges and universities are now closed for vacations. For a moment I foresee having to abandon the enquiry altogether. Maybe it's already too late? But a little encouragement restores my enthusiasm, and the final decision to go ahead is taken.

First glimpse of the terrain. We shall get the 'anti-bodies', the militant anti-Semitics, and (naturally) the victims. But far more interesting from our point of view are those persons—of either sex—who believed in the truth of the rumour, were possessed by the myth, and now are either disillusioned or believe in it still. It suddenly hits me that *this is the central point of our investigation.* How can we get in touch with such people?

Points learnt: not all shop-owners were smeared, nor are the victims those with the most typically Jewish appearance (e.g. one very hirsute North African with a great beak of a nose had no trouble at all). Only a small group of shop-owners were involved, all in the clothing business, and all young (as Monique Amrofel subsequently pointed out to us). People who believed in the rumour did not necessarily think of themselves as anti-Semitic. What strikes both Bernard Paillard and myself as remarkable is the virulent conjunction of two separate myths. In Nazi Germany, it is true, the Jew could be associated with the idea of sexual danger; and the blond Nordic Aryan racialist does have a built-in tendency to credit his opposite, the dark-skinned-Mediterranean-Jewish-colonial type, with alarmingly powerful erotic urges. But here, in France?

As we left, Bernard Paillard and I both agreed that it was the counter-attack which slotted the myth into an anti-Semitic/Nazi category. (This became even clearer as soon as I settled down to browse over the press file: a regular medieval witch-hunt.) Yet was it not just this process of schematisation (distortion) which, by supplying a pseudo-rationalising 'pattern', had enabled people to recognise, and identify, a myth which up till then had been as elusive as the rumour which carried it? Was it not this that made it possible not only to halt the myth, but to bring about its disintegration? Is it not true that the best weapon with which to destroy an evil myth is some antagonistic counter-myth, rather than a research enquiry of the sort we are about to carry out?

Throughout Thursday and Friday, while finishing the re-reading of an article on culture, I found myself increasingly preoccupied with Orléans. I rang up *L'Express* and got the address and phone-number of the lady connected with Jewish-Christian friendship in Orléans, who had written a letter to the paper. I also made contact with Colette Gouvion, the journalist responsible for *L'Express*'s investigation of the affair. She had conducted street interviews with women and girls who either still believed in the myth, or else had a second-line myth to fall back on ('It's those Jews, they did it themselves to get publicity'); but she had not established direct contact with any 'mythified person'. Sample opinions had, however, been taken in the street concerning these, and a full investigation, in depth, carried out on the victims and the 'antibodies'. We have to go about our enquiry from a completely different angle. But how?

'Did the paper receive any abusive letters?' I asked her.

'Yes, against Françoise Giroud and myself, saying we were Jewish journalists.'

'Were any of them from Orléans?'

'No, none.'

In short, the anti-Semitic reaction reveals the old classic pattern of anti-Semitism. Any new features this affair introduced flowed *ab initio* in ancient and familiar channels. Here we see the reversion characteristic of a crisis: its initial experimental phase over, the new trends settle down into old stream-beds. What we have to discover is their source.

Meeting with Hector de Galard. He doesn't know if there have been any reactions to the article on Orléans from readers. Gives me Katia Kaupp's phone-number. No answer.

Gérard rings up to say that Brun is still in Orléans, and has given me his private number. Make contact with him Friday evening, arrange a meeting for 3 p.m. Monday, and ask him to send out invitations for a 'sociological dinner' on Monday evening. Find the idea of such an *agape* most appealing: it promises a basic exercise in the techniques of group-feasting and group-drinking.

Monique Amvofel, Friday 1 p.m. Bernard Paillard also present. Key interview with a Jewish girl-student from Orléans.

She is twenty-four, a typical red-head, with big, open features and a very pleasant manner. Studying literature, and a part-time supply teacher in Orléans, but lives half the week in Paris. Parents in business in Orléans. She was brought up there.

I asked her to tell us how the affair had affected her personally; but there were numerous digressions, mainly because I could not resist asking her various questions that sprang to mind as I listened.

She said: 'I heard about it that day when the crowds gathered outside the shops in Orléans. It was the first Saturday in June, and just before a public holiday, so lots of people had come in from the country to do their weekend shopping. There were hundreds of them in the streets. The groups that gathered outside certain shops, including that owned by my parents, wouldn't let shoppers enter them. "You mustn't buy anything from the Jews, they're in the white slave trade." My parents were absolutely shattered. They called me up by phone. They knew I was in touch with various Jewish organisations in Paris. I contacted the *Cercle Bernard Lazare,* and certain other groups. *No one believed what I told them.' (My italics.)*

Her other most important points were as follows (owing
to a technical fault, no tape-recording survives):
1. The incubation period: in her opinion, this lasted about
a fortnight, prior to 30–31 May. According to the generally
accepted version (? a hypothesis on the part of the police)
which now seems to have become dogma, it began after
the publication of the article in *Noir et Blanc* (No. 6, 14
May) which provided the model for it.
2. The climactic 'day of madness', Saturday 31 May;
'everyone was talking about it,' the cleaning-woman said
that in her bus going back to an outlying village (Olivet)
the scandal formed the sole topic of conversation: 'You
work for the Jews,' she was told, 'you must know all about
it.' Crowds gathered outside six shops, all women's boutiques, all owned by young businessmen.
3. The complete ignorance of what was happening on the
victims' part until two or three days before the final outburst: symptom of a terrifying, invisible segregation. The
entire Jewish Community of Orléans remained totally in
the dark. Two or three days before that Saturday, the
principal victim (Licht?) was tipped off. By whom? He
sized up the situation. What action did he take? He went
to the police. Reaction: a practical joke. Monique A——'s
parents told their daughter on the phone: 'We've only
known about it for the last two days.' (Find out how they
heard.)
   M.A.'s sister, a teacher in Orléans, just called up. She
said: 'They'd been talking about it in my *lycée* for over a
week, and I hadn't heard a thing.'
4. The speed of the reaction: on Monday 2 June the local
press alluded to the events, mentioning 'respectable
businessmen', though without describing them more precisely. (Only one paper found a 'whiff of anti-Semitism' in
the affair.) There were short articles denouncing 'this
odious cabal' (*Nouvelle République*) and the 'campaign of
defamation' (*République du Centre*). On Wednesday 4
June, the meeting organised by the LICA took place; the

MRAP would appear to have moved into action (check this) at just about the same time. M.A.'s parents, it seems, sent letters that Saturday to the Paris dailies and weeklies, which got reporters on to the story (did AFP carry anything about it?). Articles appeared in *Le Monde* (7 June), *L'Aurore* (10 June), *Le Figaro*, *Le Nouvel Observateur* and *L'Express* (9 June). Various public statements (make list of these) by the authorities, parents of school-children, professional associations and political parties. All of them, whether tough or cautious, evasive or forthright, deny the validity of the rumours concerning Jewish shop-owners.

5.   It was, then, during this decisive period between 2 and 15 June that there took place a gigantic struggle between the word of mouth rumour and information disseminated by official sources and the mass media. This struggle led, finally, to the collapse of the rumour. It lost its virulence, underwent some sort of metamorphosis (?), and broke up (into several constituent elements). It would seem that, during its last desperate phase of resistance, the rumour had, somehow, to refute the allegations made by the Press and the authorities, and was thus forced to invent a Jewish plot *in extremis*: 'The Jews have bribed them to keep quiet.' Even before this, it would seem, the fact that these 'disappearances' were not referred to in the papers, and ignored by the police, had produced the familiar rationalisation: 'They've been bought.' People claim that the Chief of Police was paid three million, the Prefect six, and so on. (Check all this. Separate the original myth from the myth as described by the anti-myth, which only preserves the most grotesque or outrageous features of its original.)

What is the situation like today, just about a month after the affair? M.A. says trade dropped a good deal in the shops concerned (there was almost no one in Licht's on Saturday 7 June) but 'it's picking up again now'. Women are shopping there, but always escorted, either by their husband, or a child, or even, in one case, by a dog. *None of them will enter such a shop alone.* (Check this.)

The myth seems to have been weakened, but also to have gone to ground. The virulence of the anti-racialist counter-attack shook it badly, but there does not seem to have been any collaboration between the *mythifiés antisémites* and the *anti-ces-mythes* (my weakness for puns is getting hold of me again).

What was actually said at the meeting sponsored by the *Maison de la Culture*, under Guillou's chairmanship? At a guess I would imagine it added up to a rational-cum-ritual condemnation of racialism, without any attempt at endo-genous elucidation. (Check to find out whether this pessimistic theory is well founded.)

One seemingly odd fact is that teachers do not appear to have played the part of *Aufklärer* in this business—not to mention those worthy liberal-minded ladies who ad-vised their pupils against patronising some (? or all) Jewish shops. In the majority of cases the attitude taken by teachers was a passive one. The first group that got around to making a firm public statement against the rumour was a Parents' Association (Lycée Jean-Zay and CES Jeanne-d'Arc)—or, at any rate, their chairman. In my dossier I find no statement by the local branch of FEN or SNES (*Syndicat National de l'Enseignement Technique*.) Two or three sources deplore this passivity on the teachers' part, and indicate that some of them were taken in by the rumours. High-school pupils of both sexes seem to have been extraordinarily credulous! Did any spontaneous anti-myths develop among them?

I asked M.A. if her relations with people, or with some people, had changed in any way since these events. She said not. In point of fact she had few friends among the non-Jewish population. Some of her left-wing intellectual acquaintances had quarrelled with her since the Six Day War; for the first time in her life, she admitted, someone told her: 'You're only saying that because you're Jewish.'

When I see her sister, I must remember to find out just

what kinds of 'whispered rumours' led her to alert the
principal.

Suzanne. The Lusignans are just back from Washington.
During the course of conversation I told them I was going
to Orléans, and explained what the enquiry was about.
Suzanne, with a knowing air, said: 'I'm not in the least
surprised.'

Her father is an Orléanais, from a lower-middle-class
family of peasant stock (like Pompidou, emphasised her
husband). He used to detest the Jews. Suzanne has a
great-aunt who still lives in Orléans. This opens up the
possibility of gaining an *entrée* to a respectable (and perhaps anti-Semitic) Orléans family. Better still, Suzanne has
agreed to accompany us to Orléans and take charge of this
sector. She is very worried because she 'doesn't know
anything about sociological methods'. 'All the better,' I
assured her.

I explained that in sociology the main problem is not so
much knowing what questions to ask other people, as
formulating questions to ask oneself, and then letting the
problems come up naturally during the course of conversation. As I write these words I can hear superior snig-
gers from our orthodox technical bureaucrats. (Apropos,
I ran into Claude Frère yesterday evening at Colette's. He
said: 'I always stand up for you against your detractors—I
mean, those who claim I've always regarded you as a joke.'
Now there's a back-handed compliment, real bludgeon
stuff.)

Sudden revelation. Suzanne tells me that before the war
Jean Zay was a Deputy for Orléans, and Claude Lévy was
Mayor. . .

Clara. Phone-call this morning from Clara Malraux.
Talking generally (with particular reference to *Le Vif*) she
said: 'One can only advance when one has no idea where
one's going.' The phrase pleased, indeed exhilarated me,

since it embodied not only my general credo but also the
special essence of this enquiry I am about to undertake. I
told her about the affair. She said, placidly: 'There must
be witches or warlocks around, mustn't there?'

What accumulated fears, obsessions, frustrations and
furies were discharged in this way at Orléans on 31 May?
And why Orléans?

RECAPITULATION

A. Chronological recapitulation

1. Historical background to the events in Orléans

a. General socio-economic and demographical data;
political evolution since the pre-war period (and the rôle
played by Jews—e.g. Zay, Lévy—in political life): the
most recent stages of socio-economic development.
b. The Jewish Community. 'Almost all the pre-war
Jewish families are gone' (Suzanne); about a hundred
families now in residence; an invisible and peaceful type
of segregation; 'The businessmen form their own closed
society' (M.A.): what about the rest?
c. The anti-Semitic background; virulent anti-Semitism
(doubtless limited to certain sectors; what happened
during the Occupation?); evidence for latent anti-Semitism.
Testimony from M.A.: 'My friends tell me people have
said for years that the Orléans Jews were crooked';
'Jewish businessmen are good at their job, that's why
other businessmen don't like them.'
Must find this ultra-Catholic businessman who (according
to M.A.) insisted on his employees producing a certificate
of baptism, and is supposed to have fired a window-cleaner
who held a similar job with one of his Jewish competitors.
He is suspected of having played some part in the affair.

2. National historical background

a. The urban-provincial motif of white slavery and
mysterious disappearances.

b.   Localised accounts of events falling in this category,
particularly those placed in the back rooms of shops.
c.   Jewish stories of this type: Le Mans (1968), Lille,
Valenciennes, Paris (Hit Parade)?

3.   Triggering agent

The article on Grenoble in *Noir et Blanc*; some sort of
deliberate plot (? by right-wing extremists)—not *a priori*
very plausible; a hoax that got out of control (?)—but
where did its plot-line come from? In all likelihood it will
prove impossible to track down the original source of the
fabrication. The important point is the sheer virulence and
widespread acceptance of the myth as such.

4.   Incubation

This is our area of darkness. We are in the same position
as those who knew nothing about the rumour, and, the
moment they were appealed to by one side or the other,
only thought of fighting it—until, a month later, the
Jewish Social Foundation looked into the affair and had
the idea of backing a sociological enquiry, which led to the
present investigation.

It is absolutely essential to find evidence concerning this
crucial and fabulous period, when an archaic rumour broke
down every kind of resistance, and won acceptance as
documented fact.

The extraordinary thing about this period is that *the
inflation and the endorsement of the myth* apparently progressed *pari passu*. From one disappearance in a single
boutique, and then a series of disappearances (still in a
single boutique), it was only a short step to a mythological
network, linking the basements of these shops by various
underground passages, which all converged on the Loire.
The silence of the authorities was incorporated in the myth
as proof of the occult power and maleficence of these six
shop-owners, who were also, at the same time, 'the Jews'.

5. Chronology

a. Try to clarify the chronology of the days immediately preceding Saturday the 31st.

b. This Saturday (31 May) was not only the day when the scandal broke, but also the eve of the elections, a big shopping day, for all practical purposes the first day of the month, a day virtually charged with collective electricity. If it provoked a storm at Orléans, the process was already well begun.

c. Sunday the 1st: shops shut; in the morning, the elections. Counter-attack being prepared.

d. Monday the 2nd: short articles condemning the 'odious cabal' and the 'campaign of defamation' appear in the provincial press.

e. Tuesday the 3rd: publication of a statement from the parents of pupils in the Jean Zay and Jeanne-d'Arc high-schools.

f. Wednesday the 4th: letter from the UDICO (*Union des commerçants d'Orléans*) protesting against 'slanderous and defamatory statements'. Meeting of the LICA, with representatives from various political parties (check the relative dates of the various communiqués from political groups, trade associations, unions and official sources).

g. Thursday the 5th: articles in the provincial papers. Friday the 6th?

h. Saturday the 7th: article in *Le Monde*.

i. Sunday the 8th: meeting in the *Maison de la Culture*: subject, racialism. Louis Guilloux in the chair.

j. Next ten days: coverage by the Paris press.

k. Chronology after 10 June?

6. Visible consequences

a. In the Jewish Community: isolation and fear. Some people saying: 'We've got to get away' (to Israel?). Alarm at the possibility of a general reversion.

b. In the population at large: first one major mystery to explore, then another.

c.   Fresh establishment, or breakdown, of communications between Jews and non-Jews?

B.   Thematic recapitulation
1.   The composite myth

The composite character of the myth, i.e. its new character (every myth is composite to begin with, and acquires its unity by a process of consolidation) is the first thing to analyse:

a.   The fitting-room: a place with disturbing erotic undertones, where women strip themselves naked, in isolation yet not alone: mirror poses, appreciative glances, physical contact in order to correct the pose or arrange alterations, etc. Narcissistic tendency to interpret such touches as erotic advances. Potential scene of genuine erotic advances and contacts with libidinous proprietors, setting for unadmitted Lesbian eroticism. In short, the fitting-room—that mysterious private retreat—constitutes an excellent source of erotic fantasy.

b.   Drugging by means of a doped sweet or an injection, which produces a dazed condition or unconsciousness, thus facilitating rape or abduction. Here we have a motif which has been widely popularised through various media, including cheap magazines and novels, television and the cinema.

c.   The combination of these two themes in itself constitutes a news item, i.e. a possible event liable to whet public curiosity. Such, in point of fact, was the 'news item' from Grenoble (whether true or false, since when there is a lack of real incidents to feed people's obsessions, fantasies or mythologies, pseudo news items are duly manufactured): an authentic event (authenticated by the periodical in question as 'information'), but nevertheless adhering to a fantasy-pattern which may be either simple or complex, disturbingly combining several different kinds of fantasy.

d.   The disappearance of women and the white slave trade

are traditional motifs which simultaneously provide
material for (genuine) news-in-brief columns and for small-
town gossip. The disappearance of women is further linked
with the sex-fiend motif, while white slaving has underworld connections with the riff-raff of Corsica and
Marseilles (and, very often, with 'dagoes').

The new element is, clearly, the tie-up between the Jew
and white slaving, and, more broadly speaking, between
all the motifs referred to above.

e. The Jewish shop-owner. If German anti-Semitism saw
any connection between the Jew and a sexual threat, the
threat involved was a straight risk of polluting Aryan
blood. Similarly with anti-Negro racialism, where the
Negro, as far as the white woman is concerned, embodies a
direct threat of rape. In these cases Negro and Jew alike
symbolise both sexual superabundance and blood pollu-
tion. Here the myth is possibly less explicit, perhaps even
camouflaged, and in any case (failing new information)
side-tracked on to a *traffic in human flesh*, which transforms
pretty girls into so many pieces of merchandise. Nevertheless, even in this disguised and diversionary form, we can
see emerging in France the motif which connects Jews
with sexual danger. In support of this hypothesis we may
note that the shop-owners in question are young men, who
at the same time deal in women's garments, a commodity
with strongly erotic associations.

Furthermore, and by the same token, these young
businessmen are not the ones who look obviously Jewish,
i.e. obviously different, alien. Here we once more hit on a
feature of German racialism, which attacked well integrated
Jews given to hiding their otherness under a mask of
communal identity. French anti-Semitism, on the other
hand, concentrated on Yiddish-speaking immigrants,
those who both looked and sounded foreign, odd.

In Orléans, it was the Jew *without* a Jewish appearance
who became the target for attack. Just because his appearance belied his alien status, it rendered still more

irritating and enigmatic that mysterious, fascinating, obsessive and disturbing difference between him and other men.

f. Thus the Jewish shop-owner became *a focal point on which could converge all those heterogeneous fantasies* I have mentioned above. He assumed responsibility in those fantasies of rape and prostitution which are properly the dreams of innocent young girls and respectable women. In such a fantasy the girl or woman is relieved of all guilt, on two counts. Firstly, she has been drugged; and secondly, she is the innocent victim of a man who to all appearances was normal and inoffensive (a shop-owner looking more or less like any other ordinary citizen), but who in fact was carefully concealing his true nature and his real identity.

g. Once installed at the unificatory heart of the myth, as thus formulated, the Jew will soon dredge up his latent, dormant, repressed diabolical streak, and become the Jew who puts the non-Jewish innocent to sleep, with the object of taking from her her most precious possession.

h. It is the inflation of the rumour, under the impact of certain multiplying and expanding agents *the nature of which at present eludes us* (I cannot bring myself to believe that we simply have here a case of exacerbation through isolation—and where's the isolation anyway?) which facilitated the deployment and growth of anti-Semitic themes, dormant in the very nature of the Jew.

i. Another necessary condition has been the *correlative* proliferation, through an awakening of certain archaic depths in the urban imagination, of that mythology concerning the city's alleged subterranean secrets. One has only to scratch the glossy surface of this noisy, well lit, crowded modern town for the oubliette and underground passage to reappear. Indeed, during the period of its apogee the myth actually asserted that the six boutiques were linked by intercommunicating underground passages, with a common outlet on the Loire. The blood and thunder

motif of the subterranean urban tunnel, as a means of
communication employed by some hidden power threatening the town, derives from nineteenth-century pulp fiction.
What led to its recurrence here? What connection (if
there is a connection) could it have with the transformation of Orléans from a static, hierarchical provincial town
into a shapeless modern agglomeration? (Try to explore
this hypothesis.)

In any case there is a clear parallel between the anti-
Semitic myth of the Jews' hidden power, complete with
subterranean conspiracy, and the myth of that secret
underground domain over which the six Jewish shop-
owners (associated for their own nefarious purposes)
allegedly held sway. (At the apogee of the myth it was
alleged that they had already spirited away no less than
twenty-six women, and were preparing to operate on an
even larger scale, until they had absorbed every girl in town
—so much so that on that climactic Saturday the prevailing
emotion was not aggressiveness but sheer panic. The
exhortation 'Don't go near the Jews' was a kind of collective SOS, the high-point of the myth's fulfilment; at the
same time it made its ultimate decline, its reduction to
more modest proportions, a foregone conclusion.) There
was a kind of analogy, microcosm to macrocosm, between
the *Protocols of the Elders of Zion* and the Jewish plot in
Orléans, from the moment the idea gained ground that the
Jews had purchased the silence of the authorities, and—
since their cash gave them a hold on the Chief of Police
and the Prefect—were in fact the town's secret masters.

j.   Reflect on all the convergent anxieties implied by the
emergence of a theme linking the undermined town with
a triumphant Jewish conspiracy. Just think of all it
portends!

k.   The composite character of the myth—i.e. the association of various fantasy elements which hitherto, in France,
have remained scattered and heterogeneous (though from
now on we shall be better able to detect such advance

symptoms retrospectively)—explains its improbability. It
was unforeseen and unbelievable, and it still remains a
quite exceptional case. Furthermore, the way in which
each of its component elements became virulent simultaneously, combined with the overall effect (much greater
than the mere sum of its parts) which this synthetic fantasy
produced, might serve to explain its extraordinary range
and intensity. Likewise, the moment the myth took a
really hard knock, this composite heterogeneity reappeared, and the all-too-recent unification very quickly
broke up once more (the problem of fall-out or reversion is
something else again).

1. The problem here is to formulate some advance explanation of how all elements in the myth triggered off a
strain of virulence in each other. I return here to the
hypothesis that the myth's very improbability is precisely
the feature which renders it plausible. Right from the
beginning it had the plausibility of a news item: that is to
say, it is quite conceivable (provided the information is
vouched for by a reliable source) that a shop-owner should
dabble in white slaving, and be Jewish. Each individual
element of the myth can, *per se*, survive critical scrutiny,
while the conscious mind is not put on its guard by any
suspicion of anti-Semitism (which explains why so many
of the carriers had no idea they were getting involved in an
anti-Semitic myth—*which was both true and not true,
simultaneously*).

Secondly, the composite character of the myth means
that it can adapt itself to both town and country requirements. The urban myth of the high-school girl, dreaming
of being drugged and abducted from some fitting-room,
merges into the rural myth of girls who are carried off to
the big city, and wicked Jews, and so on.

In the third place, there is a link-up between the myth's
modern and archaic features. The fitting-room leads to the
subterranean dream world, just as the drug produces
drowsiness and sleep. Modern fantasies merge with those

of the Middle Ages, and, after a certain point of intensity
has been reached, actually resuscitate them. And it is the
Jew, first and foremost, who forms the common repulsive
element in all these fantasies and anxieties, whether
archaic or modern, urban or rural. *Mythologically speaking,*
he has a crucial unifying function to perform.

2.   *Can what we have here be properly termed anti-Semitism?*
This brings us to a key point in the argument. *The anti-*
Semitic features we have observed were a secondary addition
to an erotic/urban myth, but were rapidly becoming its
central element. The anti-Semitic motif appeared in response to a fantasy-anxiety (and though it may have come
from outside, its inducement was not artificial, for the
spectre of the Jew is liable to appear in our civilisation
whenever and wherever anxiety exists). *It provided a link*
between various different fantasies: and the link soon became
an integral element in the structure. From the moment the link
brings together disparate elements in any system, it becomes
part of that system's structural pattern.

This is not in any way to suggest that the process reached
its logical conclusion at Orléans, or that it will necessarily
do so elsewhere: but the tendency certainly exists. At the
moment when the Orléans incident exploded, an ambiguous stage had been reached when not only was anti-
Semitism at the service of the erotic/urban myth, but
already the myth had, *vice versa*, begun to promote anti-
Semitism. The myth, in fact, was reversible. What we have
here is a state of symbiosis, of double parasitism,
where our business is not, as yet, to diagnose the pre-
dominant element, but simply to observe the pattern of
events.

Thus the anti-Semitic elements in the myth are doubly
ambivalent. On the one hand they are bound up with a
non-racialist motif (which means that those who believe in
the myth don't realise they are being anti-Semitic). On the
other, *this motif provides anti-Semitism with certain charac-*

*teristics unknown to the ordinary anti-Semitic patterns
common in modern France,* but nevertheless observable in
other racialist or anti-Semitic constructs. Thus when an
anonymous caller rang up one of the shop-owners, Licht,
asking for free tickets to Beirut, there was obviously some
dissociation in his mind between the most typical features
of Judaism (which at the present time, through the agency
of the Israeli-Arab conflict, has brought Jerusalem and
Beirut into opposition). When another caller asked him
for twenty kilos of fresh meat, he was picking up a motif
common in archaic anti-Semitism by way of the sexual-
erotic motif.

What genuinely anti-Semitic themes can we isolate
(those that emerged progressively as the myth developed)?
a.   The feeling that in some concealed fashion the Jews
were all in league with one another (since no-one told the
other Jews about the charges made against those few
shop-owners who were the targets for the rumour).
b.   The tendency to pass very quickly from individuals to
generalities. The thing for which people criticised a specific
Jew soon became a characteristic feature of all Jews.
Hence the key phrase on 31 May: 'Don't go near the Jews.'
c.   The link between the Jew and danger—in this case the
new peril of sex. Thus association of the Jew with the
erotic, superficial at first, became increasingly profound,
until it formed the psychological substratum of the
phenomenon under consideration.
d.   The resurgence of archaic themes: hidden or occult
powers, the ritual murder of an innocent child (for which,
in this case, traffic in the young flesh of innocent girls
formed a substitute).

3.   The anti-Semitic and anti-myth reaction
It was like fighting empty air. There were no pamphlets,
posters or graffiti; no individual or group emerged as the
coordinator, much less the only begetter, of this collective
outbreak. It was essential to recognise the enemy, a process

made somewhat complex by the composite, ambiguous nature of the myth. He therefore had to be named.

Three different labels were suggested. Firstly that of a slanderous cabal or plot, which made it possible to overcome the mystery of what had been diffuse and impalpable by reducing it to conscious and voluntary action on the part of individuals or groups. In other words, *the evil was to be placed firmly on the shoulders of certain persons allegedly responsible for it, whether they had yet been unmasked or not.* Secondly, the evocation of various obscurantist practices and quasi-magical or medieval superstitions: this would make it possible to relate this new phenomenon to a known pattern which was, at the same time, both obsolete and condemned. And thirdly, patterns of anti-Semitism in its most blatant, repugnant and barbarous form, i.e. as practised under the Third Reich.

The counter-myth, in its most resolute and aggressive form, linked these three themes together, and saw the myth as an amalgam of Nazism, medievalism, and slanderous calumny.

However, the three themes were not invariably associated: they were also, on occasion, dissociated, even antagonistic. The first two made it possible to ignore the anti-Semitic issue altogether, a line which suited those who were scared that any mention of anti-Semitism would simply encourage it, and others who took a similar line over anti-fascism (i.e. left-wing extremism). This group included certain Jews, and most officials or middle-of-the-roaders.

Both Jews and non-Jews experienced this duality of reaction.

Among the Jews, the two reactions were very strongly allergised. One party felt strongly (an attitude based on considerable experience) that the less talk there was about Jews, the better for them, and therefore that one should discuss this subject as little as possible. Such people had no wish to do more than stigmatise the rumour as a slanderous

reversion to the Middle Ages—i.e. to denounce its criminal
and archaic features. The other group took a quite different
line. They were determined to make a public issue of the
scandal, by concentrating on the deadly germ encapsulated
within the myth, i.e. on the identification with Nazism,
which remains a phenomenon of nation-wide abhorrence
through its connection with the Occupation.

The former category included a large proportion of
women ('My mother was afraid, she didn't want it talked
about any more than was necessary—'M.A.), old people,
and, it would seem, the President of the Community. The
latter contained most of the younger generation (very
Israeli-minded in the sense that they identified defence
with attack), the men, and non-official persons (check this:
I have a feeling these groupings may be over-simplified).
At all events there were two alternative strategies available.
On the one hand we find that of the chameleon—fading
into the landscape—which, however, risks turning into
that practised by the ostrich, who buries his head in the
sand to avoid seeing the enemy. On the other there is the
strategy of the lion, who faces up to the enemy; this,
equally, is liable to turn into that of the bull, charging
blindly into the arena.

Among non-Jews we have the same symmetrical breakdown, but for different motives. Militant anti-racialists
attacked, and denounced as Nazi-inspired, behaviour
which they wanted both to expose and to check through
intimidation. The official authorities and the moderates
were scared of finding themselves dragged into left-wing
activities which might involve and compromise them, or
benefit their political opponents. They were also alarmed
by the prospect of slipping back into what they considered
the obsolete dichotomy of Collaboration v. Resistance,
which would reopen old differences and, in some cases,
reawaken very unpleasant memories. Consequently this
group, like the cautious Jews, preferred to rest their case
on superstition and slander.

The only line which (in the light of such evidence as I currently have at my disposal) strikes me as somewhat complex is that of the Communist Party. It vigorously denounces anti-Semitism in connection with Hitler and the Occupation, but not as a phenomenon which in some circumstances can be independent of Nazism. Thus there is no need, clearly, for it to modify its anti-Zionist position; at the same time it can firmly dissociate the Nazi-anti-Semitic virus (disseminated by Fascist elements) from the general population of Orléans, a fundamentally healthy body which merits no criticism whatsoever—an admirable attitude compounded of common sense, propriety, way-out demagoguery and sharp practice.

This fiercely positive attitude combats the myth by forcing people to declare themselves, openly, for or against Hitler, and—in the latter case—to repudiate the myth; but it also accentuates the anti-Semitic aspects of the myth as such, which still remains, in fact, intrinsically ambivalent.

The alternative approach tends to obscure, and thus to suppress, the anti-Semitic aspects of the myth, in such a manner that they founder in an amorphous flood of calumny and medievalism; but it does not constitute an active instrument of dissuasion.

Both these strategies have their strong and weak points. They were both employed simultaneously, and it is hard to estimate their relative efficacy. Nevertheless I am convinced that, on a short-term basis, the former was more effective because of its greater capacity for intimidation.

4. Antibodies and conductors (Metaphors, admittedly, drawn in the one case from biology and the other from electricity.)

Those who put up the most active and vigorous resistance against the myth are: its victims strictly considered, i.e. the six shop-owners, and, more broadly speaking, the Jews generally; militant anti-racialists: middle-aged left-wing activists (i.e. those who had personal experience of

F

Nazi methods during the war); what may be loosely
termed 'left-wing intellectuals'—though perhaps there is
some ambivalence here. Thus a young Trotskyist, according to M.A., was prepared to admit that one, or
several, of the shop-owners might conceivably traffic in
women, since for the 'bourgeois world' everything figured
as merchandise; but he rejected the myth with fierce
hostility the moment the word 'Jew' was mentioned.

Put in another way, we find certain areas and individuals
specially sensitised (in the allergic sense of that word) to
anti-Semitism; and it was these that formulated the un-
compromising counter-attack. Their response also forced
the authorities into action, though the official line (as
indicated above) was a 'soft' one. As so often happens, the
'soft' group, with their moderation and clear-sightedness,
might well have not taken any action at all, or at least not
so promptly, without the stimulus—the intimidation,
even—provided by the hard-liners.

Some elements were hesitant and equivocal. Young
'left-wing intellectuals' may well have hovered because
their traditional anti-Semitic reflex instinct came into
conflict with a new reflex brought about by the Israeli-
Arab conflict, according to which Zionism struck them as
necessarily identical with imperialism and colonialism.
This tended to make them suspicious of the Jew, who in
their eyes became an ambivalent figure: sympathetic in
his role as Nazi victim, antipathetic *qua* Zionist.

There were also the younger people, who perhaps likewise tended to forget the Nazism-anti-Semitism equation.

The teachers? If so, why?

The conductive areas, i.e. those that proved most
vulnerable to the rumour. As far as I'm concerned this is
the area of darkness. Were they girls, women? Pupils in
religious foundations, high-school girls? Lower-class
country areas? Or middle-class circles? (Personally I'd be
inclined to opt for the former, or those just recently
urbanised, where middle-class city life is still something

full of wonder and mystery, rather than the reactionary
bourgeois groups, which seem not to have recognised their
own old anti-Semitism when they met it again.)

Another of the problems to be worked out.

5. Reversions and fall-out
Our investigation should enable us to study (a) fragmenta-
tion, (b) residual survivals, (c) germs or bacteria, as undergone or left behind by this myth, both today and *for the
future*.

C. Self-criticism
On the basis of a few random and scattered *testimonia* I
have already reconstructed the overall situation. Before
even beginning enquiries *in situ* I get the impression of
having solved the entire problem. Intellectual ethylism?
I shall see in due course (when both field-work and my
fellow investigators have tested my theories) just how far
these hasty rationalisations of mine are justified. But
always supposing I have not built one fantasy on another,
the implication would seem to be that a sufficiently
knowledgable and experienced type of clinical sociology
can very quickly interpret the disparate signs of a crisis
in such a way as both to reconstruct the phenomenon itself and provide a diagnosis. (Oh dear: self-criticism seems
to be turning into self-congratulation. . .)

D. Memorandum for investigators
1. We are plunging into a regular thicket of a problem,
with extensions (and repercussions) on all sides. Right
from the beginning it is essential not to ignore *any* lead.
Experience and discussion will enable us to sort out the
most promising trails.

2. It will be necessary to *listen to* a vast quantity of
testimony, and store it all on tape. On the other hand, we
must very quickly pick out the basic centres of interest,
the key problems, and those persons, or groups of persons,

that are of the greatest strategical importance to our enquiry.

3. Points for interviews

a. Get the person interviewed to describe the events as they affected him or her personally.

b. Try to elicit information concerning his/her personal attitude—and that of others.

c. Ask him/her to define a Jew.

Leading key-persons: those who were contaminated and cured, those who were subjected to the myth, lived it, believed in it. Find out how they came to give it credence; why, in the end, they stopped believing it; and what they believe now.

Key groups: teachers, young people (the most promising field of operations, but—unfortunately—we're too late on the scene: no hope of arranging discussions and interventions in class. . .), the Communist Party, militant groups. Loyal customers of the incriminated shop-owners.

4. Enquiries to be made

External: Lille-Valenciennes (write to the Kosaks). Francine Lefèbvre (film news, Paris), Hit Parade, Paris. Background investigation at Orléans, especially on the Occupation. Collect all public statements issued concerning the affair. Try to obtain a copy of the various police reports.

Arrangements for Monday: the 'sociological dinner' on Monday evening (commensalism, get people talking). Operate sociological dragnet enquiry (women investigators should be ready with a lead-in story beginning: 'Well, I was in a fitting-room in Paris and I really thought that. . .'). Get on to the contaminated cases (and, better, those who caught the virus but are now cured) *as quickly as possible*. Have long interviews with them.

Provisional arrangements to be made on Monday at lunch. (Find a reasonably popular restaurant where we can discuss our enquiry out loud and thus provoke further contacts. Ask our first contacts to tell us where most gossip goes on, e.g. bistros, etc. Ask people what parts of the story are true, and what parts false. . .

Plan ahead with a view to the collective drafting of the final text right from the beginning. A detailed scheme with each person responsible for one part. Essential to attempt a collective draft.[1]

SUNDAY, 6 JULY
Advance programme
For Monday (tomorrow). Make contact as soon as possible with the Orléans AFP office, the *Nouvelle République*, the *République du Centre* (reporters who covered the affair, readers' letters, contacts with those who were hoaxed by the rumour).

Police headquarters (ask for contact with Le Mans). Police rationalisation of the *Noir et Blanc* article. Police reports.

Local branch of MRAP.

Communist Party.

Maison de la Culture (get facts about the Guilloux meeting).

Orléans Public Library (the town's recent history).

Teenage bars (Julia, Capulier).

Discothèques, night-clubs (every night).

Analysis of press coverage (Paillard).

Le Mans (Paillard).

When a whole town. . .
Find myself reflecting on a phrase some young Orléanais used when talking to Katia Kaupp: 'When a whole town says the same thing, there has to be something in it.' The myth was based on proof by common consensus, which is indeed the best (but also the worst) of proofs.

[1] This project was rendered impossible by the dispersal of the investigators immediately after the enquiry.

The shield

The Jew had as his shield the left-wing intellectual and
the militant revolutionary. After the Israeli-Arab conflict
it looked very much as though this shield was half lost to
him. Ever since then, it is true, in the eyes of left-wing
intellectual and militant revolutionary alike, the Jew has
become a double, indeed a two-faced being: one half Good
Persecuted Jew, the other half Bad Zionist Jew.

SATURDAY, 26 JULY

The days spent on this enquiry were so intensely busy that
I was not able, at the time, to write up the notes I accumulated for my journal. Then, after I got back, I flung
myself into the composition of the actual report, and all
my notes became grist to that particular mill. Yesterday
evening I tried to produce a retrospective account of
those days. But the whole picture had faded and vanished
beyond recall. Not the detailed points of reference, which
are there on paper still, but what constituted the life of
our undertaking: those animated conversations when
members of the team met and exchanged their findings,
the sequence of discoveries, changes of plan, and so on.

I tried to begin at the beginning, in that old middle-class
house on the Rue du Boeuf-Saint-Paterne, where we met
M. Lévy, with his thick pendulous underlip and good-
natured manner; but it's all stale now, lacking in impact;
the material has been used already. I feel as though during
the course of this investigation I broke through the sound
barrier, and that the actual noise (i.e. my personal impressions and research diaries) followed long after the
report instead of preceding it.

I was on the point of writing that all the 'juice' had gone
into the report, and what remained was not even the pulp,
but mere dried fibres. The living pulp of my Orléans adventure is now mashed up beyond recall. This confirms me
in my belief that one should try, at all costs, to keep an on-
the-spot diary, with at most a one or two day lag in entries,

as I did at Plodemet. I would have liked to evoke some of those faces, those destinies even, that we met or glimpsed: Lévy, Brun, the Abbé Séjourné, Licht, Inspector Fontan—the 'sociological dinner' held on that Monday evening at the Restaurant Madagascar—or my own observant exploration of those Orléans streets, striving to work out their secret, suddenly alert for the least sign, round the market-place, in the Rue du Chariot or the Rue de Bourgogne, an overwhelming and permanent sense of this town as an unknown quantity, the intoxicating impression of a permanent enigma matched by constant discovery. I can't, I won't, do any more.

SUNDAY, 31 AUGUST

Draft report finished. Towards the end I felt, briefly, an overwhelming sense of the weakness inherent in what constitutes my motive force. My tendency to try and explain (rationalise!) facts has ended up by turning the Orléans rumour into a straightforward, cut-and-dried phenomenon. It's true that my brand of rationalisation isn't the sort practised by those in search of a central idea, a simple structure. I have no intention of destroying the facts in order to fit a pattern. The pattern I have sought is a fluid, multiform one, where the disruption of one element will shake all the rest, and modify the overall structure. At this level, I feel satisfied with my analysis. Yet I cannot but wonder whether it has not let slip through its meshes what may well be the essence of the matter, something which—as Julia Vérone very clearly saw—is almost inexpressible: that fabulous poetic element, transmuting dream and reality, mystically associating one with, and within, the other, a poetry which habitually eludes sociological investigation, and which all speculation (as regards its origins, causes and consequences) does no more than reduce to an entity that explains everything bar itself.

BERNARD PAILLARD

WEDNESDAY, 2 JULY

Meeting at Rosenthal's with Léon Poliakov, author of a vast study on the history of anti-Semitism, and a representative of LICA, which is backing the enquiry. First general impressions:

The Orléans affair forms part of a pattern of other similar incidents in France. There was the Grenoble affair, which gave rise to an article in *Noir et Blanc* (this, according to the Chief of Police—rationalising hypothesis?—must have provided the model for the Orléans affair), with subsequent repercussions in the Mid-West (threatening letters or phone-calls to Jewish shop-owners in Tours, Le Mans and Angers), similar incidents in Lille, Valenciennes, even in Paris.

Three types of overall theory advanced:

1. Plot designed to discredit certain Jewish shop-owners, organised by an anti-Semitic group, either right-wing extremists or Arabs (hypothesis put forward by certain Jews known for their hypersensitivity to anti-Semitism). Doesn't really hold water, especially since in every case where right-wing student extremists of the 'Occident' group were accused of being the source of the myth, not a thing could be proved. Furthermore, it doesn't explain why the affair caught on so successfully.

2. Latent presence of anti-Semitism, which in certain periods of stress is liable to rise to the surface again (some-

168

one pointed out that we were in the thick of a referendum
and an election, hence a feeling of insecurity). Doesn't
explain this anti-Semitism. Why should it assume this
particular form? What we have in the Orléans affair is a
link-up between white slaving and anti-Semitism: this is
what calls for analysis.

3. Self-delusion on the part of certain hypersensitive
Jews, who saw anti-Semitism where in fact something
quite different existed. It has been pointed out that the
affair never, in fact, took on an openly anti-Semitic
character. In Orléans six shop-owners were made the
target for accusations. It is true that they were all Jewish,
and this forms the main basis for the anti-Semitic theory.
Now for one thing the other known Jewish shop-owners
(including those known to be pro-Israeli, or active propa-
gandists in the Israeli cause) have not been disturbed. For
another, it was the least obviously Jewish-looking ones
(in the morphological sense) who were accused. Provisional
hypothesis: to begin with, a relatively classic case of the
'white slave trade rumour' which sometimes occurs in
provincial towns, and the antecedents of which remain a
mystery. Should, therefore, be studied.

At this point I must digress briefly on a rumour which
gained currency in Laval. It was at the time when a certain
woman, well known as a militant opponent of the white
slave trade (she had written several books on the subject),
was going round the country, from one town hall to the
next, denouncing this invisible evil (and the failure of the
authorities to deal with it), and putting parents on their
guard. This was the period when young girls were first
struggling free of close parental supervision. (In the
provinces they were beginning to go out in the evening,
travel unaccompanied, or commute to some large nearby
town for higher studies or a job.) After this *worthy* person
revealed the danger threatening such young girls, parents
and teachers awoke to their responsibilities. At some point
either shortly before or shortly after this woman passed

through Laval, a report of white slaving began to circulate in the town, which slowed down feminine emancipation there considerably. In this case the triggering-off mechanism was quite straightforward (sensitisation by means of a nation-wide campaign) but this does not explain the rapid development of the myth. Conservative reactions in religious circles (part played by Catholic schools staffed by nuns, plus the anxiety of parents and teachers confronted by a process of emancipation which they have neither the ability nor the means to control).

One particular line of enquiry worth exploring in the Orléans affair is to see whether any connection can be found with phenomena deriving from schoolgirl emancipation since May 1968.

To return, then, to the overall theory formulated above: a white slave rumour which, for reasons unconnected with anti-Semitism (note the part played by the *type* of trade—clothing, footwear—which acted as a control), happened to involve certain Jewish shop-owners. The hypersensibility to anti-Semitism evidenced in Jewish circles, both among the victims and elsewhere (e.g. by militants of the anti-anti-Semitism movement), very soon brought in the Jewish myth as an element in the general picture. This myth was then free to develop autonomously (note the *accelerating* function of anti-Semitic groups such as *Occident*, and, in a less specific way, of right-wing extremist students generally). According to this hypothesis, there will have been inter-action of some sort between anti-Semitism and anti-anti-Semitism. According to this hypothesis there are three lines to follow up: the problem of white slaving, which recurs periodically just before the summer holidays, and is now progressively more in evidence during the winter months as well (we find campaigns denouncing this evil in journals like *Ici-Paris* or *France-Dimanche*, which pick on resorts such as St Tropez, on the Côte d'Azur, or various winter sports centres); the extra sensitisation to anti-Semitism shown by certain Jewish circles since the Israel affair; and, perhaps, anti-Semitism of a more latent variety.

What this means one should do, in concrete terms, is as follows. Firstly, study the type of campaign conducted by the militant anti-racialists. At what stage in the affair did they intervene? What sort of tactics did they adopt? Whom did they approach—the police, organised groups, the Press (local, regional, national)? Did they demonstrate in Orléans itself, and if so how? Were there public gatherings or meetings? How do *they* explain the phenomenon? (In this connection note the very revealing article in *Le Droit de vivre*, which rants on in denunciatory vein about a return to the days of the 'Final Solution', and talks in the most inflated language about certain militant anti-Semites with a special interest in promoting the Orléans affair.) Secondly, one should follow the actual development of the affair. Essential points to clarify: was the outburst sudden or gradual? what type of supposed victims? Check the background of those young people and adults involved. Just who came in on the affair—religious institutions, high-school, parents of pupils, parents generally (in the double rôle of first warning their juniors, and afterwards denouncing the myth)? What proportion played any physical part in the proceedings (threatening letters or phone-calls, gathering outside shops and picketing them, reducing their trade turnover)? Possibility that regular customers remained unaffected by the myth. Intervention by the Press, the Church, various associations (e.g. the Communist Party), leading to resorption. Pay particular attention to the appearance of anti-Semitic themes and their content—also to their disappearance. Study the part played by the kind of trade involved. Look for the sexualisation beneath the garments.

Groups to see: anti-Semitic militants, both as actors in the drama, and as a turntable for other contacts; shop-owners; teachers (contact with Jewish-Christian friendship group); young people (no contacts at present).

THURSDAY, 10 JULY

During our stay in Orléans we had no time to write; and
yesterday evening, instead of settling down to my notes I
went to see *Adalen 31*. As a result I have to go back over
the accumulated backlog this morning.

The period we spent in Orléans was brief, but relatively
fruitful. By Tuesday we got the feeling that we had examined
the question from all sides—or, to put it more precisely,
that we had covered all the existing ground. In point of
fact, given the unfavourable circumstances—the affair
had taken place a good month ago, and the anti-myth
campaign had done its work all too well (quickly re-
absorbing the myth by making people ashamed of having
believed in it); not to mention the fact that key groups
like high-school girls and teachers were no longer there to
be sounded out—despite these unfavourable circumstances, as I say, we did as much as we possibly could, and
with reasonable dispatch.

We discovered a host of aspects to the case that no one
could have suspected at the outset, and which were, more
or less, to constitute guide-lines for our better understanding of the myth's development and dynamic force.
These included the part played in the affair by young
people, and by popular milieux, in particular those
factories and offices where women congregated;[1] the political suppression of the affair; and its rationalisation in
Jewish circles, where anti-Semitism was made the central
theme, though in fact it was no more than secondary.

Finally, this incident, minimal at the outset, forced us
to explore the various strata of Orléans society, gave us a
glimpse into the political game at City Hall level, let us see
the various types of opposition: commercial, regional, in
the last resort racial. There were countless unsuspected

---

[1] A brief parenthetic note here on the rationalisation practised by certain
intellectuals, or quasi-intellectuals, from journalistic circles, who regarded themselves as left-wing, and were convinced that the myth
developed in a town where the proletariat formed a minority, and thus
could not perform its proper counterbalancing, commonsensical role.

factors which we stumbled upon, but which could not be
properly clarified in so short a time or so long after the
event (e.g. the political hushing-up of the affair, and the
numerous forms of opposition found within the context of
the local bourgeoisie—which may to some extent account
for the rationalising systems found at certain levels, and
provide a motive for the various tendencies to develop,
integrate, modify, propagate, resist, combat or ignore the
myth). One thing that emerges from these two days is that
the rationalisations given by journalistic circles are equally
mythical, and in that capacity must be assimilated to our
analysis as antidotal, shock-absorbent elements.

Another point which becomes clear is that we have two
separate areas to explore. One leads us towards official
circles, in the broadest sense of that term: the Préfecture,
City Hall, the police, local politics, and various professional, political or cultural organisations. The other
occupies a terrain which very soon becomes vague and
elusive: that of the 'non-assimilated' circles populated by
young females, a world of stenographers, of girls who live
wholly in the present, nurtured by the sensational mass
media, who have at their disposal, in reserve, a whole
collection of prefabricated scenarios, myths or legends.
Such persons, if successively activated, can produce a
series of chain reactions which give reality and substance
to myths hitherto experienced only at an imaginary level,
conjugating and multiplying them.

It is, then, the incubatory phase of the myth on which
we should concentrate, but this is just where our ignorance is greatest. All we can do is to advance a series of
more or less plausible hypotheses. When the Chief of
Police suggested that the article in *Noir et Blanc* was at
the bottom of the whole thing he only made one mistake,
that being not to realise that the real origins of the affair
lay far deeper, and that the article in question was no
more than a stimulus, or catalyst, which activated a whole
mass of reserves accumulated over many years.

Here, then, are two threads into the labyrinth which we must follow. We must trace the emergence and diffusion of the legend up to the point at which it became public—after which, passing into the sphere of officialdom, it activated a series of institutions which reacted *qua* institutions, with their own internal dynamism and individual logic.

We can now make the following provisional reconstruction of events. The legend took root in areas where semi-assimilated women predominated (recently urbanised districts, not yet taken up by unions or political parties), in factories, among office workers, junior clerks, and shop-assistants (institutions most frequently blamed were the factories, the Post and Telegraph Services, and the *Nouvelles Galeries*). Thus, initially, the period of incubation took place in circles frequented by lower-class women, who cherished a whole series of mass media myths, experienced at fantasy level, in the imagination (reading sources include illustrated romances, serial fiction, heart-throb stories and the more sensational weeklies).

It is very easy to see how the myth could take root and flourish in this particular ambience, where the predominantly female population encouraged an atmosphere of pullulating quasi-hysteria (the stories they read often serve as a setting for their own boasted conquests of men, a habit which merely serves to accentuate the rivalry between them—whether genuine or mythical). The basic question, however, in the last resort, is the transition from myth to reality (something hitherto experienced on the imaginary and fictional plane which develops a need to materialise, to come true). Here we enter the domain of full-blown hysteria, and it is this hysterical mechanism that we have to understand.

To begin with, we can certainly say that the article in *Noir et Blanc* formed the traumatising element which triggered off the process of mythic materialisation. The article in question was, in fact, an extract from a novel that had appeared at the beginning of the year; and the photographs printed beside the text were, similarly, taken from a film. Thus the piece maliciously concealed its doubly fictional character. The titles of the novel and the film were, in fact, printed—but in tiny type that could easily pass unnoticed. The fictional nature of the article was thus camouflaged, which gave the 'facts' every appearance of reality (supporting photographs). In this way fiction was transmuted into information, and could well have been passed on as such.

Here, however, we touch on an important problem. If in fact fiction can be camouflaged, with the result that the account given ceases to be imaginary and becomes informative, then fiction which presents itself as fiction can very soon also pass as 'information' if conditions are favourable. Journalistic speculations about some event, even if announced as hypothetical *ab initio*, can very easily become serious propositions for the reader. A double mechanism of trust and distrust operates here ('It's because the paper knows a lot that it doesn't make a definite statement—or at least it only makes it in this ambiguous, fanciful way'). In this way a patently imaginary article is, as it were, *decoded* in the search for some underlying factual content.

Thus it is quite easy to figure out the process by which the myth came to acquire the status of reality. Broadly speaking, it consisted of the following three phases:

a.   Supposing what happened at Grenoble were to happen in Orléans?

b.   It *is* happening in Orléans.

c.   The proof of it is that the same thing happened at Grenoble—I read about it in the papers.

The traumatic nature of the article could arouse certain areas capable of stimulating the most profound and far-reaching anxieties—areas where the anxiety thus released would be compelled to find its fixation-point in reality. This diffuse anxiety thus becomes *real*—which means that from then on one can fight it. For us, to grapple with such a problem would have meant plunging into the thick of this feminine anxiety, plumbing its depths, circumscribing it. The question remains open; unfortunately it cannot be tackled by way of research on the Orléans affair (lack of contact, at present, with the female population).

Endless rationalising theories can be advanced, but none is really satisfactory. One approach is that of modern psychoanalysis. According to this, what we would have here is an infantile fear of castration, resolving itself in the ambiguity of feminine narcissism and anxiety concerning mutilation/rape. Such a condition would naturally pre-dispose those affected by it to hysteria, thus producing the fictions of rape, abduction and—in the case with which we are concerned—white slavery. This hypothesis attaches great significance to the tendency of women to gossip and spread rumours. By diffusing, and thus generalising, their individual anxieties, they liberate themselves from them; the individual threat becomes collective, and if it is the collective group which is threatened, the individual feels that degree more secure. When danger hangs over all alike, there is less chance of any particular person being singled out.

Apart from this, there also exists the inverse mechanism of fascination. In this connection it is remarkable that the shop-owners felt, in a vague way, that the women who suffered from the most acute anxiety were all quite old (in comparison, that is, with the juvenile clientèle), and generally the plainest ones, in the thirty-and-over bracket. Furthermore, it was reported to us that the puncturing of the myth was accompanied by a certain feeling of dis-appointment: that certain young girls who regarded themselves as attractive were shocked by the fact that no one had tried to abduct them. We can detect a streak of feminine narcissism at work here. The woman approaching middle-age tries to convince herself she is still young, and her fear of adventure makes her believe she is still of an age to have it. The same mechanism operates in the case of plain women, whose fear of being abducted proves to them that they very well might be. It is also very useful for young girls, who are at an age for adventures, but perhaps have not as yet had any. Such hypotheses are *a priori* plausible enough (though further polishing and refinement of detail would be essential for their final presentation); but when we attempt to verify them, we come up against an insurmountable obstacle. One essential point we would have to determine would be which strata of feminine society were most highly sensitised. Young people without any emotional life? The feminine partners in unstable relationships? All this would have called for a far more serious investigation. If this type of motivation could predominate in lower-class or teenage circles, it could also develop in those middle-class milieux afflicted with creeping provincial 'Bovaryism'.

Orléans seems, in fact, to suffer rather more from provincialism precisely because the town lies within reach of Paris. There is a kind of *ennui Orléanais* which develops in contrast to the Parisian sparkle that everyone knows about; consequently there is a tendency to dismiss local cultural facilities (cinema, theatre) and local night-life as essentially second-rate, though the town has a fine crop of restaurants and several modern *boîte*-style cafés. Orléans' calm surface may perhaps mask various clandestine activities (one hears tales of notorious cuckolds, and of young people's surprise parties behind locked doors). Because night life is officially frowned on (open town), life remains calm on the surface, though a good deal of secret activity may be going on underneath.

A group of young people gathered in *La Rotonde* were asked whether the Orléanais were *fidèles*: when I put this question I was not thinking of conjugal fidelity, but rather of loyalty to one's country. In point of fact the discussion

had been turning on such themes as *fidélité* to Joan of Arc,
the idea of unconscious nationalism: Orléans as the centre
of France, where the most pure French was spoken. . .
With a certain amount of snickering, they promptly replied: 'Oh no, there are plenty of well known stories'—at
which point I realised the mistake I had made.

Could modern Orléans still be living in Madame Bovary's
day, with husbands visiting the Municipal Theatre once a
month to applaud sophisticated comedies which they were
unable to make head or tail of? According to this theory,
middle-class women alerted by their children reacted at
two levels. They took action to protect their threatened
offspring; but they also dreamed up adventures for themselves. (Liberal circles—e.g. doctors—are said to have been
particularly affected.)

Let us pick up the thread of the rumour's development
once more. We see that it was incubated in predominantly
feminine circles, and then canalised by the young. It
affected girl high-school students, who provided it with
its first diffusion centre, since these schoolgirls passed it on
to their parents (thus reaching the middle-class strata)
and their teachers (thus ensuring its dissemination in every
school). Women soon spread the rumour among their
menfolk, and from here it rapidly expanded through every
social and geographical azimuth (including the rural
districts) on market-days (the Saturday before, and more
especially the Saturday of these events).

Thus we can posit the following sequence of events: the
article in *Noir et Blanc* appeared during the week 8–14
May, acting as a stimulus towards the creation of the
myth. The latter had about a week's incubation period,
gradually spreading among the girls' high-schools. By the
20th it was already widespread enough for the Public
Prosecutor's Department (appraised of the affair by its
stenographers) to alert the police and ask just what was
going on. (The police were not, as it happened, in on the

picture—any more than the journalist who happened to be
tipped off by the Superintendent.) The reaction in official
circles was ambivalent. (General inclination to regard the
whole thing as a hoax, no one concerned enough to warn
the shop-owners involved.)

The latter were only put in the picture at a late stage, by
friends or other Jews—who had themselves only been
tipped off by accident. On the 20th, a minor city market-
day (but not to be compared with the Saturday one, which
brings shoppers in from all the surrounding area), the
rumour reached the entire population of Orléans, both city
and suburbs; penetrated the middle-class districts, through
the agency of maids coming back from market; and spread
to all working-class areas that had so far avoided contamination (here housewives acted as carriers). By the
23rd, the news had been disseminated in places right
outside Orléans; it may well have got as far as Tours and
Angers and Poitiers, the virus being conveyed by commercial travellers.

The week of 24–31 May saw the generalised diffusion
of this virus. No-one escaped contact with it. It infiltrated
the cafés, which became active centres of dissemination,
using teachers as their chief carriers. The latter issued
warnings to their pupils. The sheer momentum with which
the virus spread tended to annihilate its natural antidotes
(everyone had some close friend or relative with a story to
tell), all the more so since the silence maintained by
official circles could be taken as an endorsement of the
rumour. There was, so to speak, a suspension of judgment
on the authorities' part. If they had taken a positive stand,
one way or the other, this would at once have labelled the
rumour as true or false.

Those official circles which took the affair lightly
(regarding it as some sort of hoax) could not react through
normal bureaucratic channels: no department of public
administration is under any obligation to deny a rumour
when the Public Prosecutor's Department has not been

officially notified. The somewhat superficial enquiry conducted by the police had come to nothing, since they had
not been formally notified of any disappearance; thus it
did not lie within their competence to issue a denial of mere
intangible gossip. It was, very probably, during this last
period that the story took on an increasingly anti-Semitic
tone, though the anti-Semitic element still remained
secondary. (What people said, in effect, was: There's a
white slave traffic going on, and *what's more* it's being run
by Jews.) Real anti-Semitism was only grafted on to this
pattern from the moment someone added: 'Well, that's
not surprising, is it?'

On Saturday 31 May, the day of the big regional market,
what had been whispered rumour became public. Groups of
people gathered outside the *Boutique Dorphée*, which was
admirably situated to form the first target—opposite the
Nouvelles Galeries, just by the meat market, in a street
which at the time was more or less blocked for repairs.
Thus it formed a natural point at which numerous passers-
by could stop for a few moments, out of curiosity, and
exchange a few words, sometimes accompanied by open
gestures of hostility or anti-Semitic remarks. It was this
bursting of the abscess which at once triggered off a brisk
anti-anti-Semitic counter-attack: and it was the latter's
vigour, combined with the official status the phenomenon
now acquired, which destroyed its more active germs.

To some extent one can say that such a rumour is only
capable of developing in secret. The moment it becomes
generalised, it loses its real force (inevitable reaction
against its more exaggerated features, which raise doubts
as to its veracity). The moment it becomes public property—
i.e. from the time it runs out of non-contaminated areas
to infect—it tends to disappear. When it passes into its
official phase, it sets in action certain highly energetic
antidotal elements. These accelerate the process of resorption, but at the same time are not, perhaps, strong
enough to deal with all the contaminating bacteria (no

smoke without fire). There is always the possibility, in fact, that a similar type of phenomenon develops, with a different though cognate mythology, and attacking other persons. Some in fact claim that there was nothing in the rumour as far as the Jews were concerned, but think it quite possible that Orléans *did* experience, and hush up, a case of drugging or white slavery. This would explain how the rumour got started; it would then have taken the nasty turn it did as a result of popular imagination.

Here, then, in brief, we have the main processes by which the rumour was disseminated and afterwards resorbed. I have not yet dealt with the actual themes of the rumour itself, since its mythological content necessarily leads us on to some more precise analysis of those hidden tendencies which are then revealed. The first question one has to ask oneself is: what connection exists between the anti-Semitic and white slavery motifs?

10 AUGUST
Letter to Edgar Morin
General remarks

I feel there is a basic error in the overall construction of the report. This error becomes very apparent during the final chapters. After one chapter analysing the structure of the myth and the anti-myth we proceed to a fresh piece of socio-phenomenographic reportage on conductors, antibodies, and political repercussions. The entire pattern needs revising, and I no longer have the earlier pages by me for consultation.

Nevertheless, I'll do what I can.

1. A large opening section which would, in a sense, constitute our descriptive report on the Orléans affair. This could be done by bracketing chapters 4, 5 and 6 with the chapter on the rumour's development (but omitting the analysis of the intelligentsia).

2. A second, more analytical section (on the structure of the myth and the anti-myth), to which might be appended

various special problems—on the new anxieties affecting
adolescents, say, or the fight which teachers are putting up
against today's teenage feminine culture. One could then
go on to analyse the role of the intelligentsia, and give
further scrutiny to the cycle of the rumour as a whole: its
genesis in adolescent circles, its derivation from a fantasy
which reveals both the degree of segregation imposed on
these teenage girls, and just what stress-anxieties they
suffer when brought up against the new feminine culture
and modern sexual liberation. Here is a rumour which has
swamped the town and even made certain inroads on the
polis—at this point make a more detailed analysis of the
political repercussions, i.e. go beyond mere reportage and
deal with a number of questions other than that of the
town's general anxiety (what this last implies except a lack
of close analysis I don't quite see).

Such a conclusion would, I think, both improve the
structure logically and make for more effective analysis.

Another suggestion: further work should be done on the
hypotheses one can formulate about the way adolescent
girls are both attracted and scared by the modern liberation of feminine sexuality.

The Orléans affair reveals, firstly, a relatively high
degree of segregation among adolescent girls, but at the
same time suggests that communications within the group
are potentially excellent. The rumour may have 'incubated'
among adolescents, but when it began to spread it came in
contact with a number of other social milieux. Its passage
to adult circles was a slow, uphill business. We can
legitimately speak of a feminine adolescent sub-culture,
which is something distinct from juvenile culture as a
whole. Amongst adolescent boys, in point of fact, the
rumour seems to have caught on comparatively late
(segregation between boys and girls being strict enough to
prevent all communication). For example, a senior class at
the Benjamin Franklin Technical School got wind of the

rumour from a day-pupil, whose own source of information was not his sister, or some Orléanais girl-friend, but family relatives. Thus we can infer a wide area of secrecy in feminine adolescent circles, with confidences exchanged selectively between girls at varying degrees of intimacy, thus facilitating either the release of pent-up anxieties, or else the mutual communication of new experiences.

Adolescent girls are very far from being immunised against fantasies by the smattering of scientific knowledge, psychological as well as physiological, that filters through to them by way of women's periodicals. Indeed, modern developments in the sphere of feminine sexuality find them surprisingly defenceless. The repression of women's sexual instincts, based on the idea of motherhood as a great mystery (and on the fear of premature maternity), has generally lost its force, though it still constitutes a key element in sexual initiation. But the removal of this at-mosphere of mystery from the sexual-maternal function still leaves behind a dark zone of new impulses and desires—for the provocation and release of which it was itself responsible in the first place. The result has been a new world of impulses which tend to arouse profound anxieties (since they form the object of individual ex-periment and experience): this world, it would seem, has not yet been codified or recognised socially. For adolescent girls the appeal of sex no longer lies in an anxious anticipa-tion of self-fulfilment through marital bliss; instead they are seeking precocious sexual experience, pre-marital de-floration, a wider range of experiences involving several partners.

The adolescent girls most vulnerable to the myth are perhaps those who have only recently begun to move in the orbit of this new feminine sexuality. Introduced and initiated by the magazines, stimulated by the company of their friends, they take their first step towards emancipa-tion when they enter the world of teenage fashion, which presents, in outline, a strategy of seduction, realised or

desired. At the same time, however, they are held captive
by the traditional rules, under the aegis of parental
authority. Thus they have to assume a twofold and contradictory initiation: that of modern feminine sexuality on
the one hand, and the traditional social conventions on
the other. Both of them induce guilty feelings (when
dealing with their initiated companions they tend to be
ashamed of their virginity, while vis-à-vis their parents
they feel bad about having lost it); but at the same time
they do balance each other out to some extent. This double
pull can induce what might be termed mild trajectory-
wobble, with a series of sexual experiences culminating,
finally, in marriage; but the oscillations are still liable to
generate profound anxiety, and this in turn will breed
fantasies. On the one hand we find individual micro-
fantasies, in which to believe oneself desired, but to resist
temptation, removes all culpability from the desire to make
oneself desirable. On the other, there is the macro-fantasy
of the white slave trade, which has localised these floating
anxieties by embodying itself in mythic form. The extent
of the myth reveals, at a fundamental level, the depth of
anxiety generated by these newly experienced impulses
(which are beginning to run wild for lack of sufficiently
effective repressors). It is true that traditional ethics still
maintain the upper hand, and contrive to repress such
impulses. (These are expelled as being the by-product of a
new sexual slavery, that of instinct and impulse, which
turns a woman into a willing love object, a quasi-
prostitute.) But by so doing, they release various inhibitory
and anxiety-inducing mechanisms, since this strange
world of sexual instinct is something they can neither
explain nor recognise.

Thus it is at the intersection of these two worlds of
feminine sexuality that one finds the more sensitised and
vulnerable zones, perhaps hidden behind a surface display
of self-assurance.

But when it enters the world of women's workshops,

the rumour acquires another base from which to propagate
itself, since here the modern teenage girl's universe comes
into conjunction with one version of the adult woman's—
that represented by pulp fiction. Certain working-class
adolescents, steeped in the romantic and slightly old-
fashioned culture associated with this heart-throb literature, may possibly have augmented the myth with material
drawn from their own fictional reading.

These adolescent girls both inhabit a romantic world
which stimulates their imagination, and at the same time
plunge into the orbit of new-style feminine sexuality: as
a result they suffer considerable emotional disturbance,
all the more so since their initiation is, more often than
not, an abrupt one, without any cushioning by a protective
social ambience. Entry into modern adolescent culture is
often no more than an imaginary attempt to escape from
the work bench, the desire to better oneself by seducing
some student or middle-class worthy's son; and it is nearly
always accompanied by a sharp break with one's friends at
work or in the neighbourhood of one's home.

One last suggestion: the final reflections on the interplay
between archaism and modernity are either too long or too
short: too long if one simply wants to give a general idea
of the situation, too short if one's aim is to genuinely
enlighten the reader. The remarks on the future of tish
civilisation are superfluous.

The *conscience of the world* does not produce any really
decisive arguments: it leaves the major problem un-
touched. What *is* elucidation? What use is it? What aims
does it have? Why elucidate anyway? Insofar as you have
tried to answer such points I don't find you very con-
vincing. If it's true that one is perpetually passing off
rationalisations as rational arguments, a moment is bound
to come when one shelves the problem and instead
concentrates on defining the limits and terms proper to
rationalism (epistemology and logic).

Finally, it does seem to me that the analysis of the intelligentsia's rôle remains much too strongly influenced by your own special ideal of the intellectual—which allows you to take a group with innumerable internal divisions and to lump it under one category labelled 'cultivated class'.

We have to make a clear distinction between the private and public sectors of the teaching profession. In the latter, warnings to pupils mostly came from the administration, and not so much (though cases are on record) from individual teachers.

It would be desirable to make rather more of the example offered by the President of the Parents' Association, which testifies to an abrupt conversion. In his case this was accelerated as a result of the meeting with Licht, but a slower version of it was probably experienced by a sizeable proportion of the teaching body. This leads one to a double hypothesis: that people became sensitised in turn by both the myth and the anti-myth (the latter stemming from confirmation that the facts as stated were untrue). The woman I saw at the *Maison de la Culture*, though far from forthcoming, admitted to me that at first she too had believed the rumour. However, faced with its widespread prevalence and anti-Semitic character, she realised that it must be a 'Fascist plot'. Is this a case of two separate mental worlds in collision, or can one single world embrace two such contradictory reactions? In either case there is a failure to elucidate, though the explanation adheres to the ideal postulate of the rôle assumed by the intelligentsia.

Bring out more clearly the variegated and far from confident nature of the teaching body's reactions, which testify to the heterogeneity—and the critical state—of the intelligentsia today. Such characteristics can no longer be analysed in terms of the vocational rôle as 'enlightener' which the teacher used to enjoy early this century. Since then there has been a widespread tendency for teachers to become part of officialdom and the bourgeois Establishment.

The whole section on political repercussions calls for a more cautious and hypothetical diagnosis.

By far the weakest side of this report is its attempt to explain and define the reactions of various social groups. On the other hand the analysis of myth and anti-myth is excellent: it breaks new ground and raises a whole multitude of questions. Our lack of phenomenological data on the hard facts of those social relationships and conflicts which operated throughout the Orléans affair, and the extreme brevity of our enquiry, do not permit us to go far beyond the sort of generalisation that admits of more or less *a priori* verification. For this reason it might be advisable to emphasise the phenomenological and monographic character of these sections, and to set them in a framework of not particularly original general remarks. You could then put forward one or two more closely defined hypotheses, and, above all, raise a number of particular questions—e.g. teenage girls' culture (with special reference to the new sexual freedom), the problem of adolescence, the crisis in the teaching profession, urban society, local politics, and so on. It seems to me that the formulation of such hypotheses would be more useful for the reader than general speculations on our civilisation and its future in a time of crisis.

EVELYNE BURGUIÈRE

MONDAY, 7 JULY

Drive down from Paris to Orléans. During the car journey we have time to go over the background of the affair, and allot special areas of investigation. Edgar Morin will take responsibility for official interviews. V. and C. have the sort of appearance—long hair, hippie necklaces—that should enable them to make contact with young people. Suzanne is Orléanais by birth. I am to accompany her on her middle-class pilgrimage.

Arrival in Orléans. A cold, dull town. Grey sky. Walls, stones, a statue of Joan of Arc dominating the middle of the public square which is to be our rallying point. Suzanne and I set off towards her great-aunt's house. The streets we walk through are practically deserted. What are people saying to each other behind the walls of these little two-storey houses?

Mme Escalier's house: very soft, comfortable place. Carpeted floors, velvet-pile upholstery. We go through a small, yellow, silk-panelled drawing-room into another, larger, apartment. A piano, vases of flowers, photographs, a television set. In the kitchen the housekeeper is busy preparing lunch. Sink into an armchair and try to imagine what it must be like living here—the silence and solitude.

The old lady leads a very isolated existence here. In the evening her downstairs tenants come up to watch television. They tell her the latest city gossip. We discuss the affair.

How did she learn all about it? Through the neighbours, her messengers from the outside world. They must have read about it in *Le Figaro*, she said. (She herself takes *L'Aurore*, and thus saw nothing.) She shows considerable irritation. Condemns the public rumour, nourished—she says—on a parcel of old wives' tales. Also condemns the press campaign (a far from innocent one, in her view) for giving this 'nonsense' free publicity: 'Who benefits from it? The fellow-travellers.' And again: 'They engineered this situation. They've got this passion for dividing people against each other, setting them at loggerheads.' Even her housekeeper, who 'certainly has no cause for complaint', one day had the temerity to tell her 'that she didn't want to be treated like a dog'.

This is a change from the silent, inscrutable Orléanais we encountered at first. In this city rival camps and tortuous feuding are commonplaces. Suddenly the old lady brings up the underground-tunnel motif, one of the essential ingredients in the white slavery myth as applied to Orléans: 'When I was a little girl, my grandfather wanted to show me them [the secret passages]. There was a well at the end. I got frightened.' Did the old lady, quite unconsciously, recapitulate the same process of romantic myth-making that set all Orléans by the ears? Or is what we have here rather a collective legacy from the past? To judge by what she told us, everyone in Orléans knew about the existence of this underground city, a labyrinth dating from Joan of Arc's day, with tunnels extending under the Loire: a world which no one ever actually explored, because it was so scary, but which fed the darker side of people's imagination, was conjured up in order to scare oneself, or others. . .

She also described one of her neighbours, a young girl, as 'coming home sometimes with a dress she'd bought from the Jews'. Is 'the Jews' a term currently used in Orléans? It would appear so.

In her opinion the real competition with which Orléanais

shopkeepers had to reckon did not stem from the 'Jew shops' but from 'the Germans', in the shape of X's big chain-stores. Was this an unconscious shift away from anti-Semitism (socially non-acceptable) to a more convenient type of xenophobia? Or could there be a far closer connection between the two attitudes?

After leaving Mme Escalier's, I felt I had progressed a little in my knowledge of Orléans and *la vie orléanaise*: provincial boredom, endless rival factions (by no means only in the commercial field, either). Awareness of a general feeling for 'the honour of the town'. Mixed emotions: shame, a desire to erase the memory of what had happened, to minimise its importance, to lay the blame for the outburst on the imagination of the masses, to avoid any personal involvement in the event. Suspicion of the (threatening) Stranger in one's midst. A two-level town—the visible one of reality, and the secret underground one, apt vehicle for unconfessed imaginings and erotic fantasies?

Visit with Suzanne to A., one of the shops which came under attack (despite the fact of its being non-Jewish).

The proprietress told us all the various troubles she had had. There was the man (sardonic emphasis on this word) who turned up, like a representative of the town's collective terror, to inspect the entire shop before allowing his daughter to come and make purchases there. There was the woman customer who looked scared when told she could use the telephone in the back room. There was the hostile, suspicious crowd that gathered outside the shop. There was the husband of the sales-manageress ('a parachutist', she said) who had insisted on his wife leaving there and then; he wouldn't let her stay in a place where 'a traffic in women' was carried on. (Nevertheless this same woman's mother came round later and told A. how ashamed of this incident her daughter was.)

A mixed bag of intermingled reactions: suspicion,

hostility, fear, shame, even the desire for atonement. When we asked the proprietress how she thought the rumour had got started, she hesitated, unsure of her answer. Mass stupidity? Or deliberate malice?

We chatted with the young salesgirl who had arranged our visit to the shop. What about the goods sold? we asked. 'People are jealous, that's what I mean, look for yourselves—this isn't a shop for middle-aged mums.' There were, in fact, some quite ravishing things there, all in the very latest fashion.

Who formed the clientèle? 'Mostly young people—and some not so young ones who go for our style.' What about the fitting-rooms? 'All this stuff about abduction is crazy. Why, you can see the fitting-rooms from the street.' Gossip? 'Oh, people said that at the [Jewish] shoe shop young girls were injected in the sole of the foot, and then carried in a drugged stupor through the underground passages to the Loire.' (Like so many others, she firmly believed in the existence of these subterranean tunnels.)

This visit to A.'s struck us as being of considerable interest. Suzanne and I discussed its implications. All these shops are new. Suzanne told me that the boutiques she knew sold a more traditional range of clothes, and at higher prices. These short dresses and well cut pants and exotic accessories must have caused considerable alarm among Orléans' conformists.

We discussed the myth. How had it been fabricated? From what the young sales girl at A.'s told us, it looks as though the element people concentrated on to begin with was the abduction of women and the subterranean network linking one shop to another, the shoe store to the dress boutique. Before that Saturday, the rumour may have circulated widely, but its anti-Semitic implications seem not to have been recognised. It was only afterwards, when the various shops had been named, and bracketed together in the public mind, that the anti-Semitic motif was detected. If the shops were not connected by sub-

terranean passages, at least they had other common
features that linked them together: they were all owned by
Jews.

The little salesgirl talked about the 'Jewish shops'. Yet
such shops differed in no way whatsoever from the one
where she worked: they sold exactly the same sort of
dresses. Nevertheless, she imperceptibly emphasised the
fact that there *was* a difference by the mere use of the
word 'Jewish'. She did not assume this difference, but
repeated it as a leitmotiv of various conversations she had
had with her friends. 'The Jewish shops' seems to be a
phrase in current use, applied to several establishments.

Visit to D., a small manufacturer: highly dynamic
personality. Very pretty courtyard. Stone-barred windows.
Arches, the calm atmosphere of old Orléans. Valuable
pieces of sculpture. Statues, ivy, old worn flagstones.

D.'s interpretation of the events. He was out of town
when the affair took place, so could analyse it un-
emotionally when he got back. He has two theories. The
first is political. In his view, prior to 31 May the rumour
was both uncontrolled and uncontrollable. After then,
however, it was utilised for political ends. After 31 May
he distinguishes two periods: first suppression, in the
interests of the electoral campaign, and then political
counter-bidding between the two ballots. His second
theory is that the rumour was deliberately organised, but
in the event turned out to be good rather than bad publicity.
Curiosity pulled in more customers. After a fortnight's fall
in sales, business picked up and got better than ever.

The first, political, explanation suggests that the shop-
owners were the innocent dupes of electoral shenanigans.
The second makes them out to have been unconscious
beneficiaries (or, at worst, the shrewd inventors of their
own scandalous publicity: D. didn't go so far as to suggest
this, but it's the interpretation I find myself unconsciously
veering towards).

I am convinced that D. is not alone in holding the views
he put forward for our benefit. He is interpreting discussions he has had with other people in Orléans. What I
find most striking is the simultaneous desire to minimise
the incident, and to exaggerate (under a specious cover of
disapproval) the degree to which it was utilised for political
ends—not to mention the determination throughout to
sidestep any denunciation of anti-Semitism. In this context
anti-Semitism no longer possesses any tangible reality.

His sister: a spinster businesswoman in her forties.
Violent reaction against what she terms 'this shop-girls'
serial'. Takes refuge behind a barricade of reason and
common sense. When asked if she believed in the abduction story at any point, replied: 'The abduction of women
is impossible under any circumstances.'

Yet there may have been a period, between 20 and 30
May, when she too played some part in the myth's propagation by word of mouth, since she admitted that in the
middle-class circles she frequented women did discuss
the event. May we conclude from this that the rumour was
not the exclusive prerogative of 'factory girls'?

The dinner. Among those present are the various shop-
owners smeared during the affair, a number of journalists,
M. Brun, M. Lévy, Mme K., a teacher and her husband.
People only begin to talk at all freely at the very end of
the meal. M. Licht introduces us to Mme Buki (*Sheila*).
'She's been wonderful,' he says. 'She fought back just like
a man.'

Find myself seated close to her. She is a subtle, intelligent,
sensitive woman, who has been badly scarred by the
incident. Several times she was to express a desire to pull
up her roots, and emigrate to some country where anti-
Semitism does not exist: Israel, perhaps. 'Before, I was
blind. Now I see things clearly.'

For the journalists, reconstructing the myth produced
something much akin to the 'Z' affair, with its political

G

undercurrents and complexities. The very first rumour
dated back to about 10 May, and came to light in the
Public Prosecutor's office, where it was circulating among
the secretarial staff. It then assumed such proportions that
the magistrates were notified. When the affair penetrated
official circles, its anti-Semitic nature was recognised, and
energetic measures taken to suppress it. What interested
us, however, was rather everything that *preceded* the official
explosion, namely the progress of the word of mouth
rumour—not to mention the way in which certain people
brought themselves to believe in such sensational rubbish.

Mme K. told us about a teacher (Suzanne and I tried to
meet him this afternoon, but failed), an active member of
the Parents' Association, who at one point believed in the
rumour, but then, after meeting M. Licht and hearing the
facts of the case, took a leading part in the myth's des-
truction.

What was the general reaction in teaching circles?
People tell us about official statements by various associations, and give us a few adresses. Mme K., the daughter
of an Orléanais Jewish shop-owner, and herself a teacher,
emphasises the conspiracy of silence that surrounded her,
the quiet whispering campaign, the way some of her
colleagues gave credence to the myth, the complete lack
of frank discussion between them and herself. Throughout
the course of these events she was shut in a kind of invisible ghetto, though no open accusations were made
against either her or her parents.

When we asked Licht and Mme Buki to reconstruct the
climactic period of the myth for us (that is, the Saturday
and Sunday of the elections), they became tense and
uneasy once more. They could see those crowds gathering
outside the shops. Licht stressed the threatening way some
people had behaved, and the dangerous tension that built
up at certain times. Saturday is market-day, and there is
usually a crowd in the streets then. But that day, in their
opinion, the crowd was aggressive. I caught the same

intonations with them as I had noted when talking to
A.

They are not, like the people at A.'s, newcomers to
Orléans. They have friends here. 'Hardly a single phone-
call to assure us of support or friendship.' The phone-calls
they *did* get were anonymous, threatening and sarcastic.
Someone asked them if maybe they could provide tickets
to the Middle East. Some joker rang up and said: 'I'll let
you have a case of champagne if you'll get rid of my wife
for me.' Customers enquired whether they were offering
reduced price vouchers for the shoe shop by way of a
bonus, and so on.

In their eyes this aberrant episode, which kindled people's
imagination and affected even the most level-headed
individuals, is far from innocent. The plot theory reappears,
a vast net covering all France (Lille, Le Mans, etc.). It
encircles Orléans and produces a more violent explosion
there than elsewhere. They are determined to pin down
those responsible, to isolate potential political carriers.
They talk of right-wing extremist movements.

There is some retrospective relief in the air, since no
actual disappearance took place during this period. Yet
the gossip-mongers supported their claims with instances
of people who had (according to them) undoubtedly been
spirited away, this information being derived from un-
impeachable sources, i.e. a friend or a relative.

Who actually *did* spread the rumour? There seems to
have been a great deal of excited chatter in the high-
schools; but this afternoon people were talking darkly to us
about 'Post Office employees' and 'factory girls'. Which
age group are we concerned with? Adolescents or young
women? It's now being suggested to us that we ought to
investigate the ladies' hairdressing shops, those ideal
centres for the dissemination of news or gossip. There are
certain *coiffeuses*, we are informed, who believed every
word of the story. We ought to go and interview
them.

TUESDAY, 8 JULY

Share-out of special jobs. Edgar Morin suggests that Julia,
Suzanne and I should go the rounds of the hairdressers and
beauty parlours. I would like to discuss things with Mme
B.'s salesgirls.

When I arrive at the boutique, Mme B. is there. She
introduces me to her salesgirls, both of them young. They
are busy putting out dresses on hangers. I tell them what
I am investigating: the dissemination of a certain rumour.
Blank wall: no cooperation.

'We've had enough of all that,' said the blonde one. 'The
journalists twist every word you say, God knows what they
won't make up.'

'I'm not a journalist.'

'As far as we're concerned the case is closed, there's no
point in going on about it.'

I persisted. They began to get more nervous as they
hung up the dresses (especially one of them, the blonde).
It was she who had been aggressive from the start,
whereas her dark-haired companion hardly uttered a
word.

'It's just stirring up a lot of trouble. People have forgotten the whole thing.'

'No one talks about it?'

'No. No one.'

'Who talked about it before the elections?'

'Everybody.'

'Young people?'

'Young, old, the lot.'

'The old folk took it all more seriously,' said her
companion. 'They knew more than the kids. Well, I mean,
they know white slaving's a fact. They know it can
happen.'

'So they said it was possible, did they? Did they believe
in the rumour?'

'Well, yes and no. Fact is, most people took it as a joke.'

'But not old people?'

'There are always people who take that sort of thing seriously. But the moment it was clear the whole thing was moonshine, no one mentioned it any more. Best to forget it.'

'Look, you work in this shop. You were close to the source, you ought to have known the truth. Surely people questioned you?'

'Oh, people know me,' the dark-haired girl broke in. 'Sure, they asked me for information, but they didn't believe what I told them. I found out about this business through a friend of mine. She came asking me about it on Sunday the 25th, Whit Sunday that was,'

'Did you tell your employer about it?'

'I meant to talk to her on Tuesday, but we had electricians in the shop. I got around to it the next day. No, of course I didn't believe the story. Still, I was caught up in the affair a bit—I mean, after all, I work here.'

The other salesgirl had been away sick during these events, and the gossip had not reached her. Nor had her husband heard about it in the office where he worked. During our conversation the proprietress had gone out, and I now broached the theme of anti-Semitism in a more direct manner.

'Oh, people sometimes say things to me like, "You work for the Jews, you're helping them to make money".'

'What do you reply?'

'I explain that they're my employers, they're just ordinary shop-owners like anyone else.'

'*Except that they're Jews*, for the people who are talking to you, right?'

'But that's racialism. People who talk like that are stupid. You can't have a reasonable discussion with them.'

Then they both tried to define their own idea of a Jew.

'You can't, he's just a man like anyone else.'

For them, the older generation were largely responsible for the reappearance of racialism. 'Old people are hopeless. You can't change them.'

There was talk of the 'instability' of the young, and their fantasies.

'Anyway, if you want to ask questions about all this business, it's the teachers you should have gone to.'

'The teachers? Why?'

'There are kids in high-school who were talking about it.'

'You mean the teachers are responsible?'

'No, of course not.'

'Then what?'

'I don't know. But they ought to do *something*, explain things. . .'

From then on there were several interwoven themes: racialism, education and its shortcomings. . .

'I'm not anti-Semitic. Coloured men? Some of them are very nice. All the same, I can't really see myself going out with a Negro, or marrying one.'

'People criticise me because I work for Jews. I just can't argue with anyone who takes that sort of line. They're old, narrow-minded. Young people are better. You can explain things to them, change their outlook,'

Orléans is a town with some experience of foreigners. There were the Americans, for instance.

'The French don't like foreigners.'

'Seems as though they don't like Jews, either, wouldn't you say? But they're not foreigners, are they?'

'Personally, I think there's a lot of jealousy in it somewhere. Jews are such successful businessmen.'

'There are Jews who aren't successful, but people still say "Oh, they're Jews", in just the same way.'

'Because they're a bit foreign, too. They're sort of Israelis.'

'How do you mean?'

'People think of them as a bit foreign.'

'They've got an accent, you mean? And have their own way of life?' (I get a feeling that the young salesgirl who used the word 'Israeli' may simply have mixed it up with

'Israelite', but prefer to let her explain herself in her own way.)

'Well, that depends. But I'm sure it's mostly jealousy.'

A nice circular argument.

Meanwhile Mme B. has come back, and now lets us have her views. The Christian religion, she feels, is no stranger to the propagation of anti-Semitism. It was the Jews who killed Christ—even children are told that. Her allegation brings a brisk rebuttal from the dark-haired young salesgirl.

'I was brought up in a Catholic school, and no one ever told *me* such a thing.'

Her companion agreed: 'Religion doesn't seem important enough to put people against each other.'

'Especially today. People don't go to church the way they used to. There just isn't the time.'

Mme B. returned to the attack, and described certain episodes of her childhood: the daily beatings and insults she had to endure. Sheer amazement on the part of the salesgirls, who once more emphasised the importance of education.

'The schools ought to find some way of stamping out these racialist reactions.'

Mme B. recalled another, more recent incident: 'I showed you my identity card, it states quite clearly that I'm a Frenchwoman. I showed it to you while all this was going on. Did you ever doubt that I was French?'

The young salesgirls had in fact never thought of contesting her nationality. Mme B.'s gesture was provoked by a momentary fit of anger, a desire to exhibit the proof of her nationality, and by so doing to silence that charge of duplicity which public opinion tends to bring against the Jews. Jews—or Frenchmen?

The salesgirl's reply was: 'No, I never doubted that you were French (Mme B.'s foreign-sounding name might have led to some uncertainty), but I had no idea you were Jewish, either.'

Overall impressions of this discussion: our exchanges
were constrained by the presence of Mme B., owing to the
fact that she knew me, and had introduced me to her
assistants. The latter had several reasons for being wary
of me: the fact that I knew Mme B., her presence while
we were talking, the resentment they felt at being called
on to dredge up 'all that stuff' again. I couldn't hope to
get their own real evidence on, or reaction to, these events:
it was easy to predict what both would be like. What one
might have elicited, though, was the impact that the
event made on their acquaintances, the way in which they
had got to hear of it, the discussions they had had on the
subject amongst themselves, in the café with other
shop-assistants or with their boy-friends. We drifted into
a more general discussion (which it would be interesting
to analyse, if only because of its clichés, ineptitudes and
contradictions).

These two salesgirls are more mature than the young
assistant at A.'s. The married one has contacts with circles
that are no longer adolescent, and do not seem to have
played any part in spreading the rumour. On the other
hand certain individuals in them take an anti-Semitic line
of the sort she describes as 'obtuse', because it is expressed
without reason or justification, except for the jealousy
motif (several times repeated).

As for the other salesgirl, her information was in a sense
official, or quasi-official.

The most interesting point, beyond any doubt, is the
discussion we had on racialism and child education—a
discussion which, in its very banality, might well faithfully
mirror the provincial mentality. Some of the argument
was very obscure and confused—e.g. the 'old folk', we
learnt, were the most gullible, while 'the younger generation' should be regarded, not necessarily as carriers of the
myth, but rather as the victims of their elders' credulity.
Who disseminated the myth? No clear facts emerged from
this interview. The 'old folk' believed it—but who told

them in the first place? Plenty of our points which seemed quite clear yesterday at A.'s now look equally dubious.

One note on erotic fantasy. The motif of female abduction they either carefully played down ('a mere joke'), or else ignored altogether. A nasty joke, and any further reference to it was in the worst possible taste.

Nearly noon. Return to A.'s. An enlightening visit. Find she has just put an advertisement in the paper asking for a new manageress. She never did mean to stay in Orléans, she said; just long enough to launch the shop and train a manageress. But now she's got even less inclination to hang on. All very like the conversation I had yesterday evening with Mme X., who also talked of leaving Orléans.

We had a few words about the women customers who looked uneasy when they came back to the shop after the affair: 'It was the plainest ones who looked the most worried.'

Midday. Lunch with the other members of the team in a restaurant near the meat market. Julia comes straight from the hairdresser's. Then Edgar Morin, Bernard Paillard and Claude Capulier arrive, each with his own collection of anecdotes, all of which we discuss. At the end of the meal the *patronne* puts her word in: 'If I'd been attacked in the way those shop-owners were, I'd have fought back hard, I'm telling you.' Edgar Morin points out the aggressive quality in my questions: 'Let them do the talking, don't say much yourself.'

In an enquiry of this sort, here is where the difficulty lies. You don't arrive with a ready-made questionnaire: you have to pick up delicate, fleeting reactions, and must avoid scaring people off.

Afternoon. A walk round town. The 'sociological dragnet'. Rather at a loss where to go. We ought to explore some other area than the cafés, which Julia and Claude are

covering. Return visit to Mme B.—this morning I asked
the young dark-haired salesgirl to try and rustle up some
young people (not students or high-school kids) for us to
meet. Another blank. Everyone she'd seen was working
late.

Where could we meet young people on our own, then?
'Try the bowling-alley,' she said. 'Either that or the public
swimming-pool.' 'But if you want to make people talk,'
the other one chipped in, 'make a better job of introducing
yourself than you did this morning. Say what you're up
to, straight out. This morning we thought you were a
journalist. Journalists aren't popular around here.'

We don't have any real intention of 'introducing ourselves'. The bowling-alley, though not empty, is by no
means crowded. Also, it hardly seems the kind of place
where one can have a harmless chat with anyone that one
happens to meet. The tables are set well apart from each
other, and sparsely occupied. The actual alleys are reserved
for players, who prefer to concentrate on their score.
There are one or two bar-football tables which seem more
promising, with a very young lot hanging round them,
high-school kids by the look of them. Bernard Paillard
starts playing the pin-tables. A young boy catches our
eye, and we invite him over to play with us. He did, and
still does, believe in the abduction business. 'It's quite
true,' he told us. 'Some women have vanished, and some
shop-owners have been arrested.' He works here, in the
bowling-alley. The customers talked about it, too. What
sort of people were they? Oh, young folk, of course.
Broadly speaking, the sort of young folk who can afford
to treat themselves to an evening's bowling (a fairly
expensive occupation). There's a restaurant and a snack-
bar, and the prices there are pretty steep too. Shortly
afterwards we make up a party to play bar-football, and
this gives us a chance to latch onto one of the young girls.
Her friends come and watch us playing. We bring up the
affair in the course of conversation, and they all burst out

laughing. 'Absolute nonsense' is the general verdict. One of them tells us: 'I buy dresses from these shops—no one really believed all that stuff.'

So two different groups of young people rub shoulders in the bowling-alley: one that believed, or still believes, in the truth of the rumour, and another that rejects it *in toto*. Obviously this is only a superficial attempt to get at the facts; but we can't go much further in this context.

Walk back to the centre of town. We try stopping people in the street, and asking them, as though we were ordinary visitors, which are the smartest, most fashionable boutiques, with reasonable prices. No hesitation: we're directed to *Sheila* or *Alexandrine*.

Meeting with a young group, all girls. In fact we learn nothing new from them. Not one dissentient voice. The rumour was going around the high-schools. Mme Licht's sister wasn't tipped off by her friends, people just looked at her and said 'poor woman'. Even her most intimate acquaintances kept the news from her—and, it would seem, believed it themselves.

These girls provide us with a good description of life in Orléans: the cultural desert, the various closed circles. They themselves live their own separate life, gain little acceptance from other groups, are wary of admitting alien elements. The theatre? They hardly ever go, it's rather a bore. The *Maison de la Culture*? That's mostly for students. The big event in Orléans life is the Joan of Arc procession, the choice of a girl to impersonate the Virgin Maid. This choice necessitates a stern board of very religious-minded official censors. They make little jokes, with some relish, about the increasing difficulty of finding a genuine virgin in 'aristocratic', respectable, devout Catholic circles. From here, in response to a misunderstood question by Bernard Paillard, they go on to talk about the '*fidélité*' of Orléanais husbands, which appears to be somewhat dubious. We glimpse a Courteline-like world of cuckoldings, in which certain males are credited with great erotic prowess. They even crack jokes about X., the young homosexual who buys his clothes at *Sheila*.

The moment we get on to sexual problems, responses and anecdotes begin to flow more freely. The conversation, very conventional and stilted to begin with, brightens up. Here is a theme which arouses their interest.

This is the note on which our enquiry ended—a motif which underlay the affair originally, got mixed up with an unadmitted (but openly expressed) case of anti-Semitism, and recurred during our numerous discussions with various sectors of Orléans' population. Apart from the Jewish group we met, who stressed the anti-Semitic factor, the rest tended to minimise this aspect of the affair. On the other hand they often went out of their way to emphasise the sexual theme, and to separate this from the motif of anti-Semitism; sometimes, indeed, they refused to admit any connection between them at all, regarding their juxta-position as a purely fortuitous, though admittedly em-barrassing, coincidence.

What did we really record during our brief descent among the inhabitants of Orléans? Immediate reactions, like those which succeeded in forming and developing the rumour—or reactions precipitated by the rumour itself, and the countless rationalisations (Press, public state-ments, etc.) which fastened on it? Spontaneous reactions, or conditioned reactions? Both are too deeply and in-extricably entangled in the rumour for any useful or logical purpose to be served by attempting to separate them.

SUZANNE
DE LUSIGNAN

MONDAY, 7 JULY

Drove down to Orléans with Edgar Morin and his team. While reading over these preliminary notes I made a mental note that I was probably the only Catholic in the group. This vaguely worried me insofar as one of our main tasks would be to investigate anti-Semitic reactions.[1]

Began with a visit to Aunt J., now about seventy-five. She leads a fairly isolated and withdrawn life, but still takes an interest in the affairs of the town where she has always lived, and passes her time with gossip.

Her main reaction to the affair was one of sarcasm tinged with irritation. 'The whole thing's over and done with. Flimsy nonsense, blown up out of nothing by the press.' Indignant at the idea of *outsiders* taking an interest in the eccentricities and aberrations of *her* town. Alive to the 'stupid and hateful' aspects of the affair. Said she'd never believed in it, and that only ignorant fools did. Emphasised the disastrous part played in the whole thing by the Press, which by giving prominence and specific shape to an unimportant, footling incident, had simply

---

[1] *Editorial note*: In actual fact Bernard Paillard and Evelyne Burguière are both, like Suzanne de Lusignan, Catholic by birth. Julia Vérone is half-Jewish on her father's side, while Claude Capulier is half-Jewish on his mother's side. While he was in Orléans Edgar Morin did not reveal the fact that he was a Jew.

succeeded in magnifying it out of all proportion. Had got
wind of this 'tall story' some forty-eight hours before
'the Press got mixed up in it'. Furious at the thought of
anyone believing it possible that her fellow citizens in
Orléans were anti-Semitic. To prove the opposite, cited
as an example the way in which her friends the R.'s had
been assimilated by Orléans society. Certain Jewish shop-
owners from the Rue de Bourgogne who had fled during
the war were now back in Orléans again. Slipped from here
to a caveat (which contradicted what she had just said):
there *was* one kind of xenophobia which had definitely been
in the air, but this was directed against 'big German
firms'—i.e. foreigners—who ran mail-order businesses
(probably a reference to the firm *Quelle*).

This tall story was never repeated by *reasonable* people.
M., the housekeeper, believed it, though. She'd learnt it
from her 'bird-brained daughter-in-law', who spent the
whole day 'spreading gossip'.

We discussed the subterranean passages. According to
her they were an established fact. There were—or had
been, before the bombing raids of 1940[1]—a number of
tunnels which ran under the town and led to the Loire.
Orléans, as an old town, was built over underground
vaults. When she was a little girl she lived in the centre of
town. Her grandfather was always after her to go down
there. She talked of 'slippery steps', and wells, and the
risks there were in such an expedition (Mme Licht, who
likewise spent her childhood in Orléans, subsequently used
almost identical phrases). On the other hand my father,
Aunt J.'s brother, never mentioned underground passages
beneath the house when describing his childhood to me.

How did this 'report' get started? In her view, people
were quite wrong to ascribe it to commercial rivals, the
old-established houses on the Rue Royale (names? no,
of course, she couldn't recall them). But she was well

---

[1] In 1940 all central Orléans was flattened by bombs. The whole of the
Rue Royale and half the Place du Martroi have been rebuilt *in toto*.

acquainted with such people. They were 'good types', people of substance. She would be really amazed if they were capable of such a 'filthy trick' (*sic*).

Became furious and forbade me to pursue the matter any further when I told her of my intention to question V., my old class-mate ('39–'40). To do this would be to insult her (*sic*), to remind her that she was Jewish—a thing the family very much wanted to make her forget.

M., my Aunt J.'s housekeeper for the last twenty-five years, is a woman in her sixties. Repeats the basic story, that of the man who keeps waiting in vain for his wife to come out of *Dorphée*, finally goes in himself, in a temper, and after having ransacked the place from top to bottom finds his wife tied up and drugged, along with two other women. Whereupon he at once has Dorphée arrested...

Heard the story about a week before it came out in the papers. Got it 'from her son, no, her daughter-in-law' (not clear). Her daughter-in-law got it from a girl she knew who worked in the Sandoz Laboratories. She had been given specific details—the victim's name, and that of her husband. But the story had been denied. It must be false. All the same, people did say the police had been bribed...

On the other hand what was definitely *true* and had never been denied either by the police or the papers was that two young girls of Saint-Jean-le-Blanc, two 'students' they were, had disappeared.

That was a fact, people knew them, they were being looked for everywhere. On the other hand 'malicious folk' took advantage of them disappearing to make trouble for the Jewish shop-owners in the Rue Bourgogne. Why? Because the Jews in the Rue Bourgogne sold the same goods as the other shopkeepers, only cheaper. 'No one can work out how they manage on such a thin edge of profit.' Obviously it was better for a prospective shopper to buy goods from them. She herself 'hadn't the time to go there, but Mme G., who's mean as old boots, buys everything from that lot'.

The Jews on the Rue Bourgogne were settled in the
oldest part of Orléans in ancient houses that all had
cellars and underground passages: that was a well known
fact—'and if you don't believe me, just ask your aunt'.

How did she explain the affair? Undoubtedly there was
an element of truth in it. 'A really dirty business'—the
girls were drugged, and then—(expressive gesture).
Afterwards, 'to make people forget', a story was put about
that the Jews had been responsible. Because in Orléans
Jews weren't popular. It was even alleged that X (voice
lowered, confidential tone) 'was in the racket'. Now Madame
was different. Madame had never been prepared to believe
all this. She had ridiculed it. She had flown into a temper.
But you know what she's like, never credits a word anyone
tells her.

'Who mostly spread this story?' I asked. 'The younger
generation?'

'Not a bit of it! The whole town. Everyone. The old girls
in the suburbs. Everyone—and everyone believed it.'

In any case she herself must know very well that the
story was not true, certainly not that part of it which
concerned the Jewish shop-owners, since she asked M.E.,
her downstairs neighbour, a retired police superintendent,
and he got the information from his former colleagues.

Next day I returned to the attack. She told me that in
Orléans no one had anything against the Jews, at least,
not the old ones who'd been there donkey's years, but that
they were suspicious of the newcomers. To begin with they
were all ex-colonials, and in Orléans colonials had never
been very popular.

Checked this later, and was informed that only one of
the six or eight shop-owners under attack came from
North Africa.

Visit to A.'s shop, with Evelyne.

The proprietress is a blonde, trim, amiable, efficient

woman, very recently settled in. Semi-victimised (mixed up with anti-Semitic phenomena simply because the previous owner was Jewish). Nevertheless detached, since her non-Jewish status was subsequently established by the local press. Obviously satisfied and relieved to have her case dropped. No trace of that solidarity with her fellow victims that I would have expected.

Tells us the demonstrations that went on outside her doorway—the crowds of curious by-standers who lounged about there, watching them 'like inquisitive animals', the warnings given to prospective customers who knew nothing about the affair, and were trying to enter the shop, the drop in turnover, which during that black week sank almost to zero. Then, after the Press took an interest in the episode, the slow improvement in trade—though still with cases of overt hostility. One man came in, looked at himself in the mirror and 'adjusted his tie', then tore open the curtains of the three or four fitting-rooms, violently, to make sure there was no one inside, and said: 'You sell shoes and bags here?' (In fact A. specialised in dresses and coats.) 'Good, then I'll send my wife and daughters along; *make sure you get them home again!*'

Also tells a story about the manageress she was training. This girl had worked daily with her for several weeks, and had had ample leisure to observe her activities. One day, during the week of the persecutions, this trainee-manageress's husband, a former parachutist (?), came bursting in and said: 'I've come for my wife. Get your coat on, you're leaving this minute.' All the explanation he gave was: 'After what I've heard about you, *her reputation as a respectable woman is at stake.*'

People are still distrustful. Quite recently a lady came in wanting to make a phone-call (though there are several cafés in the neighbourhood). When told she could use the phone in the back room, she recoiled, terrified. The staff felt she was torn between fear, and a desire to stay longer and take a good look at everything.

The young assistant—we talked to her while the proprietress was otherwise occupied—had heard about the
'story' something like a week earlier, 'from some girls I
know', while they were all going off for their lunch-break.
People said that 'the same sort of thing was going on at
the *Boutique de Sheila*, too. They believed it because those
who told the story said it had happened to someone they
knew. At home, my parents had got to hear about it, and
were very upset.' Even her grandmother, who lived
right out in the country (Beauce), mentioned the rumour
when they went to see her that Sunday.

Oh yes, they issued denials and all that, but still. . .
Not that it could possibly have been true about *Sheila's*—
that was just tittle-tattle, 'the same as for our place'.
Still, who knows? People *say* it didn't happen, but after
all, I mean, what do we really know about these shop-
owners? Take a businessman like D.D., he 'doesn't exactly
look Catholic, now, does he?'

D., aged forty-two, runs his own business. Catholic,
educated in a religious institution. Few contacts with the
old Orléanais families. Was abroad when all this happened.
Read about it in the papers. On his return, out of curiosity,
went and questioned M. Lévy, leader of the Jewish
Community in Orléans. The latter seems to have played
down the anti-Semitic side of the affair, and to have given
the impression that it was a question of unfounded stories
without any real significance. According to M. Lévy, those
shop-owners who had initially suffered as a result of the
'affair' ended by benefiting from it, through sheer morbid
curiosity on the part of their customers. Losses were
balanced out by increased sales.

D.'s explanation for the 'incident': business rivalries.
Difficulties in the world of trade and affairs. Taxes,
company laws, the general atmosphere of 'bolshiness' and
resentment that had prevailed since May 1968. By
comparison with this picture, the newly established

Jewish dress boutiques, which dealt in swinging fashions
for young people, seemed in a flourishing state of health.
'On the surface, anyway. No one really pried into their
affairs.'

Dorphée's meteoric success story, some few years back,
astounded the entire town. Licht was by way of being a
pioneer. Since then other ready-made outfitters of Jewish
extraction have followed in his footsteps. A few 'town
shops' have tried to cash in on the trend, but they lag far
behind this little group of modern boutiques. People are
furious because they 'started from nothing'.

His sister, a thirty-year-old spinster. Heard about the
'affair' from friends, roughly ten days before the papers
got on to it. The friends had it from their daily help. She
treated this 'scandalous rubbish' with contempt. 'Absolutely typical of people in this town. Nothing better to
do. So stupid and narrow-minded you can't imagine.
Narrow minds, narrow lives.'

Had lunch alone with her the following day. She talked
about Licht. 'He hasn't the personality to organise something like that. Far too nervous.' She also described him
as a very touchy person. He had ordered goods through
them, wholesale, and was hurt when they asked him to
put down a deposit, like any other customer. All the same,
he paid the money over, in spot cash, and showed himself
extremely scrupulous in all his dealings with them. He'd
arrived in Orléans ten years before 'without a penny to
his name'. 'Not that I've got anything against people
making a fortune overnight,' she hastened to add. She
didn't believe the old adage about it taking three generations before any business could afford to be honest.

G., a druggist. My uncle J.'s best friend since their high-
school days (over fifty years ago). Can't suspect me *a priori*
of hostility against the clan. Tell him I'd like some information about the incident because it's been picked up
by the American press.

G. explodes. Furious temper. The incident's closed. 'How can an intelligent girl like you waste time on such nonsense? Just trying to stir it all up again. It's done quite enough harm already to some very respectable Jewish shop-owners. The Press got hold of it and wildly exaggerated its importance. Look, if you really want the story, you go round to the offices of the *République du Centre* and ask for that week's papers.'

I must confess that his outburst really staggered me. He had no reason at all to get so cross, and I told him so. After this he quietened down a bit.

At first, he said, there was just 'a lot of old wives' gossip' in the Châtelet (Orléans' meat market), aimed more or less at the town's Jewish business community. There were three successive stages in the affair. First people tried to suppress the entire incident: this, in his view, was the most sensible reaction. Then 'they' began to discuss it in the papers, and the whole thing got distorted and exaggerated. Finally, the 'incident' was exploited for political ends. If people hadn't been so stupid, and the Press hadn't intervened, it would never have got beyond the level of mere idiot gossip, and as such would have very soon dropped into oblivion.

Here we have the old anti-Jewish legend which recurs at periodic intervals. G. is furious and, at heart, *ashamed* the outside world's censure should have been directed against his home town.

In the evening we gather in a restaurant to meet the shop-owners who formed the target for this rumour. At first sight they impress us as a very close-knit little group, tense, scared and full of anxiety. As time goes on, however, and they gain more self-confidence, these group reactions begin to break down, individualism emerges.

Find myself at the same table as the worst-hit family, the Lichts. Realise after an hour or so that the wife was one of my philosophy students in 1955. I remember her

as one of the oldest students in the class (she must have
been twenty; I was only three years older myself), a
cheerful, rather lazy girl. Today she still retains—on the
surface at least—that placid, cheerful, smiling personality
of hers, despite the 'affair'. She radiates sweetness and
patience: talks to me about her 'streak of optimism'. The
air of placidity and nonchalance turns out to be deceptive.
She is the person responsible for the success of the shop.
To sell dresses she has to put customers at their ease,
make them *want* to buy from her. She is far more alert and
observant than she looks, never misses a trick.

Her husband explains to me that he leaves the running
of the shop entirely in her hands, and himself only deals
with the foreign business. His dynamic, forceful personality
puts me in mind of a boxer: that tense expression contrasts
strikingly with his wife's charming and attractive smile.

When he gets onto the tale of their misfortunes his
indignation becomes positively frenetic. He talks about
his success. He set up shop right in the Châtelet quarter,
near the meat market, at the meeting-point of town and
country, just when the dress-habits of those with moderate
incomes (his clientèle came from the semi-rural outer
suburbs) were undergoing a radical transformation. He is
proud of his success. But both he and his wife are very
conscious of how narrowly people watch them, how
jealous and envious they become at the least outward
sign of this material achievement. For example, their
neighbours made unpleasant comments when they traded
in their old car and bought a new one.

General themes emerging from their description of the
affair:

1. Their hurt surprise at finding themselves, as they
thought, universally hated. M. Licht was well placed for a
successful sales campaign; but by the same token he found
himself at the storm-centre of local gossip, and a focal point
for public curiosity. The mere fact of their being mixed up
in this fantastic story, for which a lot of simple, uneducated

people were responsible, did not bother them all that much *per se*. What really made them unhappy was to see the entire town unhesitatingly accept such 'claptrap' as gospel, without one single person offering them any help or sympathy at a time when, as they honestly believed, they were on the very brink of some catastrophe, perhaps even of a pogrom. The least thing, he insisted, would have sufficed to make the crowd smash their shop-window and attack them physically.

There was also the horrible hiatus between the moment when *they* became aware of the danger, a good while after the gossip had begun (they reckon the 'affair', as such, predated the first press mention by about a month), and that at which the town, the Press and various moral authorities woke up to their plight, and decided to lend them aid.

Their only friends throughout this ordeal were their co-religionists. In normal circumstances they mix with few people save their own little group of 'modern' Jewish boutique-owners ('modern', that is, as opposed to those who are older themselves, cater for an older clientèle, and employ more old-fashioned methods). Mme Licht, it is true, had various Catholic girl-friends before her marriage, but nowadays she only sees members of her husband's little group. He has a number of contacts 'in town' through the Chamber of Commerce.

They felt themselves surrounded by an atmosphere of contemptuous indifference; they were also confronted with evidence of more positive hostility, such as the anonymous caller who rang up and told them to 'reserve me twenty pounds of fresh meat'. Such attacks, they thought, were mainly the work of students. There was also the remark made to M. Licht in a nearby bistro, one where he had been drinking coffee for years: 'You lot had better just pack your bags and get out!'

2. Looking back over the 'affair', they detected some conscious, deliberately planned element in it, some sort of

cabal or plot. It was election time, and people wanted to
whip up nationalist hatred. What sort of people? Oh,
right-wing extremist student groups, members of the SAC,
and, more particularly, certain businessmen who were
actively supporting the young nationalist groups—and
also just happened to be in direct competition with the
Lichts themselves.

The daughter of another shop-owner, playing the part
of the awful-child-who-speaks-out-of-turn, at once ex-
claimed: 'Oh, you mean X.' Her mother was embarrassed
by this accusation in a public place, which could very
easily be reported to the person concerned. But the wife
of one of the victimised shop-owners (who had nevertheless been claiming hitherto that no individual person was
responsible for the accusation) nodded approval and said
to me, quasi-confidentially, that the X. in question had
openly boasted of having had an eighty per cent boost in
turnover during the week when Jewish firms were,
notoriously, being boycotted.

It occurred to me that there might be a counter-legend
as well as a legend.

At this point I made what turned out to be a most unfortunate remark. I drew a parallel with the waves of
nationalism that had scared me when, as a small girl, I
came back to France in 1939—demonstrations against
Jean Zay, young people keeping up an interminable
rhythmic chant of 'France for the French' (which struck
me as farcical, since I had been living in the United States
and felt myself half-American). This was a most frightful
gaffe. They told me, very cuttingly, that French was the
only language they spoke. He, the husband, had done
thirty months of military service, while she was born in
Orléans and had lived there ever since childhood.

Two women near me got onto the subject of fitting-
rooms. Going on about the immodesty and lack of embarrassment they tended to induce in the feminine clientèle. Exhibitionistic self-satisfaction. Some girls who wore

transparent undies to try on dresses, others who brought
their boy-friends in to watch, others again who loved
slipping into gorgeous new clothes just for the hell of it,
and never actually bought a thing. These habits diagnosed
as forms of disguise or escapism.

During our conversation Mme Licht described her
parents' house on the Rue Bourgogne, and the cellars
underneath it: slimy steps, the danger of slipping, pitch
darkness, unguarded wells and so on. She used almost
exactly the same phrases as my aunt J. It does rather look
as though, in the mind of every Orléanais, these commonplace cellars have been transmuted into an unconscious
symbol, an image of the mouths of Hell.

TUESDAY, 8 JULY

Visit a hairdressing salon in the Rue Bourgogne. The
proprietress. Claim I don't know Orléans. Unfortunately
she saw me greet Mme Licht in the street yesterday.

Was not born in Orléans. Parisian girl who'd had a
hard life. Very indignant about the rumour: 'For heaven's
sake, of *course* nothing happened.' It was all a packet of
old wives' tittle-tattle from the meat market: 'And that's
why they referred to *Dorphée* more often than not.' In
Orléans women had nothing to do with their time except
gossip. Chorus of young Orléanais shampoo-and-set girls
(it was quite impossible to make them speak in turn):

Oo, how lucky you are being able to live abroad! Oo,
if only I could get out of this dump! Orléans is a rotten,
ugly, mean-minded place. Got to find something somewhere else, doesn't matter what, anything to get out.
Orléans is *bourgeois*! The rumour was spread by a lot of
bourgeois frumps who were jealous because this bunch
made a success of their lives! (Divergence here from the
proprietress, who saw the peasant women in the market
as the source of all the gossip.) Orléans is the worst town
on the Loire. Tours is fun, Blois has possibilities, Nevers
isn't too bad. But Orléans is rock-bottom.

(An old familiar refrain: I've spent much of my life listening to the same litany from various Orléans refugees.)

Whoever got the rumour going isn't going to admit it, that's for sure. The Gaullistes are anti-Jewish, it's a well known fact. The proof of it is the way rumours like that have got started all over, in Tours and Le Mans——

The proprietress: 'Local residents have been very good. They signed petitions right away.' (Mme Licht had told me precisely the opposite.) What proved the rumour to be nonsense was that 'the husband was never in the shop, always rushing about on business'.

Call in at a lingerie shop on the Rue Royale. No suspicion here, since I really was looking for a black slip, and tried several on. In the fitting-room I tapped my foot on the ground, laughing, and asked the woman serving me where the trap-door was. She laughed too. She was a relaxed, cheerful woman in her fifties. 'Oh, you wouldn't find a trap-door in *my* place,' she said. 'I mean, I'm French, and a Catholic, and that rumour was directed against the Jews. I never believed it myself, but there's plenty in Orléans who did.' I told her I was a Catholic myself. She said she was a practising Catholic. She deplored the fact that so many Catholics in Orléans, at least those of an advanced age, were so violently anti-Jewish.

Together we went over the clan's shameful secrets. According to her, the reports were first put into circulation at La Source (the university) by 'certain student groups', and were picked up in town by 'elderly middle-class people'. She added: 'Maybe it came in handy to fix one or two competitors. It certainly fitted nicely with the elections. People *could* have spread it deliberately.'

At the townhall I questioned an old gentleman of about seventy who had known my grandfather well. Offering certain (non-existent) American students as my excuse, I asked him to put me generally in the picture about the political scene in Orléans. I said I was absolutely shattered by all the changes that had taken place in the town since my grandparents' day. He gave me a long disquisition on the subject, while I took notes, which appeared to flatter him. Before the war Orléans had been radical. Now it had become a stronghold of Gaullism (with a by no means negligible Communist minority) under the influence of the present Mayor, Roger Secrétain, himself a Gaullist.

The new population, people with modest or average incomes, was split in about equal proportions between the Gaullists and the Communists.

At La Source there was a leftist majority (and some pro-Krivine groups) which was regarded with the highest distrust and suspicion by Orléanais traditionalists. The young elements amongst the latter formed themselves into what might be termed Gaullist shock-troops; they were a highly convinced and enterprising group.

The businessmen of Orléans are traditionally conservative and right-wing, to a fault. In their eyes, no doubt, these new Jewish shop-owners are all fellow-travellers or Socialists, even though they may not publicise the fact.

Attempts have been made—unsuccessfully—to turn Orléans into an industrial satellite of Paris. Only light and medium industries have been attracted by the possibilities which this particular agglomeration has to offer. On the other hand commerce has been radically transformed. It has become centralised to a quite staggering degree, to the detriment of the small businessman. Shops such as *SUMA* have succeeded beyond the wildest expectations, and indeed far better than in many other provincial towns (howls of protest from small shopkeepers). The Leclerc chain got off to a flying start. The Orléanais at once saw where his own best interests lay, and had no hesitation about forsaking his old local tradesmen—so much so that even Jewish establishments which operated on a limited scale, such as the *Nouvelles Galeries*, found themselves at a disadvantage. The only areas in which small shopkeepers still survive are those peripheral districts, half town, half village, on the outskirts of Orléans: but even they feel themselves threatened, and are very bitter in consequence.

How are we to explain this rapid transformation in the commercial pattern? One reason, undoubtedly, is the younger generation. The young person of today spends everything he has on his clothes and car, at the expense of food and lodging. To take one example: though the population doubled, the number of bars fell almost by half. These youngsters don't believe in economising. They buy clothes on credit from the ready-made boutiques, absolutely casually, without a second's thought. Then they resent the people to whom they owe money. It's the Jewish shop-owners who started the scheme for selling clothes on credit, though in the old days they wouldn't trust a soul.

The same applies to cars. They buy some old crock at a bargain price so they can get out on the road over the weekend, nose to tail for hours on end. The cafés aren't doing the business they used to do, so *they're* complaining, too. Young people buy very little in food-stores. They bring home more money than their parents ever did, but they don't give a damn about keeping up their houses.

Now for the students. At La Source they're so divided that no pattern emerges. The Left is very active, but there are right-wing groups to provide a 'counter-balance'. Bourgeois society is coming more and more to be a minority in Orléans. The bourgeois middle-class districts aren't expanding.

Free education continues to flourish in Orléans, more than at Tours. While members of the liberal professions in Tours will send their children to the *lycée*, in Orléans it is still socially acceptable to let children—girls, at any rate—attend Saint Charles or Saint Aignan. What is more, these Orléans free schools do not even bother to modernise themselves, since they get their quota of pupils automatically.

The rumour? This tale of abduction was disseminated, and used for personal ends, by people in whose interest it

lay to slander the shop-owners involved, and thus to
drive away their custom.

M. P., a sexagenarian neighbour of my grandmother's:
a wise and mischievous old man who cultivates his own
garden and grows the most delicious raspberries.
Here is his analysis of the affair, as he gave it to me:
1. It is curious that the story should have been so
widespread, so universally disseminated, with its general
pattern taking shape almost overnight. One day no one
knew about it; then, in little over forty-eight hours (and
nearly a fortnight before the Press came into action) it had
become an all pervading topic of conversation, everywhere. This he found intriguing.
2. Plenty of people (though not all) believed in this story
about drugged girls because their informants furnished a
plethora of details about the young ladies who had
supposedly vanished.
3. In his opinion, we should look for the origins of the
rumour in La Source, where a small number of virulent
right-wing extremist groups exist, with a commando-type
organisation. These groups are very active, and have been
responsible for other seemingly irrational misdeeds, which
always reveal the same violent pattern, with a weakness
for sudden fits of brutality.

The taxi-driver who took me to my aunt's house on the
Place du Martroi. Told me he had been astonished to hear
the story on people's lips everywhere. He rang up one of
his friends in the police who told him 'it was an act of
vengeance', in his opinion probably 'an Arab job'.

Talking to high-school girls (*lycéennes*) in the café.
Realise that there have been several different versions of
the story, and that we should have asked people which
one they heard, and when. The earlier versions were far
less improbable than subsequent ones.

Thus we had a Catholic friend of Mme Licht's admitting that she had believed in the *first version* of the story, and had not begun to treat it with scepticism until she heard further supplementary details which placed emphasis on the *Jewishness* of the central figure.

JULIA VÉRONE

This is not, properly speaking, a journal which follows the temporal sequence of events, but a retrospective sampling of them in three sections, a psychological counterpart to the three-day physical sampling we undertook. Firstly, my impressions of Orléans; then, the young girls there (hysterical creatures, *mes semblables, mes soeurs*); and lastly, the rumour itself.

ORLEANS

My first surprise, on the morning of day 'one' in Orléans, was to confirm for myself the reality of what, in Paris, had struck me as an inconceivable aberration: that is, the rumour. Those young people with whom we first discussed it spoke of the matter in a serious and very far from detached manner, which we found somewhat disturbing. As regards the facts behind the affair, 'what really happened', no doubts were expressed; they 'believed it'— though without believing in it (I shall return to this point later). As far as people's views on the affair go, 'what was said', although they began by expressing contempt for 'such tittle-tattle' ('people exaggerate, something begins like this ——, and ends like *this* ————————'), nevertheless their way of discussing these events (can one speak of *an* event?) shows that they are very much 'inside' the rumour, and that their participation does not differ in essentials from that of the '*concierge* group'. Thus the 'white-slaving-cum-anti-Semitic' myth, which seems

222

so shocking and inconceivable outside Orléans, takes on a day-to-day, commonplace reality in the atmosphere of Orléans itself. As far as this affair is concerned, 'inconceivable' excludes 'Orléanais'.

When I interviewed people on street corners in Orléans, I found myself obliged, at first, if I was to keep a genuine discussion going, to talk about any and every topic as it came up. I forgot my role of 'interviewer'. I let myself be carried along. Thus, little by little, a second field of interest imposed itself on me: the minutiae of Orléanais life, what young people discuss in the cafés there, how they pass the time (time *does* pass in Orléans).

The first thing all young people will tell you, straight off, is that they're bored. This applies to the middle-class group in the *Taverne* (café on the right opposite the station) no less than to the 'proletarian' lot who frequent the *Berry* (on the left opposite the station). They are bored during the daytime, and especially bored at night (Orléans has no *boîtes*, indeed no night life of any sort: by eight o'clock the streets are deserted). When they're not working they go to the café.

I asked them if they had discussions there.

'Not really,' said a girl student in the *Taverne*.

'Not often,' said one youth in the *Berry*.

Yet young people's groups, both sporting and cultural, flourish in Orléans: there are at least five of them in existence. Even so, it would seem that the programmes they offer are insufficient to combat boredom. In the *Taverne* we were told about high-school drug-taking, with stories of fourteen-year-olds who were already on the hard stuff. In the *Berry*, it appeared that their chief amusement was taking the car out for a Sunday excursion in the country. In fact, one gathered that when there was nothing else to do their main activity was drinking. They all want to get out; only one young girl, the daughter of working-class parents, said 'Maybe it's no better anywhere else'.

They also maintain that in Orléans everyone knows not
only his neighbour, but also his neighbour's business.
There would appear to be a fast, streamlined, efficient
system of disseminating gossip or scandal by word of
mouth. Housewives and daily helps spread the word
among private families and in shops. Adolescent girls get
it circulating through the *lycées* and pass it on to young
people's groups. This system is such that a stream of
minor rumours is constantly on the move in all directions,
surviving or perishing according to just how incredible, or
old-hat, people find them. This facilitates the rapid dissemination of a single rumour with more sheer 'pull' than
the rest.

They say, too, that the atmosphere is unpleasantly in-
tolerant. 'Everyone here has a racialist attitude to everyone else,' said one young girl in the *Berry*. 'Negroes,
Portuguese, the lot.' She didn't mention Jews.

The young people of Orléans may be mildly disgusted by
the atmosphere in their town, but nevertheless they con-
tribute to it and participate in it themselves. Whether they
are for or against the gossip game as such, they all play it
(as became clear from their conversation). The girl student
we talked to in the *Taverne*—a pretty, elegant, self-assured
creature—said at one point (confidently, with a fractional
lift of the left eyebrow): '*I* know what happened—got the
facts from a really reliable source. Yes, of course there was
something in it, no smoke without fire—if the police
dismiss the whole thing, that's just because it suits their
book not to admit the truth.' It is in circumstances such
as these that gossip gets beyond the tittle-tattle stage and
becomes a full-blown rumour (might, indeed, in this case
have developed into something still worse), while collective
certainty expands to acquire a new dimension.

Another universal topic in Orléans is Joan of Arc. She
crops up in everyone's conversation sooner or later; everywhere one senses the presence of the Maid of Orléans—in
her hour of triumph, not at the stake. She is the historical

alibi for a town whose substance is little by little being eaten away by Paris.

My two spheres of interest—the rumour itself, the atmosphere in Orléans—both bring me back to the same problem: at what level of reality does a rumour operate when it is confirmed neither by official sources, nor by objective evidence (e.g. a police enquiry)?

At another level I find myself wondering how conversations that remain, inevitably, dialogues between individuals—even if one person is an 'investigator' and the other the 'subject' being investigated—can define or help to analyse a problem that concerns the 'collective conscience'? The longer I talked, the more I felt myself caught up and involved in the subject of my enquiry: it also struck me, with increasing force, that the realities of this phenomenon lay beyond the reach of all discussion. By what methodo-sociological lifeline can one struggle ashore from the murky waters of Orléans? The polls conducted by the IFOP (*Institut Français de l'Opinion Publique*)? Or the investigator's own subjective approach?

THE YOUNG GIRLS

I propose to deal with three examples only: a student, a high-school girl, and a hairdresser's assistant.

The student and the schoolgirl were convinced that 'something had happened', and—despite denials issued by the Press over a month or more—continued to assert that 'there's no smoke without fire' (in confident tones, and with an expression that hinted at unrevealed knowledge). The hairdresser's assistant, on the other hand, never believed the story for one moment. The high-school girl told how in her *lycée* no one talked about anything else: classes were even interrupted to discuss the affair, teachers issued stern warnings, she herself had been absolutely fascinated by it all. The hairdresser's assistant made it clear that the incident had not caught her interest very much at the time, and that in any case she found it

H

grotesque, alien and revolting. In her case failure to formulate an opinion on the matter reflects plain lack of interest
in it, and led her to make blanket judgments of the 'it's-
all-stupid-nonsense' variety. The schoolgirl, on the other
hand, was in a great state of excitement, and brimming
over with facts, opinions and innuendo. Her confident
knowingness did not apply so much to the anti-Semitic side
of the affair, but rather to its preoccupation with drugs
and white slavery. She said at one point: 'It's pure coincidence that all those shop-owners happened to be Jews.'
By way of contrast, an old lady in the Botanical Gardens
said that she'd 'never gone near that lot', even before the
affair blew up. As I listened to this schoolgirl talk, my
intuition told me (a far from sociological process, this) just
what sort of hysterical game must have been going on in
the corridors and toilets (where pupils smoke cigarettes
on the sly) of Orléans' high-schools for girls. Why, I
wonder, was she so sure of herself?

THE RUMOUR
I get the feeling that this rumour never had a beginning.
Nobody was at the back of it. Just as there can be no final
corroboration (when analysing its content) of the various
facts and names put forward, so there is no one person
responsible for its original dissemination. The trail leads
back to infinity: you keep on finding somebody else who
mentioned the subject a little earlier. There were no real
disappearances, and there are no hard facts (all those
confident assertions rested, in the last resort, on vague
faceless anonymities). The more indefinite the pronoun,
the stronger the certainty it inspires. One begins to
visualise this rumour echoing on to all eternity: 'No one
will ever know what *really* happened.' It exists in a kind of
timeless utopia; though bound, in the long run, to lose its
hold and its popularity, it can never be explained away,
stripped bare, exposed for what it was, reduced to a
nothingness in people's minds.

Perhaps the rumour's remarkable powers of self-perpetuation derive from the fact that what people trusted was not so much the information *per se*, but rather *the person* who passed it on, because he was known (a good friend or acquaintance on whose 'word of honour' one automatically relied). Another feature of the myth was its ability to assimilate every kind of inconsistency, whether internal or external (e.g. the submarine in the Loire). It throve cheerfully on rebuttals. By analogy one might attribute to it those characteristics which Plato bestows upon chaos: no boundaries, no shape, no meaning or purpose, and, in the last resort, no real existence. However, it may respond to certain internal mechanisms—mechanisms which though definable in the Cartesian sense (i.e. a locus from which thought is absent), can induce variations in it, and make it adapt itself to a changing situation.

APPENDIX: SOME ORLEANAIS ANECDOTES
The Orléans Botanical Gardens are full of roses at this time of year, and thronged with mothers and children and respectable old ladies. We went and sat down beside those who looked as if they might be reasonably cooperative.

Question: We're conducting a sociological enquiry (no details given). Would you be willing to answer a few questions?

Answer: (Silence.) She fiddles with her knitting.

She told us she had worked in the same hospital for the past twenty-five years. We mentioned the rumour. She said: 'I only heard about it eight days ago, from my son.'

'Wasn't it discussed in your hospital?'

'No.'

A pause.

'A month ago I saw some notices in the Rue des Carmes, didn't really pay any attention to them, they were about

H*

all that, though I don't remember the details. Anyway I
never went near those shops, even before.'

'Why not?'

'Oh, not on principle, and anyway my son's got a friend
who's a Jew.'

'Why not, then?'

Silence.

'What do you think about this business?'

'We'll never know what really happened, and anyway
there's no fire without smoke [*sic*]. It was the same in '51,
all that stuff about the Deputy being murdered.'

'Did you discuss it with the shop-owners?'

'No.'

'Who *did* you talk to?'

'My son.'

'What does *he* think about it?'

'Oh, he treats it as a joke, but then he's only a kid still.'

The lady's behaviour was as disjunctive as her conversation: she left us abruptly at this point.

Just as we were about to question another lady, the
park attendant came hurrying over to us, quite clearly in
a bad temper. 'I don't want any of that in the Gardens,' he
told us. 'Go and question people outside if you've got to,
I'm not having that sort of talk in here.' Did he think we
were police, or crooks, or what? In any case the motives
for his anger were obviously as obscure to him as they were
to us.

The hairdresser in the Rue de Bourgogne.

Surrounded by the odours of wet hair and shampoo, I
unthinkingly let myself drift into a perfectly genuine
discussion on the disadvantages of curly hair. The problem
of the rumour fitted quite naturally into our *salon de
coiffure* conversation.

'The whole thing was ridiculous. To start with, if anything had happened they'd have shut the boutiques.' This
was her sole comment on the matter. I felt that, for her,
the closing of the boutiques would have been the only

acceptable argument (though in fact it is no argument at all). She took up a position right outside the rumour, and accepted no part of it whatsoever. In any case her mind was more occupied with her holidays. She was one of the very few people who said not a word to me about how boring Orléans was. By the time we parted we were the best of friends.

Sylvie, a secretary, in the *Taverne*: 'Well, when you get bored you start making up romantic stories.'

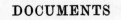

DOCUMENTS

DOCUMENTS

AN ODIOUS CABAL

For over a week now, certain rumours have been circulating throughout the town, and accusations have been levelled at a number of respectable shopkeepers on the Rue de Bourgogne and the Rue de la République.

Up till now this paper had judged it best to say nothing about the matter, since it might well turn out to have started as a mere joke—though one in the very worst of taste. But the dimensions assumed by this slanderous episode have become such that facts must be faced. What we have here is a cabal, a plot, skilfully organised by certain unscrupulous persons. Its object, clearly, is to damage the moral reputation of these shop-owners, and, by way of consequence, to severely prejudice their success in business.

At the same time, if one asks oneself what reasons can have motivated this defamatory campaign, one is undoubtedly tempted to speculate in certain quarters. As, on the face of it, there is no clear sign of any political objective, one senses behind this cabal a vague whiff of anti-Semitism, such as one had hoped to see disappear forever with the death agonies of the Third Reich.

The most disturbing aspect of the affair is the realisation that this is no isolated incident, For some time now, similar defamatory rumours, without any basis in fact,

233

have been circulating in other towns and areas. All reveal the same coordinated pattern.

But whatever their antecedents, our fellow citizens should not allow themselves to be influenced by lying accusations, mere whispering campaigns. Such behaviour is not only reprehensible *per se*, but because of all it embodies—cowardice, hypocrisy, systematic and despicable distortion of the truth.

The victims have been forced to lodge formal complaint, and the police have opened an investigation with a view to tracking down the instigators of this odious intrigue.

All citizens of Orléans should realise two facts clearly: first, that all the rumours now circulating which question the moral probity of these shop-owners are entirely without foundation; and secondly, that any person who plays a part in spreading such slanderous reports is subject to prosecution under the law relating to slander and libel.

JEAN-PIERRE IN *La Nouvelle République*

A CAMPAIGN OF DEFAMATION

For a week now a certain rumour, alleging incidents which make an odd blend of the immoral and the purely fantastic, has been circulating in Orléans. It has also implicated a number of shop-owners, men of good reputation whose names are well known locally.

The exceptionally widespread nature of this whispering campaign can be attributed in part to an all too prevalent habit of thoughtlessly passing on even the least credible pieces of gossip. However, its sheer persistence has something intriguing about it, and we cannot exclude the possibility that what we have here is a piece of calculated malice, which deliberately utilised slander as a weapon with which to damage the shop-owners in question.

Having ascertained that the reports circulating in this manner were utterly without foundation, we have hitherto carefully refrained from making the slightest reference to them. Some individuals have attacked the Press for keeping silent. Such criticisms we have received with cheerful indifference.

However, faced with the insensate and quite intolerable development of what can only be termed an offensive campaign of falsehoods, we feel it incumbent upon us to state that the fabulous tales now being bandied about have not one shred of authentic truth in them. Several victims of this defamatory campaign have retaliated by lodging formal complaints with the authorities. The police are opening an enquiry with a view to unmasking the instigators of these slanderous accusations, and it is, therefore, possible that this regrettable affair will lead to a number of prosecutions.

République du Centre

PUBLIC STATEMENTS (3 AND 4 JUNE)

A STATEMENT FROM THE PARENTS ASSOCIATION OF THE LYCÉE JEAN-ZAY AND THE CES JEANNE-D'ARC.

We have been asked to publish the following statement:

The Parents Association, alarmed by the slanderous and defamatory rumours which have been circulating widely with regard to various shop-owners in the town of Orléans, has approached the competent authorities, and in particular the police, with a view to finding out whether these rumours had any genuine foundation.

The Association is now in a position to state, categorically, that these reports have no foundation whatsoever in fact, and belong to the realm of pure fantasy. It appeals to parents to reassure their children on the matter, and to warn them against passing on information which may well be defamatory in law.

(Signed) REBAUDET, *President*

[Published in the regional press on 3 June 1969.]

MEMBERS OF THE PARENTS CONSULTATIVE COMMITTEE FOR THE LYCÉE POTHIER

M. A. Robinet and Dr A. Laruelle, members of the Parents' Consultative Committee for the *Lycée Pothier*, have asked us to publish the following statement:

We are profoundly shocked by the smear campaign which has taken place in Orléans, and even more so by the fact that willing ears were ready to listen to it. Yet an anti-Semitic campaign should not really surprise us.

1.   The Government's attitude to the Jewish Nation, as revealed by its policies, aroused anti-Semitic feelings which the nationalist organisations were not slow to exploit. Since the example was set at the highest level, we should not wonder at the fact that it has been followed.

2.   The implication of the town's teaching body in this affair has our full attention. It is true that within recent years we have been less than appreciative of those few militant teachers who took an open stand in favour of violence or against conscientious objectors. But we cannot bring ourselves to believe that any instructor would take part in so corrupt and defamatory a campaign.

The affair can no longer be hushed up. There must be an enquiry, and we await its findings with impatience. Until then, we cannot accept this attempt to cast discredit on a most worthy and respectable profession.

If it can be proved that any teachers are in fact guilty of such behaviour, we shall make it our business to inform those who played any part in this hysterical campaign that henceforth, within the profession, their moral standing will be nil, and their word worth nothing.

(Signed) ANDRÉ ROBINET, ANDRÉ LARUELLE

A STATEMENT FROM UDICO[1]

Alarmed by certain slanderous and defamatory allegations concerning the disappearance of women and young girls, said to have taken place in a number of local shops, UDICO wishes to warn the public against such malicious and utterly fantastic rumours, which prejudice the good name, not only of some highly respectable businessmen, but also of the staff employed in their various establishments, thus bringing discredit on the commercial world of Orléans as a whole.

COOPERATIVE ASSOCIATION OF MARKET-TRADERS (LE CHÂTELET)

Over two hundred traders, members of the Cooperative Association of Market-Traders based on Le Châtelet Market, are distressed to learn of the smear campaign directed against several of their colleagues, highly respectable Jewish shop-owners whom they have known for years and in whose probity they have complete confidence. They deplore this campaign in the strongest possible terms.

They are amazed that so malicious a rumour could have been spread so rapidly, in every quarter, when no one was in a position to back it up with one shred of solid evidence.

They wish to express a hope that, for the sake of the town's peace and well being, the competent administrative authorities—that is, the police and the Préfecture—who have themselves been accused of connivance in this affair, will emerge from their self-imposed silence on the matter, and publish a formal rebuttal of the facts alleged in the course of these disgusting machinations.

---

[1] *Union des industriels et commerçants orléanais.*

ASSOCIATION (LOIRET DIVISION) OF FORMER DEPORTEES, INTERNED PERSONS AND THEIR FAMILIES

The slanders must cease.

The Association of Former Deportees, Interned Persons and Families of Vanished Persons protests, in the strongest possible terms, against the slanders which, for over a fortnight now, have been circulating through Orléans, and the object of which is to discredit a number of the town's most respectable shop-owners.

We are informed that similar techniques have been employed in several different parts of the country.

This shameful propaganda campaign reminds us too forcibly of that conducted by the Nazis under Hitler, as a cover for the crimes they were planning against us.

As former Resistance deportees, we can never forget the wholesale massacre of the Jews in the concentration camps.

Those men, those women were the fathers, mothers, brothers or sisters of the people being slandered today, who themselves belong to the great brotherhood of deportation.

In the past we were powerless to stop such horrors. Today it is our bounden duty to denounce such repugnant activities as widely as possible, with all the publicity at our command. We must ask all of you, men and women alike, not to let yourselves become the accomplices of a political minority group, which has no object save revenge, and aims to bring our country to disaster. On the contrary, let these shop-owners, whose names are being bandied about so freely, feel the strength of your disapproval by making it clear to them that they still enjoy your trust and confidence.

(Signed) REBILLON, *President*

A STATEMENT BY THE COMMUNIST PARTY (LOIRET BRANCH)

An anti-Semitic campaign has developed in Orléans. It has caused great distress to the Jewish community and the whole population of the area.

It began with an alleged case of 'white slaving'. From various statements it is clear that these reports are wholly unfounded, and the merest fantasy.

The victims of this smear campaign have lodged formal complaint with the authorities.

Whatever the exact circumstances, anti-Semitism is raising its ugly head once more. This arouses grim memories: Fascism, the Nazi era, the campaign against the Jews, followed by that against the Communists. It recalls the mores of the Third Reich.

The friends of Tixier-Vignancour and Xavier Vallet are doubtless no strangers to this odious cabal.

The French Communist Party (Loiret Branch) offers its support to the Jewish Community of Orléans in its fight against anti-Semitism and racialism. It stands forward as the representative of all democrats and workers who want some light shed on this strange affair.

It has asked André Chène, Councillor, to approach the Prefect, so that this scandal may be brought to an end, and the guilty found and punished.

5 JUNE 1969

ARTICLE AND DOCUMENTS IN *La République du Centre*,

HATEFUL SMEAR CAMPAIGN AIMED AT TOWN'S JEWISH SHOP-OWNERS AROUSES VIGOROUS PROTESTS

The Loiret branch of the League against racialism and anti-Semitism met yesterday and passed a motion of protest.

The disgusting smear campaign directed against several
local Jewish shop-owners (mentioned in these columns
last Monday, with a view to denouncing its unspeakable
and repulsive nature) last night provoked a meeting of
the Loiret branch of the International League against
Anti-Semitism and Racialism. This meeting was held at
6.30 p.m. in the St-Jean-de-la-Ruelle municipal buildings,
with M. Guy R. Brun, the League's Branch Secretary, in
the chair. Several other delegates from the League were
with him.

Amongst those present were: M. Pierre Gabelle, former
Deputy; M. Violette, town councillor of Orléans; M. R.
Thinat, Secretary of the Radical Party Association (Loiret
Division); M. Breton, representing the Association of
Deportees; Mme Renée Cosson, of the Communist Party;
M. Lévy, President of the Jewish Community in Orléans;
several of the Jewish shop-owners attacked by the smear-
campaign; a representative from the *Maison de la Culture
d'Orléans*; a number of teachers; and members of the
League against Anti-Semitism.

Opening the meeting, M. Guy Brun described the ig-
nominious nature of the reports that had been going the
rounds in Orléans for over a week at the expense of local
Jewish businessmen, and told his audience how strongly
he and other members of the League felt about so reprehensible and malicious a demonstration, the origins of
which were still wrapped in mystery.

He then asked M. Henri Amrofel, himself a shop-owner,
to enlighten the audience on the precise nature of these
reports. M. Amrofel gave an account of the unpleasant
stories now circulating by word of mouth.

Their substance is well known. Police officers of the
Narcotics Squad are alleged to have found three women
in the basement of a shop, bound hand and foot and
drugged, ready for dispatch to the Middle East.

According to another rumour, no less than twenty
women (why not more while we're at it?!) are supposed to

have suffered a similar fate, being put to sleep or
anaesthetised while trying on dresses or shoes, by the
sort of methods familiar from James Bond films and the
more sensational illustrated romances.

As we stated last Monday—in order to kill a series of
grotesque slanders which far too many people seemed
willing to accept—the police (who have not received one
single complaint in the slightest degree relevant to this
fictitious affair) are only concerned with the campaign
today on two counts. They are determined to unmask its
hidden organisers, and to dissuade the gullible from giving
even limited credence to its message.

Yet despite such assurances, it remains unfortunately
true that this slanderous campaign can still produce some
extremely annoying effects. Certain excessively credulous
and naive persons persist in their attitude that 'there
can't be smoke without fire'! In such conditions it is easy
to imagine the consternation into which the victims of
this campaign were plunged; it not only caused them
severe business losses, but subjected them to a most cruel
ordeal on the moral and psychological level.

People in town have been heard asserting that 'Jewish
gold has bought the police, the Press and the public authorities', and that this is the reason for their silence
concerning the scandal! Is there *anything* people won't
believe? Obviously, it is impossible not to recall those
dark years during the last war, when—on just such
racialist-inspired charges—millions of human beings
perished in death-camps and prisons. Some of our Jewish
fellow citizens have such memories in their own families.
Confronted with opposition of a sort which they would
never have believed possible in this country, the slandered
shop-owners have now lodged formal complaint at police
headquarters.

M. Amrofel pointed out that an account of just such a
(fictitious) affair was printed in a magazine about mid-May,
and it seems possible that certain malicious persons took

this as the source of their inspiration. We may also note that similar campaigns have been reported from Lille, Le Mans, Rouen, Tours and Poitiers. Not all of them attained the proportions of that which developed here in Orléans. But such a phenomenon forces one to speculate on what started them all. In whose interests would it be to promote anti-Jewish slanders of this nature?

At last night's meeting regrets were expressed that certain members of the teaching profession should have taken it upon themselves to warn their pupils against patronising the shops in question.

The serious consequences of this absurd campaign made the regional branch of the League against Anti-Semitism decide to take vigorous counter-measures. It therefore took the matter up with several official departments, devoted a whole page of its monthly magazine *Le Droit de Vivre* to the affair, and passed a protest motion against it.

Finally, Maître Rosenthal, National President of the League, is today bringing suit, through the Seine Public Prosecutor's Department, against ——— for uttering a defamatory racialist libel.

In addition, the *Maison de la Culture* has decided to devote Sunday afternoon to a round-table discussion on 'Racialism, Slander and Defamation', which will be presided over by M. Louis Guilloux, the well known author and expert on social problems.

THE MOTION ADOPTED

The development of an outrageous and shameless campaign, based on lies and slander, and directed against certain Jewish shop-owners, who are grotesquely accused of being involved in the white slave trade—by individuals who have not even got the courage to make themselves known—has led the Loiret Branch of the LICA (BP917 Orléans RP) to pass the following motion:

Highly disturbed by the unthinking dissemination of

such unverifiable charges, the League pledges itself to warn the inhabitants of Orléans—offering proof where necessary—that the charges made are invention pure and simple; and that such charges cause grave harm to the shop-owners against whom they are levelled, men whose honesty and moral probity have never been challenged, and cannot be challenged.

The League further pledges itself to take energetic counter-measures against all such activities, which bear a singular resemblance to the ignoble anti-Semitic campaigns undertaken by the Third Reich.

The League is resolved to bring suit through the Public Prosecutor's Office against —— for uttering an unmistakably racialist libel.

The League also makes a confident appeal to the police authorities to unmask those responsible for this vicious smear campaign without delay, and put them where they can no longer cause harm to anyone.

Lastly, since the injurious accusations against these shop-owners have threatened public law and order, the League solemnly draws the attention of the responsible authorities to the need for effective intervention on their part.

ASSOCIATION OF NON-SEDENTARY TRADESMEN

The Association of Non-Sedentary Tradesmen has sent us the following statement for publication:

We wish to protest, in the most solemn fashion, against a despicable smear campaign which has been spreading in and around Orléans, and which has as its target the Jewish business community. Such a campaign can satisfy no one save the morbidly minded and the sadistic. There is no solid evidence whatsoever for the facts alleged. All this incident proves is that medieval attitudes still survive in the Space Age. It can cause nothing but harm, both to our over-gullible fellow citizens, and to the region as a whole. It is our sincere hope that the persons responsible for this slander will very soon be brought to book. Suit has already been brought against them.

ARTICLES AND DOCUMENTS IN *La Nouvelle République*
STRONG REACTION AGAINST ODIOUS ANTI-SEMITIC SMEAR CAMPAIGN
Both the LICA and six Jewish merchants who have been slandered are now taking legal action. Public authorities have been officially alerted.

During the past few days a sordid smear campaign has been going on in Orléans, and spreading by leaps and bounds.

If we are to believe this rumour—which has been passed on by word of mouth in various circles, and has even reached the Prefect's office—a vast 'white slaving scandal' is developing in our town. Young women have been intercepted, drugged and sent abroad. The official authorities, the police, the Press have all conspired to hush up the scandal; rumour does not scruple to assert that they exacted a high price for their silence.

It now transpires that all the main protagonists alleged to be behind this fantastic enterprise are—as though by chance—Jewish shop-owners in the city. Some of them are specifically said, and believed, to have connived at the use of their back rooms by these vile traffickers.

Certain members of the teaching profession, in both public and private schools, have thoughtlessly given sufficient credence to these allegations to draw their pupils' attention to the risk they might be running if they patronised such shops.

Worse still, the incriminated shop-owners have been subjected to the most abjectly insulting phone-calls—anonymous, of course. Others have been threatened in public. These were just the circumstances in which certain countries launched the pogroms, of sinister memory.

It goes without saying that the veracity of the allegations denounced in these columns cannot stand up to close scrutiny. The whole thing is like a cheap movie. Yet popular wisdom asserts, with some reason, that there is always *something* in slander; that is why we must clip the wings of this repulsive *canard* once and for all.

ACTION BY THE ANTI-RACIALIST MOVEMENTS

This is the main end to which two groups are devoting all their energies—on the one hand the victims themselves, and on the other those organisations which have as their object the combating of racialist persecution.

Last Wednesday, for example, a delegate from the Movement against Racialism and Anti-Semitism and for Peace, presided over by Pierre Para the writer, was in Orléans. Having sent a letter to M. Marcellin, Minister of the Interior, asking him to intervene, this delegate was now anxious to make contact with those persons in the city who could, in the long run, make the truth prevail.

In addition, the Loiret Branch of the League against Anti-Semitism, founded by the late Bernard Lecache, and presided over today by the former minister Jean-Pierre Bloch, held a meeting in the St-Jean-de-la-Ruelle municipal buildings, under the chairmanship of its Branch Secretary, Guy R. Brun, in order to take essential defensive measures.

Among those present were M. Pierre Gabelle, former Deputy, representing the Democratic Centre; M. Thinat, representing the Radical Party; Mlle Renée Cosson, the Communist Party; M. René Violette, town councillor; M. Georges Lévy, President of the Jewish Community; M. Louis Breton, representing the Deportees, and others.

From the debate held during this meeting it is clear that

I

these tendentious rumours are still growing apace. The
number of supposed victims of the traffic in human flesh
continues—according to the slanderers' statements—to
increase; and for the last thirty-six hours the villains of
the piece have not been just Jewish shop-owners, but
every member of the Jewish faith in Orléans.

Our fellow citizens have a reputation for moderation and
common-sense. Yet in a century which has produced the
laser beam one can only register utter astonishment at
their credulity.

So energetic measures were called for, in particular an
approach to members of the teaching profession (since it
would seem that the campaign first got under way in the
schools) to ensure that the plain truth is brought home to
all concerned.

Six of the shop-owners involved have already lodged
official complaints, while the LICA has decided upon the
following measures. It intends to reserve a whole page of
its weekly news-sheet, *Le Droit de Vivre*, to the 'Orléans
affair' (forthcoming issue). It will also disseminate the
motion it carried (text printed below) as widely as possible;
and, finally, it proposes to bring suit against —— for
uttering a defamatory libel of a racialist nature. This will
be done through the League's legal representative, Maître
Gérard Rosenthal.

The audience approved these measures. They were
endorsed, on behalf of the deportees, by M. Louis Breton,
who in the course of a highly emotional speech invoked
the memory of his Jewish comrades massacred by the
Nazis.

On Sunday at 4 p.m. the *Maison de la Culture* (Place de
Gaulle) is holding a round-table discussion on the subject
of 'Slander and Defamation'.

It is vital that public opinion should be made to take
cognisance, as widely as possible and by every available
means, of the gravity and the appalling consequences of
this most regrettable incident.

THE LICA'S MOTION

The development of an outrageous and shameless campaign, based on lies and slander, and directed against certain Jewish shop-owners, who are grotesquely accused of being involved in the white slave trade—by individuals who have not even got the courage to make themselves known—has led the Loiret Branch of the LICA (BP917 Orléans RP) to pass the following motion:

Highly disturbed by the unthinking dissemination of such unverifiable charges, the League pledges itself to warn the inhabitants of Orléans—offering proof where necessary—that the charges made are invention pure and simple; and that such charges cause grave harm to the shop-owners against whom they are levelled, men whose honesty and moral probity have never been challenged, and cannot be challenged.

The League further pledges itself to take energetic counter-measures against all such activities, which bear a singular resemblance to the ignoble anti-Semitic campaigns undertaken by the Third Reich.

The League is resolved to bring suit through the Public Prosecutor's Office against —— for uttering an unmistakably racialist libel.

The League also makes a confident appeal to the police authorities to unmask those responsible for this vicious smear campaign without delay, and put them where they can no longer cause harm to anyone.

Lastly, since the injurious accusations against these shop-owners have threatened public law and order, the League solemnly draws the attention of the responsible authorities to the need for effective intervention on their part.

AN APPEAL BY THE ASSOCIATION OF NON-SEDENTARY TRADESMEN

We wish to protest, in the most solemn fashion, against a despicable smear campaign which has been spreading in and around Orléans, and which has as its target the Jewish business community. Such a campaign can satisfy no one save the morbidly minded and the sadistic. There is no solid evidence whatsoever for the facts alleged. All this incident proves is that medieval attitudes still survive in the Space Age. It can cause nothing but harm, both to our over-gullible fellow citizens, and to the region as a whole. It is our sincere hope that the persons responsible for this slander will very soon be brought to book. Suit has already been brought against them.

(Signed) HENRI AMROFEL
on behalf of the Association of Non-Sedentary Tradesmen (Orléans District)

SLANDER AND DEFAMATION, SUBJECT OF A ROUND-TABLE DISCUSSION ON SUNDAY AT THE MCO[1]

In Germany, in 1932, the windows of Jewish-owned shops were smashed, their premises looted. The anti-Semitic violence provoked by a smear campaign leads, ultimately, to Belsen and Buchenwald.

Earlier, we had the Dreyfus Affair; later came the suicide of Salengro. On each occasion slander attained its ends; and in every case the man in the street ('decent people', as they say) sided against the victims on the basis of mere hearsay, without ever bothering to verify the accusations.

It is this hellish chain of events which may be released amongst us today or tomorrow: that same sequence which drives the five young actors appearing in *Jeanne de Toujours* to become, despite themselves, caught up in an irreversible pattern of licensed butchery.

It is with this in mind that Olivier Katian and the performers in his show will present (Sunday next, 8 June, at 4 p.m., in the MCO's *Théâtre de Poche*) a montage on

---

[1] *Maison de la Culture d'Orléans.*

various 'defamatory affairs', to be followed by a discussion under the chairmanship of Louis Guilloux. Entry free.

8 JUNE 1969

TEXT OF A ROUND-ROBIN MANIFESTO, TO BE SIGNED BY CITIZENS OF ORLEANS, DRAFTED BY LOUIS GUILLOUX (GRANDPRIX NATIONAL DES LETTRES, CODIRECTOR OF THE MAISON DE LA CULTURE D'ORLEANS ET DU LOIRET).

For some time now certain highly repugnant rumours have been influencing public opinion at Orléans and elsewhere. Their purport is that certain shop-owners are allegedly involved in the white slave trade. The origin of such rumours naturally remains obscure; but what is very clear is that they are directed exclusively against *Jewish* shop-owners.

Without making any direct accusations ourselves, are we not justified, given these facts, in detecting some deliberate aim, perhaps even a coordinated plan? At the same time one dares not ask oneself to what end, or for whose profit, since it seems barely credible that anyone in the world could have recourse to such methods for any purpose whatsoever. To blame mankind's perennial folly, stupidity and malice (not to mention cowardice) is no more satisfying, and leads to a similar process of rejection on our part.

Must we recognise what has happened here as a resurgence of the old familiar anti-Semitism which claimed so many million victims only a few years ago? The power of slander is, as we know, immense. Did not Voltaire say that if he was accused of having stolen the towers of Notre-Dame, he would make a bolt for it at once?

Perhaps, though, such a *bon mot* does not convey the best advice one could have in the present situation. We must, on the contrary, show ourselves firm, sensible and

cool-headed. We must reassure the victims of these loath-
some accusations that they have friends here who are
always ready to spring to their defence. We must demand
that their accusers reveal themselves—if they have the
courage to do so.
                                              Signature
If you are willing to let the fact of your having signed this
document be mentioned in the Press:
Name:
Profession:

THE CHURCH

LETTER FROM THE BISHOP OF ORLEANS
Monsieur le Secrétaire National,
I did indeed receive your letter, and your invitation for 8
June. Unfortunately, it reached me too late for me to take
action on it.

I have taken cognisance through the local press of this
odious cabal. And you will realise how fervently I am
praying that it may soon be brought under control.

I remain at your disposition for any help I may be able
to give you towards this end.

Your devoted and humble servant,

                                    Bishop of Orléans, 9 June 1969.

THE PARIS PRESS

ARTICLE IN *Le Monde*, 7 JUNE 1969
'DISAPPEARANCE' OF WOMEN IN ORLEANS: PLOT OR HOAX?
Scene: a women's dress shop on a main shopping street
somewhere in the provinces, late one afternoon. A couple
appears. The man decides to wait outside on the pavement
while his wife goes into the boutique on her own. After a

while the husband gets tired of waiting, goes into the establishment himself—and is informed that no person answering the description he gives has crossed the threshold of the shop. Confronted with this stubborn and obstructive attitude on the part of the staff, he goes to the police. Some time later the latter discover three women (including his wife) down in the basement, bound, gagged, chloroformed, ready to be shipped off abroad: a clear case of 'white slaving'.

This odd story is a complete fabrication. Yet though it is about as murkily fantastic as the plot of a bad thriller, it spread through the entire town in a matter of hours. Today it lies at the heart of every kind of fear and anxiety; it nurtures old resentments, acts as a spring-board for unacknowledged feelings of hatred, encourages folly and dissipates boredom. For nearly three weeks now Orléans has been living through a period of denunciation and calumny. No less than twenty-six women have already 'disappeared', while six shop-owners, all of them Jewish— the one constant factor in this affair—have brought suit against —— for defamatory libel.

Deliberately whipped up by a public with an enthusiastic taste for such things, the farce is now turning into drama. After the shoulder shrugging period comes the time for public statements. Parents, commercial groups and, most recently, the League against Racialism and Anti-Semitism, have registered vigorous protests against 'all such activities, which bear a singular resemblance to the ignoble anti-Semitic campaigns undertaken by the Third Reich'. An appeal has been issued 'to the police authorities to unmask those responsible for this vicious smear campaign without delay, and put them where they can no longer cause harm to anyone'. Further, 'since the injurious accusations against these shop-owners have threatened public law and order', the attention of 'the responsible authorities' has been solemnly drawn to 'the need for effective intervention on their part'.

In Orléans, it is very clear, the joke has ceased to be funny. Everyone suspects everyone else, anonymous letters are continually arriving at police headquarters (sometimes accusing the police themselves), headmistresses issue stern warnings to their girls, the 'suspect' shops are deserted, old scores are being paid off all round, and a collective psychosis of unparalleled dimensions is developing.

As far as the police are concerned, the affair remains peculiarly elusive. Obviously no case of genuine disappearance has been reported to them. No pamphlets have been distributed. No slogans have been daubed on walls. There has been nothing which could give even the faintest grounds for suspecting an organised anti-Semitic campaign: merely rumours—rumours, and artful innuendo. For during these three crazy weeks, the most astonishing allegations have been made. They include the accepting of bribes by the Chief of Police, wholesale suppression of the facts by the Press, and statements that this or that person (named) has disappeared—though when investigators hurried round to check up they found, to their astonishment, that the individuals in question had never so much as been away from home.

It now seems that as far as this frenetic spate of false news is concerned, the sky's the limit. To seek an explanation for it is clearly a hazardous undertaking. The idea that we have a case of latent anti-Semitism being exploited in a purely fortuitous manner is conceivably true; but it does not altogether explain this collective abandonment of reason. Other factors have clearly been at work here, though those investigating the matter are baffled as to their precise nature. One of the explanations they give seems to derive from observation rather than from any analysis of the basic motives activating this town—a town of over 100,000 inhabitants, for over five centuries now devoted to the cult of Joan of Arc.

In the issue of the weekly *Noir et Blanc* for the period

8-14 May, under the headline 'The Odious Snares of Traffickers in Human Flesh', there appeared an 'enquiry' which took the reader into the back room of a Grenoble shop, specialising in ladies' accessories—and in 'white slaving'. The story presented here presents numerous parallels with that which served to launch the 'anti-Semitic cabal' in Orléans. Should we then regard this incident as the work of a sick practical joker, or (the view advanced by the Movement against Racialism and Anti-Semitism) as heralding the appearance of 'a new species of malicious gossip, whose activities involve not just a few individuals, but an entire community'? In the latter case it might help to give some prominence to another hypothesis: 'One recalls that during the events of May 1968 in Orléans both fascist and racialist groups showed signs of intense activity.'

In any case there is nothing, as things stand at present, to justify any direct connection between the attack on the University campus of Orléans-la-Source (17 June), and the agitation of mind which led some people to say: 'You'd think we were back in the Middle Ages, when they accused Jews of sacrificing children.'

ARTICLE IN *L'Aurore*, 10 JUNE 1969

A SMEAR CAMPAIGN

At Orléans 'they' started a rumour that women were disappearing from certain shops. And, as though by chance, the owners of these shops were all Jewish. . .

Do you know Orléans? It is a town of 100,000 inhabitants, situated 100 kilometres from Paris. Very soon the Orléanais will be able to take trips into the big city by the most modern form of transport known, the monorail train. Already you can see its track, running beside the main road on a series of concrete pillars. Orléans also has a university campus and a number of important factories.

This, it is said, is a town that looks to the future, that is
assured of rapid expansion; a reassuring sort of place, which
twentieth century civilisation has thoroughly penetrated,
sweeping away those irrational superstitions and fears
engendered by obscurantism. Yet under this veneer of
civilisation, the Middle Ages still survive, and the least
thing will suffice to make them emerge once more. A few
careless words, a crazy rumour without any solid foundation, the sheer improbability of which a few seconds'
thought would have sufficed to demonstrate—and in
forty-eight hours the slander (as in *The Barber of Seville*)
had blown itself up out of all proportion, and had got a
hold on the entire town.

It all started on 23 May. On that day, everywhere in
Orléans, in shops, in offices, in cafés, in schools (particularly
the last, it would seem) a really appalling and terrifying
story began to go the rounds by word of mouth. A local
woman had disappeared while making purchases in a
lingerie shop on the Rue du Chariot. Her husband was
waiting for her outside. When she failed to appear, he got
uneasy, went inside, and asked where his wife was. The
proprietor's uncooperative attitude sent him straight
round to the police. A few hours later his lost wife, together with several other young ladies, was found bound
and gagged in the basement of the shop.

'Naturally this rumour came to our ears,' says the Chief
of the Criminal Investigation Department in Orléans.
'However, we had no reason to investigate it further—no
complaint had as yet been lodged, no one was reported
missing, and the police had not been called in. Imagine
what it'd be like if we followed up all the rumours that
circulate in a provincial town!'

DRUGGED

The only thing was that as time went on, the rumour, far
from dying down, continued to gain strength. It reached

its apogee on 31 May, which was both a market day and the eve of the elections. The streets of Orléans were crowded, and 'the affair' was the sole topic of conversation on everybody's lips. The number of women who had been spirited into thin air while out shopping had risen from three to twenty-six. While no specific name was mentioned, the report had it that among those missing was the wife of a police inspector. According to general rumour, responsibility for these disappearances lay with about a dozen shop-owners, all well known figures and hitherto regarded as pillars of respectability. All these shop-owners' premises, it was said, had cellars that were linked with one another by specially excavated underground passages, all of them opening on the Loire!

The unfortunate victims were supposedly drugged and carried down to these dungeons, then transported to the river's edge and embarked at dead of night on boats sailing for Caracas, Buenos Aires and other places well known for the frenzied rate at which they absorbed women from France's cities and countryside. It was even alleged that one of these shop-owners made his customers try on shoes in which a drug-laden hypodermic was concealed, and overcame their defences in this way. In their cheerful way the inhabitants of Orléans made the sickest thriller look pusillanimous by comparison. In point of fact, no person had recently been reported missing from Orléans, and that by itself was sufficient to kill the rumour stone dead; however, this very simple idea seems not to have occurred to anyone. Or at least, those who did think of it found it welcome rather than otherwise, because they had at once found a really smart comeback: the police were deliberately hushing the whole thing up. Why? Because they were getting a heavy rake-off in hush-money from the white slavers.

'It was alleged,' the Chief of the Criminal Investigation Department tells us, 'that I had made *ten million* francs this way. I suppose the more exaggerated and extravagant

a story is, the more people are likely to believe it. Even
the nuns who taught in one school issued a warning to
their pupils, telling them they would be well advised to
keep away from the boutiques in question.'

ORGANISED

But, it will be asked, why were these particular shop-
owners made the special target for such slanderous allegations? They have something else in common apart from
their profession: all of them are Jewish. Furthermore, they
are convinced that they have been made the victims of a
well organised anti-Semitic campaign.

M. Licht, who was the first to be singled out by the
rumour, says: 'It's because we're Jews, and for no other
reason. It seems incredible that only twenty-five years
after the Nazi concentration camps this sort of thing can
start up again. On Saturday groups of people were milling
about outside one shop shouting "Don't go in there, that's
where they abduct the women!"'

Mme Buki, the owner of a ready-made dress boutique, is
of the same opinion: 'I can't find words to express my
disgust. Such a filthy, cowardly trick! The whole episode
has given me plenty to think about. I realise now that
you're not what you are, but what other people think you
are.'

Mme Buki has a daughter of fifteen, who attends the
lycée and has heard people applying all the horror stories
reported above to her own mother. What is more, not
only Mme Buki and M. Licht, but all the other victims of
this rumour have suffered a very considerable drop in
their turnover. People are either scared or suspicious,
and therefore take the precaution of shopping elsewhere.

Six shop-owners thus attacked have brought suit for
defamatory libel, and an investigation has begun.

'Nevertheless,' the Chief of the Criminal Investigation

Department says, 'I'm not very optimistic. We haven't a single solid clue to go on, and, if you ask me, we never will.'

EXECRABLE

When a slanderous rumour has taken possession of an entire town, spreading into every corner of it like a mist, how can one track down its original instigator? The victims feel convinced that they are up against a power-fully organised plot: yet there is no real need of an organised force to disseminate poisonous gossip—gossip which in the Middle Ages (not so remote as people used to think) could, literally, kill. The 'Orléans cabal' may have been started by a small group of right-wing extremists—or merely by some schoolgirls with over-vivid imaginations, who, feeling constricted by their life in Orléans (between the Rue de la République and the Rue Royale) found relief in the concoction of this execrable piece of fiction.

ARTICLE IN *Le Figaro*, 11 JUNE 1969

THE 'CABAL' AGAINST JEWISH SHOP-OWNERS IN ORLEANS: INDIVIDUAL ACTS WHICH DO NOT REFLECT THE GENERAL MOOD, SAYS THE PREFECT OF THE LOIRET.

Orléans, 10 June. (From our own correspondent.) The strong feelings aroused by the smear campaign in Orléans, against certain Jewish shop-owners accused of being white slave traffickers, has driven the Prefect of the Loiret, M. Graeve, to make a statement concerning this 'unpleasant affair', the purpose of which, he claims, is to whip up 'unhealthy agitation'.

'I observe,' he writes, more particularly, 'that the shop-owners victimised by these fanciful accusations were not,

in the first instance, specifically referred to as Jews; which
leads one to doubt whether this affair was anti-Semitic in
character *ab initio*. One's doubts are reinforced by the
fact that the rumours circulating were just as ready to
smear officials and other well known persons; indeed, it
also would seem to have been claimed that the Prefect
himself was hushing up the affair, in order to protect
certain individuals.'

He also states: 'If it is true that these Jewish shop-
owners have received numerous phone-calls and letters,
all of a threatening, slanderous and insulting nature, such
acts are the work of isolated individuals, acting under the
cover of anonymity. They do not in any way reflect the
general mood of the population.'

STUPIDITY AND MALICE

This public statement by M. Graeve comes in response to a
request addressed both to him and to the Minister of the
Interior by the Representative Council of French Jews.
The Council asked 'that all possible measures should be
taken to identify those responsible, and that the sanctions
prescribed by law should be duly enforced'.

The Jewish Union for Mutual Aid and Resistance,
strongly moved by these events, made a similar plea to
'the competent authorities to do everything in their power
to put an end to this abominable propaganda, so unpleasantly reminiscent of the Nazi occupation'.

Furthermore, in a second statement, issued this evening,
the Prefect makes a somewhat sharp attack on the
Fédération de l'Education nationale in general and its
Loiret branch in particular. The latter had openly asserted
that the victims were asked to keep quiet until after the
first round of the Presidential elections. M. Graeve now
challenges this professional association to produce solid
evidence in support of its 'malicious insinuations', and
concludes: 'In this affair, stupidity and malice strive to

outdo each other. Let the inhabitants of Orléans draw their own conclusions.'

SUPPLEMENTARY NOTE
THE ROUEN RUMOUR

Geneviève Serreau has sent us information concerning an episode oddly similar to that which took place in Orléans.

A certain shop-owner, Mme L., and her two daughters, who together ran a luxury boutique in Rouen, were rumoured to be engaged in the white slave trade. The affair simmered on for a while; then, towards the end of 1966, it boiled over, assuming very considerable proportions in the process. After a few days the one woman originally said to have been abducted was multiplied to no less than *three hundred*. There was talk of chloroform, of girls being spirited away to Lebanon by freighter, of underground tunnels linking the shop with the port. Threatening phone-calls became a commonplace. One night someone put a bullet through the shop-window.

The proprietress filed a formal complaint, and the authorities opened an investigation. The Press, which had been very uneasy about the affair, was officially informed that no person had been reported missing, and that the only action contemplated was that taken by the shop-owner herself, as a result of the smear campaign against her, for defamatory libel. Press intervention[1] in fact merely served to make the atmosphere still nastier. Groups of people gathered outside the shop. Some even spat at the shop-window.

Mme L. had to get out of town. She tried to establish a new business in Savoy, but even there she continued to be

[1] In the form of two articles: (a) *Paris-Jour*, 10 December 1966: 'The whole town was playing poison-tattle', and (b) *Paris-Normandie*, 11 December 1966: 'Have three hundred women vanished in Rouen ?'

hounded by persistent slanderous allegations emanating
from Rouen, in despite of all official denials. Finally she
sold her business. Her two daughters decided to emigrate.

The resemblances between these two affairs are obvious.
Two points in particular deserve our attention. Firstly,
Mme L. set up her business in Rouen after the war. She
had various initial difficulties, but finally made a going
concern of it. Our earlier analysis laid considerable emphasis on the catalysing role played by the ready-made
dress shop (here a luxury boutique for ladies'-wear); the
similarity of the type of establishment aimed at in each
case should not cause surprise. However, Mme L. is not
Jewish. The absence of an anti-Semitic motif in this
instance suggests that we should *modify our hypothesis
that if such a rumour is to catch on in the provinces it needs a
Jew.* The Jewish factor may accentuate receptiveness,
but—as we can see from the Rouen affair—it is not essential for the proliferation of the myth.

Some other points to note. Firstly, this affair provoked
no political counter-movement, perhaps for lack of a
potential anti-Semitic angle. The Mayor of Rouen intervened, it is true, to issue a public denial of the rumour.
Yet despite his rebuttal, and those of other administrative
and judicial authorities, not to mention Press ridicule, the
rumour became more and more virulent. It was as though
a battle royal were taking place between the official information services of the *polis*, and the psychological-cum-
mythological realities of the town.

From such information as we possess, it would seem that
in Rouen too young people acted as the chief carriers and
disseminators of the rumour.

This dossier reached us too late for us to make any
adjustments to our general analysis in the light of its
findings. Yet though it weakens certain points in our
theory (e.g. the part played by anti-Semitism), it confirms
others in the most striking manner (e.g. the role of

adolescent girls as carriers). It shows to what extent occurrential sociology (*la sociologie de l'événement*), if it is to perform its function adequately, must keep its hypotheses flexible, must reach beyond the unusual and the exceptional to construct open-ended, revisable models.

EDGAR MORIN:

THE PRINCIPLES OF 'CONTEMPORARY SOCIOLOGY'

EDGAR MORIN:

THE PRINCIPLES OF 'CONTEMPORARY SOCIOLOGY'

There is a clear antithesis between our own sociological technique, as exemplified here, and that associated with strict specialisation, which—despite its regularity of method, and reliance on statistics—never succeeds in achieving the degree of scientific verification which makes experimental work possible. Our approach concentrates on the phenomenon rather than on any concept of discipline; it concerns itself less with variable factors than with the event as such, and is more interested in a crisis than in regular statistical patterns. The antithesis can likewise be traced, not only on the plane of empirical methodology (where we tend to accord priority to observation and intervention), but also on that of epistemology and general theory. Here we tend to concentrate our efforts, not in the multidisciplinary field, or on so-called structural formalisation, but rather on a type of phenomenal logic (the structured study of social phenomena in their own time-and-place context). At the theoretical level this must be meshed in with an anthropo-socio-historical system. At this level (as we make very clear) the antithesis between our concept and the rest becomes complementary. What we advocate is a multidimensional grasp of phenomena, which forces itself to assimilate the findings of *all* disciplines and *all* methods. It follows that we do not in any

265

sense reject statistics or the use of questionnaires. We simply refuse to let sociology become bogged down by them.

THE PHENOMENON

A phenomenon is that which appears, which emerges into social reality, as a relatively isolable datum (or group of data). It may be, e.g. an institution, a town, an opinion-trend, a myth, a fashion, and so on. The strict categorising approach cuts a section through any phenomenon, describes the angle from which it is to be studied; in a sense by so doing it *disintegrates* the phenomenon in question, since the latter can be, at one and the same time, geographical, historical, economic, sociological, religious, psychological and much besides in its implications. Furthermore, the main point of setting up multi- or inter-disciplinary teams is for the better understanding of phenomena as such. We believe this process should be taken still further. It is vital to break away from the disciplinary big battalions, to envisage new special fields, to cultivate polycentricity and certain types of anti-specialisation (over-specialisation, in the evolution of living species as in that of science, is a deadly peril) that facilitate adherence to the two polarisations brought about by any study of phenomena—i.e. on the one hand specific concrete data, and on the other, speculative theory. It is, moreover, no accident that the sociology which prevails today lies in a 'middle range' between theory and facts, being poor in one and liable to mutilate the other. Our task then, beginning from the phenomenological impulse, is to breathe some life into theory and facts alike, both of which have suffered conjointly from atrophy, under-development, and suppression.

Furthermore, the sociological approach now in fashion is well aware of the need for a phenomenal substratum, if only to give interpretative direction to those working models, equations and general or relative patterns which it finds itself driven to extrapolate. With this in mind it pounced eagerly on the concept of industrial society (or civilisation), which it set up as a kind of diptych with the notion of traditional society (or civilisation), cheerfully lumping whole millennia of complex history together in this all-embracing terminological category. Today it has hastened to add a third panel, that of post-industrial society (or civilisation); but this speculative phenomenological triptych is very thin stuff.

In our view, contemporary society (or civilisation) is a multi-conditioned complex, in which to retain the industrial determinant as one's sole essential criterion strikes us as a wholly arbitrary process. Furthermore, this economically orientated concept either suppresses, or discards as irrelevant to sociology, various conflicts, crises and events which might well shed some light on the inner nature of this world we now inhabit.

THE EVENT OR HAPPENING

Sociology reduces a phenomenon to the restrictive level of industrial (or post-industrial) society, circumscribes the concrete particular in descriptive monographs, and simply eliminates the event, as such, altogether.

An event, or happening, is regarded as something accidental, contingent, which must be set aside if we are to appreciate the true social realities, these being associated with repetition, regularity and, more often than not, with structural pattern.

We believe, however, that an event must be treated, first and foremost, as informative evidence—i.e. as a new element which not only infiltrates the sociologist's mental outlook, but affects his social assumptions as well.

Even if we restrict ourselves to a strictly cybernetic model of social life, the event-as-information is precisely what enables us to understand the nature of the system's structure and functioning; it is, in fact, a kind of feedback, a process by which information is assimilated (or rejected), and modifications brought about—either in the system, or by it.

To make a biological analogy; the event is that stress or disturbance which triggers off rebalancing processes in an organism. This may be achieved either by repression/annihilation, or by integration/evolution—that is, by modification and change.

Thus the event constitutes an active test of any system in which it intervenes; and, furthermore, it enables us to approach a problem which—whether looked at theoretically or phenomenologically—is of prime importance for the scientific knowledge of every society, and above all for those in the modern world: that of change.

In point of fact, after we have eliminated, as a matter of course, those events which follow a statistically regular pattern (e.g. suicides, car accidents, delinquency), we find that the rest *do* intervene, decisively and over a wide spectrum, in human history. This applies equally to events that are originally outside the pattern of social life (e.g. natural cataclysms, climatic changes, etc.); social in origin, but external to the society under consideration (invasions, acts of aggression, wars); and internal to a given society (political events, social conflicts or crises).

These two latter types of event are so important that they are what gives society its distinctive historical character. The implication, from our point of view, is that we must not allow ourselves to pick and choose in the field of social reality, emphasising only 'balanced systems' and ignoring the rest. Such systems should be regarded merely as 'utopian rationalisations'—to borrow a neat, and still not fully appreciated, phrase of Max Weber's—that is, as useful instruments, but not to be taken literally or regarded as 'true' models of social reality. The latter, when set against these pseudo-models, reveals rather more of a functional-dysfunctional syndrome. It consists of a permanent dialectic between those factors which tend towards the establishment of balanced systems, and counter-tendencies liable to disrupt the equilibrium thus attained. This dialectic—the source of all modifications, whether evolutive or involutive (the latter, in their own way, evolutive too)—is effectively shaped by events, which present themselves to us, partly as enigmatic messages, and partly as warnings: that is, as significant revelations.

We are still only at the beginnings of an occurrential sociology. Here I would just like to raise two points which may be of some methodological interest. Firstly, the attention given (as already stated) to those processes of modification and resorption provoked by the event. Secondly, the attention given to the triggering off of other events or new processes through a synchronisation of dynamic forces hitherto independent but now brought into juxtaposition, and/or adjusted to the same wavelength as various isomorphisms that had remained latent only so long as these heterogeneous distinctions were maintained. Thus, the student riots of 3 May 1968 immediately synchronised and stimulated certain competitive, quasi-sporting tendencies present or latent in various categories of adolescent (high-school students, young workers, those on the verge of manhood); it activated various juvenile isomorphisms, while the corresponding heteromorphisms entered on a period of latency. In their second phase, and in a still more remarkable manner from the viewpoint of the 'contemporary sociologist', the student riots (this time involving young workers as well) both synchronised and activated an isomorphic opposition between those who submit to authority and those who exercise it. This phenomenon lasted for several weeks, despite differences in background and every other sort of heterogeneous discrepancy.

The study of what we may term 'occurrential virulence'— the violent, exaggerated outburst in any form—cannot be kept separate from the ordinary processes of communication associated with events *per se*, and the symbolic, indeed the mythological characteristics they acquire as soon as they enter the social communications-system.

CRISIS

That complex of events which constitutes a crisis is, for any social system, at one and the same time the most disturbing and the most informative phenomenon known to it. A crisis, in its original medical sense, is a disturbance which facilitates diagnosis. A basic clinical datum of physiology and psychology, the crisis should also, as we see it, be an equally basic datum for clinical anthropo-sociology—as indeed is already the case as regards the two great metadisciplinary, phenomenal and anthropo-socio-historical doctrines of our day, those of Marx and Freud.

We may restate here two heuristic postulates which both Marx and Freud assumed. A crisis is a significant indicator of latent or subterranean realities (whether systematic or developmental): this effectively predicates the importance of the submerged, latent, unconscious element in the social universe. A crisis is a significant indicator of those conflicting realities which play a life-and-death role within the fabric of every society; this predicates the importance of the conflicting and dialectical element in the social universe.

But a crisis is not merely an indicator; it also initiates action. It leads to what we may term 'problematisation', i.e. the questioning, in those sectors affected by the crisis, of what had hitherto been taken for granted, as something natural and self-evident. This 'problematisation', by effect and counter-effect (uneasiness or anxiety) triggers off a process of rationalisation, i.e. vigorous ideological (or mythological) activity aimed at plugging the 'problematical' breach. Such a process also involves magical, immolatory developments ('guilty persons', etc.) and eventually, when the crisis is resorbed, a process of psychological repression which rapidly assumes the form of amnesia.

At a deeper level, a crisis activates two different processes: on the one hand a regression to the *status quo ante*, and on the other a modificatory chain-reaction (along the lines worked out above while discussing the *event*) which may lead, ultimately, to transformation. From the interaction of these regressive and transforming processes there emerges a conflictive-associative dialectic which can translate itself in the form of phenomena leading to stabilisation, regulation, evolution or revolution.

Their sociologically paroxysmal nature means that crises bring out the elements and developmental processes of innovation/evolution; but at the same time they also resurrect an underlying archaic substratum of myth and magic—brilliantly illuminated by Freud in respect of the neurotic individual (magic and the world), and now requiring further clarification as regards its historico-sociological dimension.

Only through crisis can one apprehend both change and the resistance to change.

SOCIAL TEMPORALITY

In this way we integrate sociology, at the deepest level, with the processes of involution and evolution. We make a fresh examination of how such processes develop; we are moving towards the establishment of a second marriage between sociology and history. The first marriage was that in which—during the first half of this century, under the influence of Marxism and encouraged by the *Ecole des Annales*—history moved in the direction of sociology. But during this same period, sociology was turning its back on history. We must now move back towards history, not only in order to restore such phenomena as accidents, ruptures, happenings and crises to where they belong (i.e. within the context of sociological research), but also in order to understand that the so-called irrational factors (a happening, a crisis) which sociology has rejected possess their own logical structure. Such a course of action will lead us to assume *that the process of becoming has its own structural patterns*—a concept which simultaneously generalises and eclipses the tendency commonly known as structuralism.

Let us take the argument one step further. By seeing in history a permanently pathological condition of disequilibrium, indeed of hysteria, we are not plunging into the irrational, but rather adopting that clinical perspective which enables us to apprehend, not merely the dialectical structures of becoming, but also (by way of various phenomenal manifestations) the hysterical structures of anthropological man.

CLINICAL SOCIOLOGY

All this leads us to posit the need for what we may term 'clinical sociology', i.e. a discipline which bases itself on direct observation of accidental or contingential occurrences, of the extreme or pathological incident, the crisis above all. All that orthodox sociology rejected as insignificant—i.e. anything imponderable or statistically negligible, anything that disturbed the structure or the system—we find, on the contrary, of the greatest significance, whether as indicator, activating agent, enzyme, ferment, virus, modifier or catalyst.

Clinical sociology acquires a quite extraordinary slant through the contemporaneity of subject (researcher) and subject-object (of the research). Hitherto no-one has attempted to penetrate beyond the scientifically disturbing aspect of this relationship. The historian would justify the scientific validity of his claims by a temporal 'distancing' between his own scrutiny and the object of his studies (historical perspective, 'standing back'). The sociologist tried to prove his scholarly *bona fides* by avoiding any concrete contact with his material—i.e. any dialectic between subject-researcher and the subject-object under investigation.

It looks today as though the more advanced sciences,

such as microphysics, are rediscovering the problem posed by the indissolubility and intercontamination of this subject-object duality. Until methods of simulation are evolved which make it possible to develop analogous substitutes for the experimental method, humane sciences will remain in bondage to this dialectic, which states— very precisely, from the methodological viewpoint—that science is an art and art is a science, that sociology resembles the clinician for whom art and science fuse in the act of diagnosis.

One further point. If it is true that the science of man-in-society suffers from an inability to conduct rigorously controlled experiments, could it not also be a fact that the only approach to such experimentation is that provided by the one laboratory at our disposal—the world around us in its living historical context? Should not our aim today be to refine the comparative method by henceforth treating isomorphisms with an even greater degree of flexibility than we previously applied to analogies? Should we not realise (aided by an adequate semiology, and the awareness that *all* symptoms in our social life have significance) that such symptoms constitute spontaneous social checks or test cases, with a wealth of enigmatic meaning awaiting our elucidation? The road lies open before us, but as yet we have taken no more than the first step down it.

THE 'FIELD OF THE PRESENT'

As regards the 'field of the present'—i.e. the actual presence of the investigator-researcher at the phenomenon/event being studied—we should extract what advantages we can from those well known scientific inconveniences that arise from over-close proximity to the concrete, and palliate the inconveniences themselves as far as possible. First of all, that is to say, we must exploit—in depth and from every available angle—the possibilities opened up by the presence of the investigator in the actual process.

We can do this by maximum use of on-the-spot observation, not only through the utilisation of all available recording-devices (tape-recorders, cameras, etc.) but also by increasing the number of observation-points (emphasis on team-work). Avoid repression, rather exploit the investigator's personal sensibilities: what I have elsewhere labelled sociological Stendhalism or Balzacism—Proustism, even. Another way in which the investigator can make full use of his presence is by actual intervention. This could range from a series of questions going beyond the ordinary questionnaire, with the object of provoking specific social reactions (not merely of opinion but also of behaviour) in any given situation, to what might be termed 'maieutic' interventions. The latter would either dynamically activate the field of enquiry, or else adapt themselves to a pre-existent dynamic situation. By so doing they could give the investigation a peri-experimental twist, while at the same time attempting to help the human group caught up in the situation or process under investigation.

Such practices are, obviously, both uncertain and hazardous. It follows that an investigation in the 'field of the present' will necessitate self-correction and self-regulation—not to mention art, initiative and flexibility. These cannot be attained except by breaking away from the context of pre-programmed, techno-bureaucratic, managerial investigation, and by setting up working teams of a somewhat unconventional kind.

Furthermore, an inquiry in 'the field of the present' could not be limited to, or contained by, the normal descriptive monograph. It must take as its terms of reference both a phenomenological view of the contemporary world and a general theory: not merely in order to extract guidance and endorsement from them, but also to question their assumptions. The more an investigation poses an empirical problem, the more it poses a theoretical problem too. Thus our experience suggests that studies on the events of May–June 1968 inevitably circle back, boomerang-like, to that general theory of society, the blind spots in which coincide with the main focal points of this present crisis.

CONCLUSION
Thus we take up a position at the dialectical mid-point between event and theory, history and sociology, the contemporary and the anthropological, and—more specifically in this case—between phenomenon and discipline, crisis and system, the actual and the potential, trend and counter-trend, evolution and involution, the innovating and the archaic.

Within the context of the 'Contemporary Sociology' section of CECMAS, our activities have taken the following form:

Phenomena
L'Esprit du temps (a general study of the mass-culture system), Grasset, Paris, 1961. New edition scheduled for 1970.
Plodemet: Report from a French Village, Allen Lane the Penguin Press, London, 1971; Fayard, Paris, 1967.
Nouveaux courants de la culture de masse (research in progress).
Konzerns culturels (research in progress).
Néo-archaïsme et néo-modernisme rural (cyclostyled publication), CECMAS, 1968.
Vacances et clubs de vacances (research in progress).
Le Phénomène national (general survey, to be published shortly).

Happenings/Phenomena
Enquêtes flashes (by various members of CECMAS in collaboration), 1960–2.
'Salut les copains' (a study produced by the 'Nuit de la Nation' in June 1963), first published in *Le Monde*, 7 July,

1963, and reissued in *Arguments politiques*, Le Seuil, Paris, 1965, pp. 213–20.

'Une télé-tragédie planétaire: l'assassinat du président Kennedy', in *Communications 3*, 1964, pp. 77–81.

'Planète et anti-planète', in *Le Monde*, 1–2–3 June, 1965.

L'exposition internationale 'Terre des Hommes' de Montréal en 1967 (unpublished research).

La Marée Noire, by Bernard Paillard, 1967 (unpublished).

La Mort de Che Guevara dans la presse française, by Bernard Paillard, 1967 (unpublished).

Crises

We have attempted to make some progress in our handling of crises on the basis of our communication, 'Notes méthodologiques sur l'internationalité des révoltes étudiantes' (Milan, Centro di Studi Lombardi, March 1968), and our articles 'La commune étudiante' and 'Une révolution sans visages' in *La Brèche*, by Morin, Lefort and Coudray (Fayard, 1968). 'Pour une sociologie de la crise', in *Communications 12*, 1968, pp. 2–16. *Interprétation des interprétations de mai-juin 1968* (Research seminar, 1968–9, in collaboration with Bernard Paillard and Raymond Laffargue). 'Culture adolescente et révolte étudiante', *Annales, 3*, 1969, pp.765–76. 'La Crise' (issue of *Communications* in preparation).

Research problems

'Le Droit à la réflexion', in *Revue française de sociologie* 6 (I), 1965, pp. 4–12.

'De la méthode: une démarche multidimensionnelle', in *Plodemet: Report from a French Village, op. cit.*, pp. 278–87.

'Interview dans les Sciences de l'Homme et à la radio-télévision', in *Communications 7*, 1966, pp.59–73.

Finally, reference to our anthropo-sociological postulates may be found in *Le Vif du sujet*, pp. 69–95, 139–82, 183–85, 332–41 (Le Seuil, Paris, 1969).